Charity

Charity

*The Place of the Poor in
the Biblical Tradition*

GARY A. ANDERSON

Yale

UNIVERSITY PRESS

New Haven and London

Published with assistance from the foundation established in memory of
Philip Hamilton McMillan of the Class of 1894, Yale College.

Yale University Press books may be purchased in quantity for educational,
business, or promotional use. For information, please e-mail sales.press@yale.
edu (U.S. office) or sales@yaleup.co.uk (U.K. office).

Set in New Caledonia Roman type by IDS Infotech, Ltd.
Printed in the United States of America.

Library of Congress Cataloging-in-Publication Data

Anderson, Gary A., 1955–. Charity: the place of the poor in the biblical
tradition / Gary A. Anderson.
pages   cm
Includes bibliographical references and index.
ISBN 978-0-300-18133-3 (cloth : alk. paper) 1. Charity—biblical teaching.
I. Title
BV4639.A53 2013
241'.4—dc23
2013000923

A catalogue record for this book is available from the British Library.

This paper meets the requirements of ANSI/NISO Z39.48–1992
(Permanence of Paper).
10 9 8 7 6 5 4 3 2 1

For Lisa
matrimonium hoc magna caritate compaginatur
—Augustine, Homily on Psalm 88

Whoever is kind to the poor lends to the Lord,
and will be repaid in full.
—Proverbs 19:17

Rabbi Zeira observed: Even the ordinary conversation of the people
of the land of Israel provides the occasion for the study of Torah. How
might that be? A poor person will, on occasion, say to his neighbor:
"Acquire for yourself a merit [in heaven], through me."
—Leviticus Rabbah 34.7

It is impossible, though we perform ten thousand other good deeds, to
enter the portals of the kingdom without almsgiving.
—John Chrysostom, Homilies on the Gospel of John

Contents

Charity

CHAPTER ONE

The Challenge of Charity

Once upon a time there was a peasant woman and a very wicked woman she was. And she died and did not leave a single good deed behind. The devils caught her and plunged her into the lake of fire. So her guardian angel stood and wondered what good deed of hers he could remember to tell to God; "She once pulled up an onion in her garden," said he, "and gave it to a beggar woman." And God answered: "You take that onion then, hold it out to her in the lake, and let her take hold and be pulled out. And if you can pull her out of the lake, let her come to Paradise, but if the onion breaks, then the woman must stay where she is." The angel ran to the woman and held out the onion to her. "Come," said he, "catch hold and I'll pull you out." He began cautiously pulling her out. He had just pulled her right out, when the other sinners in the lake, seeing how she was being drawn out, began catching hold of her so as to be pulled out with her. But she was a very wicked woman and she began kicking them. "I'm to be pulled out, not you. It's my onion, not yours." As soon as she said that, the onion broke. And the woman fell into the lake and she is burning there to this day. So the angel wept and went away.

—Fyodor Dostoevsky, *The Brothers Karamazov*

This book is, in many respects, a natural outgrowth of my previous publication, *Sin: A History*. In that work I argued that a major shift in thinking about human sin occurs at the end of the Old Testament period. The predominant metaphor for sin, which had been that of a weight that an individual must bear on his back, became that of a debt that must be repaid. This concept is classically expressed in Daniel 4:27, when King Nebuchadnezzar is told that he should

1

be charitable to the poor in order to "redeem himself" from his state of spiritual debt slavery. The idea became quite prominent in the New Testament as is reflected in the words of the Our Father: "Forgive us our debts as we forgive our debtors" (*debts,* not *trespasses,* being the literal translation of the Greek original). Though I spent a couple of chapters outlining the importance of almsgiving in the Judaism of the Second Temple period (from the late sixth century BCE [or BC] until the late first century CE [AD]), the amount of material at hand was far larger than I could do justice to. In this book I will examine in far greater depth the origins of almsgiving as a highly privileged religious act within the nascent religions of Judaism and Christianity. When I began this project, I had hoped to carry the investigation into the early rabbinic and patristic period, but that proved to be much too ambitious. The material mushrooms in the early Christian era, and a much lengthier second volume would be required to deal with it fully. I will leave that project to another more able hand in early Christian sources. The present book will stick to the Bible and the early history of its interpretation, subjects that I happen to know quite well.

A significant number of books and articles have appeared in recent decades on the subject of early Jewish and Christian almsgiving.[1] I have benefited tremendously from the fervent interest this topic has occasioned. But two things in particular have been underplayed in this rich literature. First, the predominant focus of scholars has been on the practice itself. As a result these studies have often been social-historical in nature. My own interests, however, are more theological. What concerns me is what the writers of this period thought almsgiving told us about the identity of God and the peoples who claimed to worship him. Though this is clearly the dominant interest of our textual sources as well—ancient Christians and Jews wrote so extensively about almsgiving because they thought the practice said something crucial about the character of God and the world he created and sustains—it has been surprisingly understudied. The other element that is lacking is a proper appreciation for the way in which rabbinic and patristic conceptions of charity are grounded in the Second Temple Jewish sources from which they emerge—in particular, the books of Tobit and Ben Sira and the Synoptic Gospels. In this book I intend to redress these two holes in our present knowledge.

The absence of a theological focus in current treatments of almsgiving is probably traceable to two problems. The first concerns the fact that almsgiving funds a treasury in heaven, a treasury that can pay down the debt owed on one's sins. Because this is a fundamental aspect of nearly every ancient work on the subject, it leads many to worry that almsgiving is grounded in the self-interest of the donor. As a result, many morally sensitive persons find it difficult to take this theological proposal seriously. The second challenge follows from the presumption that if almsgiving funds a heavenly treasury, then the hand of the poor provides a privileged port of entry to the realm and, ultimately, being of God. In short, there is a deeply sacramental character to the act. The poor become a necessary and indeed nonnegotiable point of access to the Kingdom of God. This idea, as I will explain below, was hotly contested during the Reformation and led to the overturning of many charitable practices that had been part of the Christian tradition for more than a millennium. Since the field of biblical studies has been shaped to a large degree by Protestant sensibilities, it should not be unduly surprising that traditionally Catholic understandings of the sacramental character of charity would be overlooked by such scholars, either by intention or simply by ignorance. Let me begin with the first problem.

Charity and Self-Interest

Many people find the construal of charity as a means of funding a heavenly treasury something of an embarrassment. It is troubling that assisting the poor seems to be motivated by blatant self-interest. More than one person has wondered whether these texts do not lead inexorably to the rhetoric of the so-called "prosperity Gospel," which preys on the gullible by claiming that tithing will allow one to buy a BMW and pay off one's mortgage all at the same time.[2] Most people are far more comfortable with the teaching of the ancient Jewish sage Antigonus of Socho (second century BCE), who said: "Be not like servants who serve their master on condition of receiving a gift."[3]

But lest we come to a premature judgment, let's examine more fully the scriptural bases of this tradition. They derive for the most part from the book of Proverbs, a central pillar in what biblical scholars are wont to label ancient Israel's "wisdom" literature. To interpret any proverb well, one must be sensitive to the context in which it is to be applied. The challenge for the reader of these wisdom sayings is to determine the specific dimension of human life that they are trying to address. For our purposes the most important proverb of all reads: "The treasuries of wickedness provide no benefit, but almsgiving delivers from death" (Prov 10:2).[4]

The question that stands behind this proverb is how we ought best save for the future—a question that has concerned human beings for centuries. Imagine that by some happy accident you have become heir to an enormous sum of money. Rather than giving in to the urge to spend it immediately, you ponder how these funds might be invested to provide an endowment for the future. In front of you are two advisers: one is a conventional financial analyst who urges you to invest in a broadly diversified set of index funds that would stand an excellent chance of providing you with a secure retirement at the age of sixty-five. The other person is a religious saint, or tsaddiq, who argues that God created the world out of charity and as a result true prosperity depends on finding a way to ride with those currents. Fund your heavenly treasury by being generous to the poor, he advises. Though it is technically correct that this religious person would be building on your natural inclination for self-preservation, the act of funding such a treasury could hardly be considered self-interested in the simple sense of the term. Compared with what the financial analyst can promise, imitating the generosity of God would seem to be fraught with far greater risk. Lending to God in this fashion might better be conceived of as a means for the religious believer to enact what he professes, putting his money where his mouth is.

I would like to suggest that this way of reading these proverbs provides us with a deeper set of insights about the world than that of Antigonus of Socho. For however salutary it may be to serve a master without thought of a reward, most of us would want to know what kind of master we are called to serve who would merit such dedication. There is a deeper human desire to know and believe that the world is a place formed and guided by charity, that giving to one's neighbor is not just a Kantian "duty" but a declaration about the metaphysical structure of the world itself. Charity, in short, is not just a good deed *but a declaration of belief about the world and the God who created it.*

Why is it, one might ask, that the life of Mother Teresa moved so many people?—and not just Christians, but Muslims, Hindus, Jews, and even nonbelievers. I would suggest that her popularity rests in the fact that she enacted the sort of faith that most can only dream of. But I would also want to contend that it is not just her faith that attracts our admiration, but the statement that her life makes about the nature of the world. Though all appearances would suggest that it is the financial markets that make the world go round, saints like Mother Teresa make a powerful counterclaim. In serving the poor, they not only provide concrete material help to the down and out, but they reveal to us the hidden structure of the universe.

Steven Pinker, a professor of psychology at Harvard, wrote an article in the *New York Times Magazine* to express dismay that the world showers such esteem on Mother Teresa in light of the far greater good that Bill and Melinda Gates have done.[5] Gates, Pinker writes, "crunched the numbers and determined that he could alleviate the most misery by fighting everyday scourges in the developing world like malaria, diarrhea and parasites." Pinker never explained how he knows that the Gateses established their foundation on such utilitarian considerations. Perhaps the Gateses' motivations were quite different.

But whatever the case might be, utilitarian value is not the only index for measuring the accomplishments of charity. For however much the Gateses might give away, their daily life remains, by and large, unaffected. They remain, in spite of this enormous donation, one of the wealthiest couples in the world. Mother Teresa, on the other hand, gave up everything to serve the poorest of the poor.

Pinker wisely concedes that it is unlikely that his praise for the Gateses will win them more admirers than those of Mother Teresa. But, he claims, this is not because of the profundity of her sacrifice but because "our heads can be turned by an *aura* of sanctity, distracting us from a more *objective* reckoning of the actions that make people suffer or flourish" (emphasis mine). Mother Teresa, he asserts, "was the very embodiment of saintliness: white-clad, sad-eyed, ascetic and often photographed with the wretched of the earth." But this is an amazing reduction of the supreme gift she gave her followers. In Pinker's eyes, the world has been taken in by mere appearances: her simple white vestments and the "photo-ops" in which she appears with the poorest of the poor. Amazingly, he lacks any insight as to the true gift she has given the world.

When Mother Teresa started her religious order, the entire premise of the organization was the gift of one's *total self* to the poor. She refused on principle to establish any kind of endowment that would have relieved the sisters of the order of a total reliance on God and of identifying completely with the poor whom they served. Every day she and her sisters put the success of their work in the hands of God. One well-educated Indian professor of sciences, when asked about her admiration for Mother Teresa, said: "I am an unbeliever, but I feel I need an anchor. Mother Teresa is an anchor."[6]

Whether we are believers or unbelievers, I think it is fair to say that most of us want an account of human goodness that goes deeper than utilitarian calculation. We want to believe that the world is good and, at least in the long run, rewards a life of charity. The holy men and women of the synagogue, church, and mosque help us to do just that. And that is the deep reason why the financial metaphor of funding a treasury in heaven became so significant for ancient Jews and Christians. The important point was not so much what they would gain from charity but what acts of charity say about the character of the world God has created.

Charity as Sacrament

By far the most important text for the early church is found in Matthew 25. It begins at the moment of the last judgment, when all the nations are gathered around the Son of Man and he separates the sheep from the goats. To those at his right he says: "Come, you that are blessed by my Father, inherit the kingdom prepared for you from the foundation of the world; for I was hungry and you gave me food, I was thirsty and you gave me something to drink, I was a stranger and you welcomed me, I was naked and you gave me clothing, I was sick and you took care of me, I was in prison and you visited me." The righteous are taken completely by surprise and cannot imagine when they had attended to Christ in such a fashion. Christ explains: "Truly I tell you, just as you did it to one of the least of these who are members of my family, you did it to me." Two points should be gleaned from this text: first, charity to poor has the power to deliver one from eternal damnation (recall the epigraph to this chapter from *The Brothers Karamazov*), and second, charity acquires such power because one meets Christ through this concrete action of showing mercy. For early Christians this was not just a metaphor; the church proclaimed that one actually encountered the presence of God in the poor. This is evident from the famous story of St. Martin of Tours. One day, as he approached the city Amiens, he was confronted by a beggar. Seeing his ragged condition, Martin was touched and promptly drew his sword, cut his cloak in two, and gave half to the shivering man. That night, he beheld Christ in a dream, and to his astonishment Christ was wearing the portion of his cloak that he had donated out of mercy. In some versions of the story, when Martin woke up the next morning he found the cloak miraculously restored. Portions of the cloak subsequently became highly revered relics that reminded worshipers of this act of mercy and probably prompted them to act similarly toward the needy they encountered.

As the practice of charity took hold in both synagogue and church, it quickly became much more than an affair of righteous individuals. Confraternal organizations took root that assumed responsibilities for various classes of needy individuals. This will come as a surprise to many in our own day who think of organized programs of relief for the poor as the domain of government. But before the early modern period, lay confraternities assumed this role. An enlightening account of the effectiveness of these efforts can be gleaned from Maureen Flynn's excellent book *Sacred Charity: Confraternities and Social Welfare in Spain, 1400–1700.*[7] These confraternal organizations were diverse, some dedicating themselves to the sick (mentally and physically) and to wayfarers, others to orphans, and still others to young women bereft of a dowry. Perhaps the most famous of all of these is the hospital, an institution unknown in the Roman world and one that owes its existence to the religious virtue of charity. Even today, the legacy of these institutions can be seen. In Judaism, for example, one thinks of the *hevrah kadisha,* or burial society, that is in charge of attending to the remains of the dead.[8] Many members of this confraternity raced to lower Manhattan after the terrorist attack of September 11, 2001. And in almost any city within the United States one can glean from the names of the various hospitals that some originated (and sometimes are still operated) on religious grounds.

Modern people tend to think of charity to the poor in terms of overall efficiency and effectiveness. Governmental programs are designed to solve an immediate need but also to redress the circumstances that brought about the poverty in the first place. In large part that derives from the significant changes in political thought that emerged just a few centuries ago. There can be no question of the benefits of these developments and the interests many nations and international bodies have in ameliorating the effects of poverty and economic underdevelopment. But because our focus is so singularly set on these sorts of factors, one often misses the crucial variable that drove much of Christian history for its first fifteen hundred years: the promise that scripture provides that one could meet God in the face of the poor. Charity was, to put it briefly, a sacramental act. That is, an act that established a contact point between the believer and

God. To think of poverty as a social problem that could be solved was not really imaginable in the mindset of premodern man.[9]

Early in the development of the church, the giving of alms was linked to the celebration of the Eucharist. The connection is easy to understand; both acts celebrated a display of mercy. In the Eucharist, one re-presents the love Christ showed the world by the self-offering of his life. In alms-giving, the layperson has the opportunity to participate in this divine act by imitating that mercy in his or her daily actions. It is not accidental that the Eucharist and almsgiving were the two privileged means of channeling grace and dealing with the baneful effects of human sin.

The Reformers, as most are aware, rejected the Catholic teaching about the nature of the Mass. The Mass, in their minds, was not a sacrificial act that remitted sins. That, Luther and Calvin asserted, had been done once and for all at Calvary. To be sure, they would insist that the celebration of the "Last Supper" was sacramental. But the concrete "materiality" of the rite would, for the most part, be set aside. The Eucharistic elements would not be venerated apart from the Mass, there would be no Eucharistic processions, nor would there be any need for fasting or auricular confession before receiving the elements. Moreover, and perhaps most important, the Mass no longer played an ongoing mediatory role in the salvation of humankind. A Protestant, for example, would never ask that a Mass be said in the name of a beloved family member because the Mass could not add anything to salvific power of Christ's atoning death many centuries before. And similarly for the rite of almsgiving. The distinctively sacramental sense of Matthew 25 was uniformly rejected. Begging was discouraged, and the poor were no longer special guests at funerals on the grounds that their prayers were the most likely to be heard. As to the corporal acts of mercy of Matthew 25, Calvin declared: "It is foolish for monks and pinhead disputants of that sort to invent six works of mercy (as Christ mentions no more): as if even children could fail to understand that in synecdoche, all duties of love are being praised."[10]

The charitable deed lost, in the sixteenth century, its central role making God present to the believer and became simply a sign of the underlying personal faith of the believer. Bereft of this sacramental sensibility the donor no longer had any reason to meet the beggar in person. The needs of the indigent could be more ably assisted by civic organizations. To be sure, Protestant reforms of contemporary charitable practices were probably quite effective. A number of modern scholars have continued to make this point with great passion. Recently the great historian of the Reformation, Stephen Ozment, wrote an opinion piece in the *New York Times* praising the efforts of the young Luther:

> He made the care of the poor an organized, civic obligation by proposing that a common chest be put in every German town; rather than skimp along with the traditional practice of almsgiving to the needy and deserving native poor, Luther proposed that they received grants, or loans, from the chest. Each recipient would pledge to repay the borrowed amount after a timely recovery and return to self-sufficiency, thereby taking responsibility for both his neighbors and himself. This was love of one's neighbor through shared civic responsibility, what the Lutherans still call "faith begetting charity."[11]

Donations made to the poor anonymously through contributions to a "common chest" lessened considerably the possibilities of showing mercy to concrete human persons. But it was this virtue of the personal display of mercy that almsgiving was to intended to assist. On this point, Pope Leo the Great (d. 461 CE) was clear. Almsgiving, he claimed, was "so important that, though the other virtues exist without it, they can be of no avail. For although a person be full of faith, and chaste, and sober, and adorned with other still greater decorations, yet if he is not merciful, he cannot deserve mercy. For the Lord says 'blessed are the merciful for God shall have mercy on them' (Matt 5:7)."[12] In addition, Leo claimed that Christ's becoming man entailed a double impoverishment. In the incarnation, he not only entered into solidarity with humanity at large but identified himself specifically with the poor. To give support to the poor was a means for the believer to enact his faith in the Christological mystery. As God had deigned to condescend to the unimaginable depths of the mortal person, so those who would claim to be God's people must similarly condescend to the poorest of the poor. It is in the concrete act of assisting a poor person that one meets Christ. Taking revulsion at the misery of the poor implied a rejection of God's self-impoverishment in the incarnation. The two were inextricably bound.

This deeply sacramental understanding of the poor person as mediator of the Godhead put a high value on the act of begging. But it was precisely this activity that was getting out of hand in the sixteenth century. As the population of early modern Europe grew, increasing migration to urban areas eventually swamped the traditional means of handling poverty. The powers of the confraternities were stretched to their breaking point. Pressure to reform traditional practices was growing. Begging, as a result, became a matter of controversy even in Catholic areas. Eventually the confraternities had to cede their ground and allow charitable activities to become part of the public sector. Civic authorities could enact policies that were far more economically efficient than those found in voluntary religious organizations.

But one should not downplay the religious differences that still remained. Maureen Flynn's account of the Catholic reforms in Spain in the wake of the Reformation and the Council of Trent make this very clear. If we had to boil them down to a single factor it would be the role that human action would play in the channeling of divine grace from heaven to earth. Protestants worried about the value of good works as compromising the grace that God had shown in Christ, whereas Catholics insisted that one must participate in that salvation through the sacrament of the Eucharist and the doing of almsdeeds. The differences are well repre- sented in the will of the Protestant Edward Hoppay (1548), where we read of his insistence that the merits of Christ alone have secured his salvation. As far as the "wealth of his soul" is concerned, "the faith that I have takyn and reherced is sufficient, as I believe, without any other man's work or works. . . . I accepte non in hevyn, neither in earthe, to be my mediatour betwixt God and me, but he onlie." Later in the will, when he touches on the funds to be disbursed as charity, he prays that they "be accepted as the fructes of faithe" and not be conceived as merit-worthy, for his merit "is faithe in Jesus Christe only." How different this is from the will of Henry VIII himself (1547), who left a considerable sum of money for the poor in hopes that they would pray "heartily unto God for remission of our offenses and the wealth of our soul."[13]

This somewhat lengthy discussion of Reformation attitudes toward charity may seem out of place for a book dedicated to the biblical period. But I will claim that one must always keep one eye cocked in this direction when studying the theology of charity in these early sources because frequently modern historians read the Bible through the lens of their various confessional and modern prejudices. The great historian of Greco- Roman religions Jonathan Z. Smith once observed that the "pursuit of . . . the questions of Christian origins takes us back persistently to the same point: *Protestant anti-Catholic apologetics.* . . . The same presuppositions, the same rhetorical tactics, indeed, in the main the very same data exhib- ited in these early efforts underlie much of our present-day research."[14] And nowhere is that more true than in the subject of almsgiving as a merit-worthy deed. In large part this is because the sacramental aspect of almsgiving allowed it to play a leading role in the doctrine of purgatory. And purgatory was, of course, one of the most hotly contested items of the early modern period. It is my contention that our contemporary lack of appreciation for the sacramental side to charity has been occasioned by the ramifications of these reformation debates. They continue to hamper what even Catholic scholars are able to see. When we turn to the biblical teaching about the treasury in heaven, we must bracket those debates and enter a world in which the poor were thought to be, unarguably, the central portal to the wealth of God's kingdom. One should not undervalue the literal sense of Matthew 25:31–46 for the early church.

PART ONE

Charity as an Expression of Faith in God

CHAPTER TWO

Charity as Service to God

The one who returns a kindness offers choice flour,
and one who gives alms sacrifices a thank offering.
—Ben Sira 35:2

You honor this altar indeed, because it receives Christ's body [at the Eucharist].
But the poor man, who is himself the body of Christ, you treat with scorn. . . .
You can see this altar lying around everywhere, both in streets and in market
places, and you can sacrifice upon it every hour; for on this too is sacrifice
performed.
—St. John Chrysostom, Homily on 2 Corinthians

In his book on generosity in the Greco-Roman world, Paul Veyne asks
his readers to imagine themselves in an airplane flying over the ruins
of a large Roman city. The public buildings erected by means of charitable bequests include the public theater, the baths, and various basilicas
devoted to governmental functions. So enormous are the visible remains
of these great institutions that the observer might conclude that they cover
more ground than that allotted to domestic housing. If, on the other hand,
we flew over a great medieval city, the picture changes considerably.
Instead of theaters and baths, one sees the roofs of convents, hospices,
orphanages, and soup kitchens for the poor.[1] Charitable activity left an
enormous and visible footprint on the design of the evolving Christian city.

Though the social scientist might be tempted to understand the buildings of the two towns as serving one purpose—the redistribution of

15

wealth—this conclusion would be false. Generosity in a Christian context, Veyne contends, differed considerably from its pagan counterpart. What made the charitable works of the church distinctive was their religious grounding and singular focus on the abject poor. In contrast, Greco-Roman benefactors had little interest in helping the lower social classes and did not think of their donations as having a religious function. Homes for the elderly, orphanages, and hospitals, Veyne observes, are institutions that appeared suddenly in the late Roman era and always in the wake of the expansion of the Christian church.[2] New words, in fact, had to be invented in both Latin and Greek to identify these charitable organizations, a sure sign that they had no precedent; they were the fruits of this new religion.

In this book, I want to explore the biblical grounds for the emergence of these distinctive religious practices. To begin that exploration we need to take a slightly different starting point from that of Veyne. Though his study provides us with an accurate picture of the contrast between Greco-Roman and Christian modes of public benefaction, it is important to be clear from the very start that the distinguishing marks of the church were the result of the inheritance it received from the synagogue. My story will thus begin with the picture of charity as it is found in the books of the Hebrew Bible and in early Judaism.

It would be difficult, in fact, to overemphasize the importance of charitable deeds in the Jewish tradition. Nachmanides, a well-known Jewish thinker from the Middle Ages, once said that he had no need to provide specific references to the subject of charity in earlier rabbinic writings because they are chock full of examples.[3] One way to gauge the evolving importance of the subject is simply to consult a Hebrew dictionary. As any Jew or student of biblical languages will know, the word for commandment in Hebrew is *mitsva*. During the biblical period the meaning of this word was centered on the idea that God had given a set of rules to Moses at Mount Sinai that Israel was expected to observe. Each one of the rules—whether it concerned matters of ritual purity, kosher regulations, or instructions regarding ethics and morals—could be identified as a mitsva. In postbiblical Jewish texts, however, the term undergoes a radical transformation. It develops the secondary meaning of "charity." Thus the well-known expression *bar mitzvah*, whose primary meaning is "one obligated to keep the commandments," could also mean "a generous person." Charity toward the poor had become the commandment that towered above all others. One rabbinic text puts it succinctly: Giving alms is equal to keeping all the commandments in the Torah.[4]

But the importance of charity is not limited to texts; it also shaped the practice of Judaism, and its near relation Christianity, in the first few centuries CE. This is evident from the writings of the Roman Emperor Julian (fourth century), known as "the Apostate." Raised in a Christian home, Julian witnessed the brutal murder of his father and other family members at the tender age of six. He subsequently blamed this tragedy on the Emperor Constantius, a man who professed to be a Christian. Forever turned off to the claims of this religion that had only recently become licit, Julian embarked on a campaign to revive traditional Greco-Roman religion. In one of his letters he exhorts a pagan high priest in Galatia to provide food for the poor in order to combat the success of his Jewish and Christian competitors. Having allocated enormous supplies to the province of Galatia, he gives specific orders that "one-fifth of this be used for the poor who serve the priests, and the remainder be distributed by us to strangers and beggars. For it is disgraceful that, when no Jew ever has to beg, and the impious Galilaeans support not only their own poor but ours as well, all men see that our people lack aid from us."[5]

Charity as Service to God

Julian not only confirms the observation of Veyne that the church took a decided interest in the plight of the poor, he also recognizes that this interest was a direct result of a perceived *religious* obligation. For the student of comparative religion, the striking feature of Julian's letter is the stress he puts on the duty of *priests* to distribute food to the poor. This was a radically new idea in the Greco-Roman world, for pagan religion was primarily a cultic affair concerned with service to the altar, maintenance of standards of purity, and other ritual decorum. The plight of the poor was not felt to be a major concern of the gods.[6] It was presumably for that reason that Julian's attempt to transform the pagan temple into a food depot never got off the ground. Religions are, for the most part, deeply conservative in nature, and when innovation arises, there has to be some sort of continuity with the past.

Yet Julian's desire for reform did not emerge out of nowhere. He clearly saw that the commitment of both the church and the synagogue to the care of the poor was a very effective means of solidifying support for their respective religions. For in Jewish and Christian thought, charity to the poor was not simply a kind thing to do. It was *avodah,* a privileged means of serving God.

Let's pause for a moment on this thought. Most religious persons consider charity to the poor a natural outgrowth of their faith, something like the correlation between a good education and success in a career. In both cases what is primary, service to God / service to mind, has some beneficial but still secondary effects, love for the poor / advancement in society. But this is precisely what I don't mean when I say that providing for the poor is avodah. By the close of the biblical period, service to the poor had become *the* privileged way to serve God.

One can see this in two of our earliest sources for the importance of almsgiving, the Jewish apocryphal books of Tobit and Sirach. (Though both books were written in Hebrew, they did not become part of the Jewish Bible.) The former was probably written in the third or second century before Christ and the latter in the second.[7] Though the full form of Tobit was best preserved in Greek, we do possess fragments of both an Aramaic and a Hebrew version of the work. Scholars differ as to which of these two was the original.

Tobit opens with a brief account of the exile of the Northern Kingdom in 721 BCE. Tobit is among those individuals who were carried away to Assyria. Once the narrator has provided this background, Tobit's own voice takes up the story line. In his very first words, Tobit puts special emphasis on the acts of charity that he performed among his brethren:

> I, Tobit, walked in the ways of truth and righteousness all the days of my life. I performed many acts of charity for my kindred and people who had gone with me in exile to Nineveh in the land of the Assyrians. (1:3)

But before being provided with any details about those "many acts of charity," we are given a brief flashback to the life Tobit once led in the land of Israel.

> When I was in my own country, in the land of Israel, while I was still a young man, the whole tribe of my ancestor Naphtali deserted the house of David and Jerusalem. This city had been chosen from among all the tribes of Israel, where all the tribes of Israel should offer sacrifice and where the temple, the dwelling of God, had been consecrated and established for all generations forever. All my kindred and our ancestral house of Naphtali sacrificed to the calf that King Jeroboam of Israel had erected in Dan and on all the mountains of Galilee. But I alone went often to Jerusalem for the festivals, as it is prescribed for all Israel

by an everlasting decree. I would hurry off to Jerusalem with the first fruits of the crops and the firstlings of the flock, the tithes of the cattle, and the first shearings of the sheep. I would give these to the priests, the sons of Aaron, at the altar; likewise the tenth of the grain, wine, olive oil, pomegranates, figs, and the rest of the fruits to the sons of Levi who ministered at Jerusalem. Also for six years I would save up a second tenth in money and go and distribute it in Jerusalem. A third tenth I would give to the orphans and widows and to the converts who had attached themselves to Israel. I would bring it and give it to them in the third year, and we would eat it according to the ordinance decreed concerning it in the law of Moses. (1:4–8)

Once this flashback has been completed we return to the story of Tobit among the exiles in Assyria. As a result of this special devotion to the Torah (vv. 10–11), God grants him considerable favor with the Assyrian king (vv. 12–15). He rises to a position of considerable prominence in the royal court. At this point Tobit returns to the theme of charity:

In the days of Shalmaneser I performed many acts of charity to my kindred, those of my tribe. I would give my food to the hungry and my clothing to the naked; and if I saw the dead body of any of my people thrown out behind the wall of Nineveh, I would bury it. (1:16–17)

What is striking about these two verses is that they pick up so clearly the content of Tobit's opening words (*"and I performed many acts of charity* to my kindred and my people who had gone with me in exile to Nineveh in the land of the Assyrians" [v. 3]). A historical critic might be inclined to see the account of Tobit's devotion to the temple in Jerusalem that is found between these two sections (vv. 4–9) as a textual insertion because the narrative had opened with an observation about Tobit's devotion to Torah in the Diaspora, only to return to the same point once it had informed us of Tobit's devotion to the temple.[8]

I do not believe, however, that this is a good reading of our text. The reason for our author's peculiar form of narration derives from the content of what is narrated. In our outer frame (v. 3 and vv. 16–17) we find what will become one of the most important themes of the book: the virtue of acting charitably (*gemilut hasadim* in rabbinic parlance), in which pride of place will go to the giving of alms (*tsedaqa*). Within the inner frame (vv. 4–9) we find an account of Tobit's punctilious responsibility toward his sacrificial responsibilities in Jerusalem. Whether at home or abroad, Tobit distinguishes himself in Torah observance: at home by service to the altar, abroad by deeds of charity.

Our author understands charity as a fit alternative to sacrifice. It is striking to find this concept already in a work dating to the third or second century BCE because many believe that this idea comes into focus only once the temple was destroyed by the Romans in 70 CE. One recalls the famous story about Rabbi Yohanan ben Zakkai, who comforted his disciple Rabbi Yehoshua after the Roman invasion. Rabbi Yehoshua lamented the sorry state that Israel was in due to the loss of the temple, where sins were atoned. Rabbi Yohanan famously replied: "Be not grieved, my son. There is another equally meritorious way of gaining ritual atonement, even though the temple is destroyed. We can still gain ritual atonement through deeds of loving-kindness. For it is written, 'deeds of charity I desire, not sacrifice' (Hosea 6:6)."[9]

Yet before one concludes too hastily on the strength of Tobit and Rabbi Yohanan that charitable deeds assume this value only in the absence of an altar, one should consider the evidence of Ben Sira. For this writer not only lived while the temple was still standing but also lauded its liturgical rites. Some scholars think he was a priest himself. Be that as it may, we find within the writings of Ben Sira vivid testimony that charity and sacrifice were comparable deeds.[10] Consider the following:

> With all your soul fear the Lord,
>   and revere his priests.
> With all your might love your Maker,
>   and do not neglect his ministers.
> Fear the Lord and honor the priest,
>   and give him his portion, as you have been commanded:
> the first fruits, the guilt offering, the gift of the shoulders,
>   the sacrifice of sanctification, and the first fruits of the holy things.
>
> Stretch out your hand to the poor,
>   so that your blessing may be complete.
> Give graciously to all the living,
>   do not withhold kindness even from the dead.
> Do not avoid those who weep,
>   but mourn with those who mourn.
> Do not hesitate to visit the sick,
>   because for such deeds you will be loved.
> In all you do, remember the end of your life,
>   and then you will never sin. (7:29–36)

In these two adjacent units, Ben Sira compares two different classes of people through which one can demonstrate one's reverence for God: first the priests ("With all your soul fear the Lord and revere his priests . . ."), then the poor ("Stretch out your hand to the poor . . ."). Fearing the Lord means both honoring the priest—that is, providing him with the requisite temple donations—and stretching out one's hand to the poor. Only with both priest and poor in view, Ben Sira teaches, may "your blessing be complete."

The comparison of almsgiving to a sacrificial offering is met frequently in the book of Ben Sira. Clearly, it is basic to his religious worldview. For example, in 35:1–2 it is stated that

> The one who keeps the law makes many offerings;
>> one who heeds the commandments makes an offering of well-being.
> The one who returns a kindness offers choice flour,
>> and one who gives alms sacrifices a thank offering.

It is worth noting that a thank offering is simply a special type of an offering of well-being, and that choice flour, because it is the most inexpensive of the sacrificial objects one can bring, is something that can be brought *many* times. What Ben Sira teaches us is that the acts of charity toward the poor became the equivalent of temple sacrifice even while the temple was standing. In other words, Tobit's high valuation of such acts of charity should not be explained solely on the grounds of its setting in the Diaspora.

It is not simply the case that the opening chapter has enveloped Tobit's devotion to the temple with an account of his generosity. There is a larger parallel in terms of plot as well. For prior to the invasion of the Assyrians, Tobit fulfills the mandate to serve God in Jerusalem at considerable cost to his person. Three factors make that responsibility difficult. First, in order to travel to Jerusalem he is forced to violate the policy of the state which mandates that all such sacrifices be brought to one of the northern cult centers in Dan or Bethel (1 Kings 12:25–33). Violating such state policies would have put Tobit's very life at risk. Second, because Tobit hails from the tribe of Naphtali, which was located at the far northern end of the kingdom, he has an extremely long journey in order to deliver his offerings to Jerusalem. Third, because Tobit is unique among his peers in making such a pilgrimage to Jerusalem, he must have become something of a pariah among his neighbors. All three of these factors highlight Tobit's high degree of commitment in fulfilling the demands of the Mosaic Torah.

After his exile, Tobit renews his commitment to Torah by devoting himself to deeds of charity that include the giving of alms and the burial of the dead. This commitment also comes at considerable personal cost. Not only does the burial of the dead go against the policy of the state, but Tobit perseveres in the practice of these deeds even when his own life is threatened (1:18–20). Finally, to make matters worse, he has to endure the taunts of his neighbors while he fulfills his religious obligations (2:8). Whether it is the obligation to offer sacrifice or to provide charity, Tobit goes to extreme lengths to demonstrate his piety and devotion to God. In sum, the book of Tobit has created a strong parallel framework between the obligation to deliver one's offerings to Jerusalem and to act charitably in the Diaspora.

The theology that begins in the books of Tobit and Sirach has an extraordinary afterlife in both the church and the synagogue. As we have already observed, the pagan emperor Julian felt that charity was the defining marker of Christian and Jewish identity. One visible testimony to the longevity of this idea can be seen in medieval art. Consider, for example, a painting from about 1400 by Andrea de Bartolo of Siena (figure 1). This painting is now on display at the National Gallery of Art in Washington, D.C., and has been slightly mislabeled *Joachim and the Beggars*. In Christian tradition, Joachim is the father of the Blessed Virgin Mary and is considered to be a very pious Jew. One can, indeed, see Joachim distributing goods to the poor. Nonetheless, the labeling is incomplete because it fails to mention that Joachim's wife, Anna, who is standing right beside him, is donating a jar of grain to the priest. Through the hands of this couple, God is served in two ways: by a direct gift to the temple and by the giving of alms. Service to the altar and the poor is a correlative activity.

Though Joachim and Anna lived in biblical times, their piety is not just of antiquarian interest. We find the correlation between almsgiving and service of the altar to be a standard theme in other medieval paintings that depict contemporary Christian life. Consider an image from a Book of Hours in the collection at the Walters Art Gallery (figure 2). The central thematic concern of this painting is the freeing of souls from purgatory. Notice that souls are painfully paying the price for their sins on earth at the bottom of the image while angels assist their departure for heaven at the far left. Yet at the central and focal point of the image, we see a priest who has ascended several steps in order to offer the Eucharistic sacrifice at the altar, while immediately to the right a man distributes goods to the poor. As Stephen Greenblatt has noted, there are many images from the Middle Ages like this one.[11] They graphically depict the theology derived from

Figure 1   Andrea de Bartolo of Siena, *Joachim and the Beggars,* ca. 1400
(Courtesy of the National Gallery of Art, Washington, D.C.)

Proverbs 10:2, that charity toward the poor delivers one from eternal
perdition—a subject to which we shall return in Chapter 4.

In pondering visual images like these, it is hard for me not to link them
to a well-known homily of St. John Chrysostom from late-fourth-century

Figure 2   Correlation of the sacrifice of the Mass and almsgiving; detail
from a Book of Hours with Paris Calendar, 1450–60 (Courtesy of The
Walters Art Gallery, Baltimore: MS W.274, fol. 118)

Antioch. He begins by acknowledging the honor that his congregation shows toward the altar in his church. The altar is worthy of such veneration, he explains, "because it receives Christ's body." But this is not the only altar to be found in Antioch. "Whenever then you see a poor believer," out on the streets of Antioch after Mass has ended, "imagine that you behold an altar. Whenever you meet a beggar, don't insult him, but reverence him."[12]

A Tithe for the Poor

Though most of us have been raised to think that God is beyond any sort of material need, the concept of a temple requires that we temporarily suspend these assumptions in order to understand the anthropomorphic language of the Bible's authors. The temple is the place where God "dwells" and is provided with a throne for sitting, a lamp for seeing, and an altar where his savory food is prepared. The altar is that spot whereby meat, grain, and oil can be directly transported to the divine realm. To be sure, the Bible elsewhere will qualify these straightforward claims as to how the temple "contains" God (see, for example, Isaiah 66:1: "Heaven is my throne and the earth is my footstool; what is the house that you would build for me, and what is my resting place?"). But the priestly literature I am speaking about takes the divine indwelling of the temple with deadly seriousness. Encroaching on the divine domain could cost you your life (Lev 10:1–3).[13]

So what happens when we take this anthropomorphic image and carry it over to almsgiving? If the altar has the special capacity of being able to convey food to God, then the hand of the poor, similarly, must be able to transfer funds from earth to heaven. Jewish beggars in Late Antiquity used to address their potential patrons with the words *zeki bi*, literally: "acquire a merit through me," or, more periphrastically, "make a deposit to your heavenly treasury through me."[14] In speaking this way they were simply repeating a common wisdom tradition that had already appeared in the books of Sirach and Tobit. The idea of a "heavenly bank" was born, and along with it the idea that making a deposit to this bank was like making a loan to God.

But here I get a bit ahead of myself. Let's return our focus to the issue of correlating service of altar and service to the poor. That they are correlated has been well illustrated in the books of Tobit and Ben Sira, but why did such a correlation emerge in the first place?

The best place to turn for an explanation is the book of Deuteronomy, a work that deeply shaped the book of Tobit. The hero of that tale distinguished himself at the beginning of the work by refusing to bring his offerings to the two provincial cult sites that the King Jeroboam had set up several centuries earlier when he separated from the kingdom of Judah and its capital city, Jerusalem. Thrice annually, during Israel's pilgrimage festivals, Tobit made the long trek to Jerusalem to fulfill the central command of the book of Deuteronomy—to offer his sacrifices at the altar in Jerusalem. "Take care," Moses had commanded, "that you do not offer your burnt offerings at any place you happen to see. But only at the place that the LORD will choose" (Deut 12:13–14).

At the end of the law code embedded in the book of Deuteronomy (chapters 12–26), Moses returns to the issue of gifts brought to the temple. In this memorable chapter that brings the laws to a close, he teaches the Israelites what they must declare when they bring their first fruits to the temple (26:1–11). He then turns to the subject of what will become known as the "tithe for the poor" (vv. 12–16). According to Deuteronomy, one must bring a tithe to the sanctuary during years one, two, four, and five of a seven-year cycle (14:22–27). That tithe was to be consumed by the donor and his family in Jerusalem during the days of the festivals. In addition, a portion of that tithe was to be shared with the Levites, who had no arable land of their own. In years three and six, this regular festival tithe was replaced by a tithe for the poor. (In the seventh year the fields were fallow; no tithes were brought.) What is distinctive about this tithe is that it is not brought to Jerusalem and given to the personnel at the temple (cf. Numbers 18) but stored and redistributed locally:

> Every third year you shall bring out the full tithe of your produce for that year, and store it within your towns; the Levites, because they have no allotment or inheritance with you, as well as the resident aliens, the orphans, and the widows in your towns, may come and eat their fill so that the LORD your God may bless you in all the work that you undertake. (14:28–29)

Mandating that the tithe be stored in a local town, rather than taken to a sanctuary, was a radical innovation in Deuteronomy. Tithes were normally thought of as *sacred* offerings because of the way they were treated—they were brought to a temple. But the Deuteronomic law code represents a dramatic innovation in Israelite religion. Before this book was promulgated as authoritative writ in 621 BCE, during the reign of King Josiah,

Israelites regularly brought their tithes and offerings to various local sanc-
tuaries. When Deuteronomy commanded that every sacrifice be brought
to Jerusalem alone, some legal adjustments had to be made in order to
accommodate this practice. One of them had to do with gifts to the poor.
It would have been highly impractical to require every Israelite to bring
monies dedicated to the poor all the way to Jerusalem only to redirect
them back to the far-flung provinces. In order to facilitate the distribution
of these goods to the poor, Deuteronomy enacted a law that allowed the
Israelites to store these tithes within their local province. "Every third
year," Moses commands, "you shall bring out the full tithe of your produce
for that year, *and store it within your towns.*"

But the original sacral sense of this tithe was not eliminated altogether.
This becomes evident in the way in which this tithe is treated at the close
of the law code of Deuteronomy. Having just articulated the liturgical
declaration that the Israelite was to pronounce when he brought his first
fruits to the temple, the chapter adds a declaration that must be made
when paying one's tithes:

> When you have finished paying all the tithe of your produce in the third year . . .
> giving it to the Levites, the aliens, the orphans, and the widows, so that they
> may eat their fill within your towns, then you shall say before the LORD your
> God: "I have removed the sacred portion from the house and I have given it to
> the Levites, the resident aliens, the orphans, and the widows, in accordance
> with your entire commandment that you commanded me; I have neither trans-
> gressed nor forgotten any of our commandments:
>
> I have not eaten of it while in mourning; I have not removed any of it while I
> was unclean; and I have not offered any of it to the dead. I have obeyed the
> LORD my God, doing just as you commanded me. Look down from your holy
> habitation, from heaven, and bless your people Israel and the ground that you
> have given us, as you swore to our ancestors—a land flowing with milk and
> honey." (Deut 26:12–15)

It is striking that this text continues to refer to the tithe as a "sacred
portion"—language normally reserved for donations to the altar—even
though it is never taken to Jerusalem. It is also striking that the Israelite
must declare that he has not eaten any of it while in mourning, nor removed
any of it while he was unclean. As Gerhard von Rad observed:

> These precepts are based on the very ancient idea of the material effect of the
> unclean on the clean. . . . The main concern of these precepts is therefore to
> make sure of the undefiled ritual cleanness of the tithe offering. *All this can*

surely only be understood as indicating that the solemn profession was recited
originally when conveying the gift to [Yhwh] and not to the poor of the locality.[15]

The value of Von Rad's insight should not be underestimated. Already in
the law code of Deuteronomy we see the beginnings of the sacralization of
gifts to the poor. One might have thought that allowing the tithe to be
stored in local cities away from the temple would have spelled the end of
its status as a sacral donation. But on the contrary, the public declaration
about the tithe taught the layperson that this donation to the poor was a
sacred gift and so subject to the laws of purity that pertained to the altar.

It is worth recalling that in the first chapter of the book of Tobit, when
he recounts his dedication to the temple in Jerusalem, he begins by
mentioning the obligation to bring the first fruits ("I would hurry off to
Jerusalem with the first fruits of the crops and the firstlings of the flock")
and ends with the tithe he distributed to the poor—presumably in the
environs of Naphtali ("A third tithe I would give to the orphans and widows
and to the converts who had attached themselves to Israel. I would bring
it and give it to them in the third year"). In describing his actions this way,
Tobit was taking care to fulfill the obligations that Deuteronomy 26 had
put in place. In other words, even when he still resided in the land of
Israel, Tobit was a dedicated servant of the poor, and he considered this
obligation as sacral in nature.

A Loan to God

Deuteronomy emerges as a key book for the story that I would like to tell.
On the one hand, in a completely unintended fashion, it prepared the way
for important developments that would take place during the exile (and
even after the final destruction of the temple in 70 CE), for, by putting the
temple at such a great distance from the daily life of the average Israelite,
it brought into being forms of religious devotion that did not require a
temple. One of the ways it did this was by retaining the sacral notion of the
poor man's tithe even when it was not brought to an altar. Tobit is a key
piece in this larger puzzle because, on the one hand, he looks forward to
the development of a temple-less rabbinic religion (as we noted with Rabbi
Yohanan ben Zakkai earlier). But if one looks backward in time, his actions
can be construed as simply a natural development of the logic found
already embedded in Deuteronomy 26. He begins his account of his

former obligations to the temple with the matter of first fruits (vv. 1–11) and concludes with the tithe for the poor (vv. 12–15). This conclusion is surprising, of course, because it speaks not to his devotion to Jerusalem per se but to his devotion to serving the poor outside the temple, exactly the position in which he finds himself in the Diaspora.

But I have left one item unaccounted for. I began by making a simple comparison: just as the altar is a conduit for food, so the hand of the poor is a conduit for money. What I have not done justice to is the question why the gift was understood as a loan. If we can presume for the moment that the idea of the loan has a logical grounding in Israelite culture, the next question would be, why did the concept of a loan become so immensely popular in early Judaism and Christianity? Why would the words of a common beggar in the streets of Israel in Talmudic times have been: "Make a deposit to your heavenly treasury through me"? Clearly the notion of a heavenly bank had sunk deeply into the soul of postbiblical religion.

No doubt part of the answer is grounded in the fact that non-interest-bearing loans were one of the primary means to assist the poor in biblical times. A habit, we might add, that continued into postbiblical Judaism as well.[16]

But another part of the answer is related to the phenomenology of religious life itself. To be obedient to the demands of the covenant presumes a high degree of faith in God. But the same is true, at a different register, to be sure, for the world of banking. As every creditor knows, to give someone a loan also requires an ample sum of trust. Ben Sira was not naïve about such matters when he informed his students that "many will regard their loan as a windfall and cause trouble to those who help them" (29:4). Though they speak deferentially when requesting the money, they become indignant when repayment is due. As a result, Ben Sira concluded, "many refuse to lend, not because of meanness, but from fear of being defrauded" (29:7).

If these warnings are true of borrowers even in the best of circumstances, then one would expect Ben Sira to be even sterner when it comes to making a loan to the truly down and out. But his stance is just the opposite. He commends his students to disburse their funds without a moment's forethought. "Lose your silver for the sake of [the poor]," he exhorts, and "lay up your treasure [in heaven]," for there "it will profit you more than gold" (29:10–11). A puzzling piece of advice for one who is so sober minded about the risks that attend a loan. Whence this confidence?

The answer lies in what the Jewish tradition calls a midrash, that is, a commentary on a portion of the scriptural text. In this particular tradition, Rabbi Gamaliel is approached by a Roman citizen and questioned about the rationality of his holy book. Can it be true, this gentile asks (quoting Deut 15:7, "loan liberally and be ungrudging when you do so"), that your God commands you to give to the poor without a moment's hesitation? Someone who conducted his affairs in this fashion would be out of money within days and in need of assistance himself! To which Rabbi Gamaliel responds:

> "What if a man appeared out of nowhere and asked you for money, would you give him it?"
> He replied, "No!"
> "But what if he brought you a deposit?"
> He replied, "Of course!"
> "Okay, but what if he brought you a commoner to cosign [literally, to go surety]?"
> He replied, "No."
> "But what if the governor himself cosigned?"
> He replied, "By all means!"
> "Well then, isn't the scriptural commandment logical: If you will issue the loan when the governor cosigns, how much more willing should you be when 'He who spoke and made the world' agrees to cosign. For scripture says, 'Whoever is kind to the poor lends to the LORD, and will be repaid in full'" (Prov 19:17).[17]

It would be difficult to exaggerate how important this verse from the book of Proverbs was for Judaism and Christianity (and eventually even Islam).[18] Among early Christian writers, this saying became one of the most cited sources in support of charitable giving. Indeed, the references are so numerous and diverse in approach that one could write a dissertation on the history of the interpretation of this verse alone. In this book we will merely scratch the surface. But one text deserves special mention because it is a near contemporary to our rabbinic tale. It originates from the pen of St. Basil, one of the most formidable theologians of the early church and a man who spent a good part of his life in Caesarea, the great Roman port just north of modern day Tel Aviv. Though he knew no Hebrew and probably was unaware of the story about Rabbi Gamaliel, astoundingly he sounds many of the same notes.

Basil begins by observing that when one assists the poor, one both offers a gift and issues a loan. It is a gift, Basil explains, "because of the expectation of no repayment, but a loan because of the great gift of the Master who pays in his place."[19] Basil goes on to say that though God has received mere "trifling things through a poor man," he will, in the end, "give great things in return." This is a remarkable text, for it underscores what I have been calling the *sacrificial* character of charity. One might think that the poor man alone benefits from charity and that God, residing in heaven, takes note of the good deed done to another and lays aside the requisite reward. But Basil says something quite different. It is not merely the poor but God himself who receives these "trifling things." God, as it were, resides (becomes incarnate) among the destitute. The vertical nature of this exchange recalls what we learned earlier from the words of the Jewish beggar: "Acquire a merit in heaven through a gift to me."

It is precisely the portrayal of the poor man as a point of linkage between heaven and earth that leads Basil to cite Proverbs 19:17 and to echo the words of Rabbi Gamaliel. Basil puts this question to his congregation: "If one of the rich men in the city would promise you payment on behalf of another, wouldn't you accept his pledge?" The implied answer, as in the midrash, is undoubtedly "Yes!" Who wouldn't make a loan that was guaranteed by a man of means? This leads Basil to his main point: "Yet you don't accept God as surety for the gift you would give to the poor." In exasperation over this lack of faith, Basil urges his audience to show faith in God and open up their pocket books: "Give the money, since it is lying idle, without weighing it down with additional charges, and it will be good for both of you. There will be for you [the donor] the assurance of the money's safety because of [God's] custody; for [the poor] who receives it, there is the advantage of its use. And, if you are seeking additional payment, be satisfied with that from the Lord. He Himself will pay the interest for the poor. Expect kindly acts from Him who is truly kind."

If we move just a few hundred miles to the east, into that portion of the Christian world that spoke Syriac (a dialect of Aramaic very similar to the Aramaic of rabbinic Jewry), we find a strikingly similar set of ideas. Let me illustrate this with the figure of St. Ephrem, a fourth-century Christian who lived in eastern Syria. In his hymns in praise of the holy man Abraham Kidunaya he wrote the following:

> Two heroic commandments: to love one's neighbor and God. You bore them like a yoke. Between man and God you sowed a beautiful deposit.
>
> You listened in order to act. You acted in order to issue a loan. You issued the loan so as to believe. You believed so as to receive. You received so as to reign.

> Your alms and prayers are like loans; in every location they enrich those who take them, while to you belongs the capital and interest. What you offer as a loan returns to you.
>
> The alms of the giver are like a loan that the just give. For it is in the full possession of both the borrower and the lender. For it returns to him with interest.[20]

Just like the rabbis and Basil, Ephrem understands the charitable deed in terms of an economic metaphor. The alms that Abraham Kidunaya gives are likened to loans. On the one hand, they require faith. "You acted in order to issue a loan," Ephrem observes, but "you issued the loan *so as to believe.*" On the other hand, they provide some unusual economic benefits. Whereas the collection of interest normally benefits the creditor and harms the debtor, just the opposite is true for the divine economy. The debtor owes no interest while the creditor collects it just the same. This is because the giving of alms is not just a horizontal, this-worldly affair. When one treats the poor kindly, one finds oneself before the altar of God.

My account of charity in this book will divide into two parts. First, we shall take a look at the scriptural sources for the notion that charity is a loan made to God. As I mentioned in Chapter 1, the tradition of understanding charity in this fashion has not been well received in the modern period. I will contend that a major reason for that has been the tendency to focus too narrowly on the moral status of the donor. What we shall see in the book of Proverbs and in Ben Sira—the ultimate sources of the idea that almsgiving is a loan to God that funds a treasury in heaven—is a very different set of concerns. For these writers, the concept of a heavenly treasury is used in order to describe the type of world that God has fashioned. The emphasis, in other words, is not on moral agency but on the nature of the created order (in other words, a matter of *ontology*). Because the Holy One of Israel is a God of mercy, the world that he has made is an expression of that mercy. Benefiting from charity isn't so much about advancing one's self-interest (though this cannot be completely factored out of the equation) as it is about giving testimony to the love of God inscribed in the natural order.

Though these ancient writers do not share the secularizing dimensions of modern life, they were well aware of the counterintuitive nature, even in their own day, of the claims they were making. For ancient persons did not instinctively view the world as ordered to the flourishing of those who were generous. For them, just as for many evolutionary biologists, the world often manifested itself as "red in tooth and claw."[21] It took a considerable amount of faith to act as though things were different. The writers we will examine spend so much time on the problem of charity because they are well aware of the startling nature of the claims they are making. A key feature in the material we will be examining over the first several chapters of this book is that of faith. Using the books of Ben Sira and Tobit as our guides, we shall plumb the depths of charity as a claim about the character of God that calls forth such faith.

The second half of the book approaches from a slightly different angle the matter of charity as a loan to God. If the charitable deed is understood as a form of "currency" that is received by God, then there must be a location in heaven where it is stored. In Second Temple Jewish texts this spot came to be called the "treasury in heaven." In later rabbinic sources this idea was closely related to the concept of *zekut avot* ("the merits of the Fathers") and was comparable in many ways to the Catholic "treasury of merits." But whatever the terminology, the idea is the same—charitable deeds constitute a storable commodity whose benefits can be withdrawn at a later date. Though the development as I will trace it appears natural and hardly surprising, the concept of storable good deeds that can be drawn on later became one of the flashpoints of the Reformation. Especially controversial was the claim that reward due on a good deed could be transferred to another after his or her death—an idea that was fundamental to the doctrine of purgatory. As a result of conflicts like this, many of the texts that we shall encounter in the second half of this book have been sites of bitter contestation over the past several centuries. We will need to be sensitive to the profound theological problems to which these texts give witness. But our purpose is not merely a toleration of fundamentally irresolvable differences. Rather we shall propose new ways of reading these controverted texts that we hope will take us beyond the highly volatile disagreements they have occasioned.

I should add one more point of clarification about the use of the term *charity* in this book. Its primary sense is that of providing material—often monetary—help for the poor. This is, in fact, what the Hebrew term *tsedaqa* means in late biblical and postbiblical Hebrew. This will remind some of the ubiquitous tsedaqa or poor boxes in the synagogue and church, respectively, into which congregants deposit their alms. But the word *charity* can also have a more general sense of any act of mercy shown to the helpless, a concept that is often expressed by the Hebrew word *hesed* in the expression *gemilut hasadim.*[22] The evidence of the Greek translation of the Hebrew Bible is important to note because it often uses one root term (*eleos, eleēmosunē*) to translate both Hebrew words when they mean charity for the poor. In other words, in the early postbiblical period *tsedaqa* and *hesed* were nearly synonymous. They referred to such actions as visiting the sick and burying the dead: in brief, what the Christian tradition identifies as the seven acts of corporal mercy.[23] But because charity was fundamentally construed as an act that funded a treasury in heaven, most of the sources we will be looking at put a premium on the idea of *monetary* assistance to the needy even as they allowed for other acts of mercy to fall under the umbrella of charitable action.

CHAPTER THREE

A Loan to God

crēdo: "to trust or believe in"—originally belonging to the language of business, "to give as a loan . . . " Hence, *crēditum,* "a loan."

—Lewis and Short, *A Latin Dictionary*

"Whoever is kind to the poor lends to the LORD, *and will be repaid in full"* (Prov 19:17). Had it not been written in scripture, it would have been impossible to say it!

—Babylonian Talmud, *Baba Bathra* 10a

If any would be benefactors to their souls, they should entrust (*crederet*) their goods to that one who is a suitable trustee of the poor and a most generous payer of interest. . . . But you, dearly beloved, who have believed (*credidistis*) the promises of the Lord with your whole heart, flee the foul leprosy of avarice and make a holy and wise use of God's gifts.

—Leo the Great, Homily 17

Almsgiving became such a prominent feature of Second Temple Judaism because it not only fulfilled a religious obligation to help the needy but provided a means of declaring one's belief in God. This will not be obvious to most readers and requires some unpacking. For those who have been raised in the church, belief in God is often thought of in terms of the creeds. Consider, for example, what the Nicene Creed says about Jesus Christ: "I believe in one Lord Jesus Christ, the only begotten son of God, born of the Father before all ages, God from God, Light from Light, true God from true God, consubstantial with the Father." Those

raised in the synagogue might recall the thirteen articles of faith formulated by the great medieval philosopher and Talmudist Moses Maimonides.
This famous summary of the Jewish faith is regularly recited during the
Sabbath service. Regarding the authority of the Jewish scriptures, it reads:
"I believe in complete faith that the words of the prophets are true, that
the prophecy of Moses our teacher, peace be upon him, was true and that
he was the chief of the prophets both of those who preceded and of those
who followed him."

For those raised outside the church or synagogue, these creedal affirma-
tions will sound audacious. How does one know that Jesus is truly consubstantial with the Father (granted that there is a divine Father!), or that
every word the biblical prophets spoke was true? If we start at the level of
established creed, believing in God may appear, as the White Queen put it
in *Alice in Wonderland*, like "believ[ing] six impossible things before
breakfast." True, such belief is within the realm of human possibility, but
why would I stake my life on what appears to be an arbitrary mustering of
the will?

The Jesuit priest Gerard Manley Hopkins (1844–89), one of the most
celebrated of the great Victorian poets, must have had similar feelings when
he sat down to write his dear friend Robert Bridges. In a famous passage
from this lengthy correspondence, Hopkins confesses his desire that Bridges
come to know the truth of the Christian faith. Strikingly Hopkins begins not
with doctrine but with the suggestion that Bridges give alms. "I daresay
indeed you do give alms," Hopkins adds, but "still I should say give more."
How much would be sufficient? Up to the point of personal inconvenience.
Why such hardship? Because the difference in mind between one who has
all the comforts of home at his fingertips and the man who is "pinched by his
own charity is too great for forecasting, it must be felt." The power of charity
should not be underestimated. "It changes the whole man," Hopkins
contended, "not his mind only but the will and everything."[1]

In his return post, Bridges suggested that telling him to give alms to the
point of personal inconvenience was like advising him to put on a hair
shirt. Hopkins countered this objection by saying that there is a big difference between being "short of money" (full stop) and being "short of money
for charity's sake." He concludes with these words: "And I take leave to
repeat and you cannot but see, that it is a noble thing and not a miserable
something or other to give alms and help the needy and [to] stint ourselves
for the sake of the unhappy and undeserving."[2]

It is important to observe that Hopkins is by no means original in the connection he draws between the act of giving alms and the disposition of having faith in God. Faith, we shall discover, is not reducible to mere *intellectual assent*, it is also a specific way of *enacting one's life* in the world. And it is from this pattern of enactment that a metaphysical portrait of the world begins to take shape.

Creditor as Believer

In a famous collection of ethical maxims known as *Pirqe Avot,* we encounter a story that speaks precisely to this point. In this tale Rabbi Yohanan ben Zakkai (one generation after Jesus) asks his disciples to characterize the difference between good and bad paths of living (*Avot* 2:9).[3] Rabbi Eliezer, the first to respond, contrasts a generous man with a miser; Rabbi Joshua says the difference is being a good or poor friend, whereas Rabbi Yosi focuses on being a good or poor neighbor. All of these comparisons are quite clear and need no elaborate commentary. But then Rabbi Shimon, a student whom his teacher has just characterized as one "who stood in fear of committing a sin" (*Avot* 2:8), breaks the mold of posing conventional moral dispositions. He declares that the good path is the ability "to see into the future" whereas the bad is "to borrow money and be unable to repay the debt."

At first blush, this is a surprising comparison. But a careful scrutiny of the process that goes into issuing a loan will cast considerable light on Rabbi Shimon's teaching. The person who borrows money does so in the expectation that in the future he will secure the means to repay his creditor. Thus the good path is the one that allows a person to see into the future. A person on such a path can borrow money in confidence that he will be able to repay what was loaned. The bad path allows no such knowledge. Though the person may have had the best of intentions, unforeseen contingencies (a sudden loss of employment, for example) may prevent him from paying off his debts.

But given that the future is unknowable, why, we might ask, would anyone issue a loan? The Bible shows how one could lessen the risk either by threatening to take a valuable object from the borrower and not returning it until the loan was repaid or by finding a friend or associate to provide a personal guarantee. The biblical idiom for the latter was "to go surety for someone," and it was essentially an act of being a cosigner to the loan.[4] Should the primary borrower not make good on the debt, the one who had gone surety would be responsible for the balance. Of course a third category also existed—that of charging interest for the loan. In this case, the risk of potential nonpayment was compensated for by the possibility of a very rich return. In the Bible, though, lending money at interest was allowed only if the loan was made to a foreigner.

The close relationship between issuing a loan and believing that it can be repaid can be illustrated from our present market situation as well. When we fill out an application for a loan, we are asked to disclose where we work, what we make, and how long we have held our job. These details provide a record that the bank takes as evidence about the stability of our income. Because loans involve risk, the banker who issues a loan must *believe* that the customer will be able to repay. The bank becomes your *creditor* (literally: one who *believes* in you) only when it delivers the money. That a bank establish reasonable grounds for such a belief is essential for the health of that society. For if enough people default, some banks will become insolvent and set in motion a freeze on credit ("belief") that would threaten the very viability of the market as a whole.

James Surowiecki, the financial correspondent for the *New Yorker* magazine, captured this dimension during the financial crisis of 2008 beautifully. Like the White Queen in *Alice and Wonderland,* too many bankers had believed six impossible things before breakfast:

> Fraud is a boom-time crime because it feeds on the faith of investors, and during bubbles that faith is overflowing. So while robbing a bank seems to be a demand-driven crime, robbing bank shareholders is all about supply. In the classic work on investor hysteria, "Manias, Panics, and Crashes," the economist Charles Kindleberger wrote that during bubbles "the supply of corruption increases . . . much like the supply of credit." This is more than a simple analogy: corruption and credit are stoked by the same forces. Cheap money engenders a surfeit of trust, and vice versa. (The word "credit" comes from the Latin for "believe.") The same overconfidence that leads investors and lenders to underestimate the risks of legitimate investments also leads them to underestimate the likelihood of fraud. . . . But in the past few years besotted investors were willing to believe lots of foolish things—like the idea that housing prices would just keep going up.[5]

Surowiecki begins with what many commentators have judged to be a leading cause for the near depression that the United States, Iceland, and much of western Europe entered at the close of 2008. In the years leading up to that debacle, banks had extended credit to a whole host of borrowers

whose creditworthiness was suspect, to say the least. Part of the justification for doing so was the belief that housing prices, as a finite commodity,
would continue to rise in price as the number of homeowners swelled.
The banks and other lending agencies presumed that this view into the
future made sense: should some of the riskier borrowers default on their
loans, the danger of financial loss would be minimized by the ability of the
bank to foreclose on a home that had appreciated in value. Thus, even if a
homeowner simply walked away from the property, the bank could resell
the home and reclaim the funds that it had lent in the first place.

Yet as the sources of credit began to expand, so did corruption. Spurred
on by a surfeit of trust, banks began to repackage and resell the loans they
had held in the form of mortgage-backed securities, all in the guise of both
minimizing risk and enhancing the yield for potential investors. Lulled into
complacency by the rating agencies that evaluated these new investment
vehicles, investment advisers happily sold these financial instruments
to hundreds of thousands of investors. In the middle of 2008, when home
prices began to fall, the catastrophe set in. As home prices dropped below
the levels of the mortgages themselves, a stampede began to unload such
properties. Entire suburbs in some parts of Florida became near ghost
towns.

The abandonment of these properties led to dramatic losses in the huge
volume of mortgage-backed securities that had been sold to unsuspecting
investors. Some large investment houses on Wall Street collapsed. As faith
in the housing markets fell, so did the faith of the lending institutions that
remained. At one point in the fall of 2008 there were even worries that so
many banks might become insolvent that the credit markets would freeze
up entirely. I remember listening to a commentator on National Public
Radio suggest that we could wake up one morning and go to the gas station
only to find out that none of our credit cards worked. The specter of 1929
hung over the country for several weeks. Though the worst was avoided,
some have said that it may take as much as a decade to return the credit
markets to where they once were.

What I learned from all of this was how much of our economy depends
on the good faith of the participants. When everything is functioning well,
we hardly reflect on this. Credit cards are simply handy financial instruments that free you from the need to carry cash. But in the depths of the
near depression of 2008, we learned that credit cards are true to their
name—they require belief. Every time I make a purchase using one, the

bank extends me credit. It *believes* that in the future I will repay. Should the banks lose this confidence in the ability of its clients to repay, the economy will come to a grinding halt, with devastating consequences.[6]

I already mentioned that a creditor can get some control on this risk by investigating a client's credit history. But as Surowiecki astutely observes, banks decided to cut corners on such matters on the presumption that housing prices would continue to rise. Rabbi Shimon noted, however, that predicting the future is not a simple task, and whenever the need for such wisdom is suppressed it is always to one's peril. Confidence games depend on the credulity of the public. Over the past decade investors came to believe many improbable things, and the result was the near collapse of the banking industry and the threat of a worldwide depression.

As luck would have it, just as this financial crisis was at its very nadir, I was reading a seminal article in German by Isac Seeligmann on the topic of loans in the Bible and the ancient Near East. In the course of reading this marvelous essay, I came upon a sentence in which Seeligmann describes the disreputable types of persons that assembled around David in the wilderness of Judea when he was a fugitive from the court of Saul. Let me translate this sentence into English save for one word: "In 1 Samuel 22:2 it is reported that those who were in distress as well as 'anyone who had a Gläubiger' came to David as he was in flight from Saul."[7] I have left *Gläubiger* untranslated because when I first came upon this word, I could not figure out how it fit into the sentence. The verbal root of this nominal form is simple. *Glauben* is one of the first German words I ever learned—it means "to believe." Accordingly, the clause in question, if rendered literally, would mean: "anyone who had a *believer* came to David." I knew that could not be right, so I turned to my dictionary and learned that this vocable had taken on a secondary meaning, "creditor." At first I was puzzled by this explanation— why would a creditor be thought of as a believer? But it was just then that I stumbled upon the same etymological insight as James Surowiecki—the English word *creditor* comes from the Latin root, *credere*—"to believe."

Even in English, then, a creditor is a believer. But it must be said that this simple philological truth works even better in German. For we do not need a Latin mediator to explain the relationship; it's built right into the language. Compare these two sentences:

Ich glaube an Gott den Vater den Allmächtiger. . .
I believe in God the Father, Almighty. . .
and

Der Gläubiger glaubt dem Schuldner dass er seine Schulden zurückzahlen wird.
The "Believer" believes that the debtor will repay his debt.

Or consider this brief excerpt from the nineteenth-century German poet and essayist Heinrich Heine. While reflecting on the difficulty of learning French, and not wanting to appear to be a *bête allemande* ("a German animal") in front of his tutor, he writes:

> There were many harsh words, and I remember as if yesterday how I got into trouble because of *la religion.* I must have been asked six times: "Henri, what is the French word for faith (Glaube)?" And six times, more tearfully each time, I answered, "It's *le crédit.*" And the seventh time, the enraged examiner, cherry-red in the face cried: "It is *la religion*"—and blows rained down, and all my schoolmates laughed. Madame! From that time on I have never been able to hear the word *religion* mentioned without my back turning pale with fright and my cheeks going red with shame. And quite honestly, in my life *le crédit* has been more use to me than *la religion*—It suddenly occurs to me that I still owe five dollars to the landlord of the Lion in Bologna—and truly, I undertake to owe him another five hundred dollars on top of that, provided I never need to hear the unhappy word *la religion* again in this life.[8]

It is not just Western languages such as English and German that reflect the logical connection between belief and money lending. The same thing can be found in Hungarian and Akkadian, the language of ancient Mesopotamia. Consider, for example, the Akkadian word *qâpu,* whose primary meaning is "to believe" or "give credence to." One finds this sense in sentences such as this: "So until we received definite information, we did not believe it (*la niqīp*)." Or, "As for the words So-and-So spoke to you, you said thus: I do not believe them (*ul qīpāku*)." But alongside such conventional descriptions of belief, one also finds examples that show how easily this word slips into a financial register: "A woman tavern keeper who made a loan (*iqīpu*) of beer or barley cannot collect anything that she has loaned out (*mimma* ša *iqīpu*) [during the year that debt remission is declared]."[9]

The Wisdom of Ben Sira

Having established the close relationship between belief and loans, we can now return to our original question: Is any of this relevant to the practice of charity? The Jewish book that we shall attend to is that of Sirach (written by Ben Sira and sometimes called Ecclesiasticus). This Jewish work was written early in the second century BCE. Though the full form of the book is extant only in the Greek Old Testament, we do have a good percentage of the work in Hebrew. Strikingly, the book is occasionally cited authoritatively in rabbinic texts even though it did not make it into the Jewish canon. Most of our Hebrew copies (medieval in origin) of the work were found in a synagogue in Cairo, providing evidence that it continued to be studied by Jews even though it was not in their Bible.

Ben Sira took considerable interest in the subject of charity. One of the earliest references that we possess for the giving of alms to the poor is found in the twenty-ninth chapter of his book. As Bradley Gregory has shown, the section on almsgiving (vv. 8–13) is strikingly sandwiched in between two accounts (vv. 1–7 and 14–20) that document why one ought to be wary when making a loan. The first pertains to the risks involved in both making and receiving a loan, while the second deals with going surety ("cosigning" for a loan in antiquity) for another person.[10] In order to appreciate this remarkable choice, we must begin with a careful consideration of Ben Sira's teaching on loans themselves.

Ben Sira's opening remarks about loan-giving divide neatly into two rather different pieces: some general observations about the obligation to issue loans (vv. 1–3) and then some pointed remarks about the specific dangers that attend this ancient social institution (vv. 4–7). The first section reads:

> The merciful lend to their neighbors;
>> by holding out a helping hand, they keep the commandments.
> Lend to your neighbor in his time of need;
>> repay your neighbor when a loan falls due.
> Keep your promise and be honest with him,
>> and on every occasion you will find what you need. (29:1–3)

Though it may seem rather unremarkable to describe one who provides money to a neighbor in need as one who is "merciful," this identification will have an extraordinary afterlife. The term for mercy in Greek (*eleos*) will provide the foundation for what will emerge as the standard word for almsgiving in Greek texts of Jewish and Christian origin, *eleēmosunē*.[11] This word will then come into Latin as *elimosina/elemosina*. In fact, the modern English word *alms* is nothing other than a further transformation of this Greek original (the Latinized form of the word *elemosina* became *aelmysse* in Old English and was further shortened to *almes* and finally *alms*). Another remarkable feature of this opening verse is the presumption that making a loan to a neighbor in trouble is considered an act of obedience to a divine commandment. As such a loan is not just a good thing to do, it is *merit*-worthy—that is, it improves one's standing with God. Though the Bible contains several laws regarding the making of loans, its concern is with the way in which such a financial arrangement is handled (forbidding the exacting of interest), not with the obligation to provide a loan in the first place (e.g., Exod 22:24–26). The only place in scripture where loans are actually commanded is Deuteronomy 15:1–11, though there the context is the Sabbatical year of remission.

Ben Sira continues his discussion by dropping his oblique, third-person discourse ("The merciful lend . . . ") and addressing his students directly: "Lend to your neighbor in his time of need . . . " In these verses Ben Sira balances the obligations of the one who makes a loan with those incumbent on the recipient. The lender is exhorted to give aid at "the time (*kairos*) of his [neighbor's] need" while the borrower is correlatively urged to repay this loan "when a loan falls due" (literally: "at the proper time [*kairos*]"). The lesson for the borrower is clear: if you keep your word and are faithful with your creditor, then should you find yourself in dire straits in the future, you can be confident that you will find help.

Having opened with a generally approbatory tone directed to his students, Ben Sira abruptly changes direction in verses 4–7 and dedicates the remainder of his opening section to the various dangers that await the person who puts his money out on loan.

> 4. Many regard a loan as a windfall,
>   and cause trouble to those who help them.
> 5a. One kisses another's hands until he gets a loan,
>   and is deferential in speaking of his neighbor's money;
> 5b. but at the time for repayment he will delay,
>   and pay back with empty promises, and find fault with the time.
> 6a. If he can pay, his creditor will hardly get back half
>   and will regard that as a windfall.
> 6b. If he cannot pay, the borrower has robbed the other of his money,
>   and he has needlessly made him an enemy;
> 6c. he will repay him with curses and reproaches,
>   and instead of glory will repay him with dishonor.
> 7. Many refuse to lend, not because of meanness,
>   but from fear of being defrauded needlessly. (29:4–7)

He begins by remarking that there are many unscrupulous sorts that will view a loan as a sort of "windfall"—as though they have just happened upon an unclaimed treasure—and pay no heed to the person who assumed a risk on their behalf.[12] Though the borrower will speak very respectfully when appealing to a creditor, upon receipt of the money things can change dramatically. The time set for repayment is delayed and inquiries about the matter lead to indignation. In the end, the lender will be lucky to get back half. The initial deed of generosity ends with disgrace—the creditor is repaid not with money but with curses and reproaches. Ben Sira closes this section with an astute observation about the social implications of such behavior: "Many refuse to lend, not because of meanness, but from fear of being defrauded needlessly."

As the ancients well knew, it is hard to forecast the onset of difficult economic times. One of the means by which the dangers of temporary impoverishment were ameliorated was through loans such as these. But if enough reckless borrowers appeared and exploited such generosity for personal gain, there would be little incentive in the future for others to do the same.

The third section of this chapter (vv. 14–20) concerns the act of "going surety" for a friend. This guarantor had two roles to play. First, he ensured that the borrower would not flee and leave his financial obligations unmet. As the Bible notes, those who fled society because of unpaid debts often ended up outside the control of established political authority. Thus when David had to flee Saul's court out of fear for his life, he went to a small fortress outside of Jerusalem to seek sanctuary from his adversary. We are told that "everyone who was in distress, and everyone who was in debt . . . gathered to him; and he became captain over them" (1 Sam 22:2). Obviously, it was in the interest of the common good to prevent borrowers from fleeing. The second obligation was far more risky for the one who went surety: he would be asked to stand in for the borrower and make good on the obligation should the borrower default. Because the guarantor assumed the full risk of the loan, his situation would be quite precarious. Biblical writers strongly cautioned against the practice:

> Do not be one of those who give pledges,
>> Who become surety for debts.
> If you have nothing with which to pay,
>> Why should your bed be taken from under you? (Prov 22:26–27)

Ben Sira, at first blush, looks very different from this more mainstream view because he understands going surety just as he views giving loans—it is part of the obligation of the well-to-do toward those who have fallen upon hard times.[13] Accordingly, the section Ben Sira devotes to surety is structured very much like the section on loans. He begins with a general observation expressed in the third person about the institution itself ("a good person will be surety . . . ") but then abruptly addresses the reader directly as though he had just found someone to go surety for him ("Do not [*you*] forget the kindness of your guarantor").

> A good person will be surety for his neighbor,
>> but the one who has lost all sense of shame will fail him.
> Do not forget the kindness of your guarantor,
>> for he has given his life for you. (29:14–15)

Having dispensed with these introductory remarks, he then returns to the third person in order to recount some of the specific sorts of dangers that attend this sort of behavior.

> A sinner wastes the property of his surety,
>> and the ungrateful person abandons his rescuer.
> Being surety has ruined many who were prosperous,
>> and has tossed them about like waves of the sea;
> It has driven the influential into exile,
>> and they have wandered among foreign nations.
> The sinner comes to grief through surety;
>> his pursuit of gain involves him in lawsuits. (29:16–19)

Ben Sira, however, does not end his account of going surety with this list of dangers. Because giving assistance to those in need is a divine command, going surety must be described in a way that is intelligible to those who wish to serve their God. So Ben Sira urges the practice but also warns those who would heed his counsel to proceed with due caution:

> Assist your neighbor to the best of your ability,
>> but be careful not to fall yourself. (29:20)

Up to this point most of what we have seen in Ben Sira is in keeping with biblical precedent. Taking his cue from biblical law, he is aware of the need to provide loans to those who find themselves in desperate straits. Also in line with wisdom traditions, Ben Sira warns his students of the many dangers that attend this act of compassion. But at least two elements of his presentation are novel. First, he is attentive to the risks that a lender undertakes, whereas earlier biblical texts worried about the borrower.[14] Second, whenever the book of Proverbs dealt with the matter of surety, it always urged caution. Ben Sira is also cognizant of the dangers, but because his discussion of loans and surety is couched in terms of aid to the poor, he cannot be so dismissive of the institution itself. Though going surety has its attendant dangers and must be entered into with due caution, it remains a fundamental obligation of the Israelite toward his neighbor.

The Giving of Alms as a Loan Made to God

So far we have treated the two bookends of our chapter, Ben Sira's opening unit on loans (vv. 1–7) and the closing unit on surety (vv. 14–20). It is striking that the treatment of almsgiving (vv. 8–13) is set in between. This arrangement suggests that almsgiving has been categorized as a type of loan.

The novelty of this position should not be missed.[15] Biblical texts, as is well known, have a very special interest in the plight of the poor. The prophets in particular were the champions of the poor and held Israel's ruling elite responsible for how they were treated. But neither were biblical law codes mute with respect to this issue. In those rules that pertained to donations made to the temple—the ordinary means of taxation in ancient Israel—specific imposts were designated as means of assisting the plight of the poor. As we saw in Chapter 2, Deuteronomy mandates that the Israelite farmer donate his tithe every third year to resident aliens, orphans, widows, and Levites—persons who had no regular source of income (Deut 14:28–29). In addition to this, during the harvest season Israelites were not to reap their fields entirely but had to leave the corners untouched. There the poor could enter and glean freely to satisfy their needs (Lev 19:9–10; Ruth 2).

But Ben Sira does not link the obligation to give alms to any of these legal precedents; rather he understands the gift of alms as a sort of loan. This raises all sorts of questions. If giving alms is a type of loan, and if making a loan involves great risk even in the best of circumstances ("One kisses another's hands until he gets a loan, and is deferential in speaking of his neighbor's money; but at the time for repayment he will delay"), why would one grant a loan to someone who is terribly impoverished? In other words, the choice to place almsgiving in this particular location seems to focus attention on the risk it entails. What possible rhetorical gain could emerge from that? Before turning directly to this question, let's look closer at the text itself.

> Nevertheless, be patient with someone in humble circumstances,
>   and do not keep him waiting for your alms.
> Help the poor for the commandment's sake,
>   and in their need do not send them away empty-handed.
> Lose your silver for the sake of a brother or a friend,
>   and do not let it rust under a stone and be lost.
> Lay up your treasure according to the commandments of the Most High,
>   and it will profit you more than gold.
> Store up almsgiving in your treasury,
>   and it will rescue you from every disaster;
> Better than a stout shield and a sturdy spear
>   it will fight for you against the enemy. (29:8–13)

The discussion of alms follows immediately upon that of the dangers of making a loan (vv. 4–7). As I noted above, that section closes with a notice about the terrible damage that fraudulent borrowers inflict on society as a whole. Because of the needless defrauding of those well disposed to help, Ben Sira observes that many "have refused to lend." It is striking to see that, given the gravity of this worry, Ben Sira immediately introduces his injunction to lend to the poor. "Nevertheless," he begins—that is, in spite of all I have warned you about—"be patient with someone in humble circumstances, and do not keep him waiting for your alms."

The urge for patience may come as something of a surprise. The Hebrew idiom (erek *appayim*) that underlies the Greek (*makrothumos*) is often used to express God's patience in the face of human wrongdoing. Thus, when Moses tries to assuage God's anger over the rebelliousness of Israel in the wilderness, he exhorts God to remember that he is a God who is slow to anger—that is, *patient* in the face of the gravest sort of sin (Num 14:18). If we remember the mood that was established in the immediately preceding verse ("Many refuse to lend, not because of meanness, but from fear of being defrauded needlessly"), we can see why the caution to be patient is apt. Given that many have been defrauded, the natural human response would be to grow angry at the request of yet another seeking funds. So Ben Sira shifts direction and counsels being patient rather than curt. Yet lest one think that patience might imply taking one's time and assessing the creditworthiness of the recipient, he is quick to add: "don't keep him waiting for your alms." Throw caution to the wind and provide what he needs right away!

But why should one be so eager to act so imprudently? Is Ben Sira retracting the sage counsel he had provided just a few verses earlier? In his view, the requirement to lend to the poor is grounded in the Torah itself: "Help the poor for the commandment's sake, and in their need do not send them away empty-handed." We already saw a linkage between almsgiving and the keeping of commandments in the first verse of the chapter. What is new in this verse is the injunction not to send the poor away "empty-handed." The diction of this verse draws on the laws governing the obligation to make a triennial pilgrimage to the Temple on the requisite festival days: "Three times in the year you shall hold a festival for me. . . . No one shall appear before me empty-handed" (Exod 23:14, 15). As we saw in the previous chapter, both Ben Sira and Tobit understood the gift of alms as a form of sacrifice due at the altar of the Lord. In this verse, Ben Sira gives voice to the sacral nature of charity by linking it back to the festal legislation of the Torah.

It might be worth mentioning at this point that the text of Sirach is often difficult to determine and translations can often vary considerably. M. H. Segal, for example, has argued that the second half of verse 8 is to be read not as "do not keep (the poor) waiting for your alms" but instead as "extend the time due on the loan." Though this reading would fit nicely with the opening verse of the chapter, which grounds the virtue of showing mercy in the obligation to make such a loan ("one who shows mercy, lends to his neighbor"), it is unlikely to be correct. For if lending on generous terms were the focus of the command in verse 9, it would be quite difficult to understand the next line: "*Lose your silver* for the sake of a brother or a friend, and do not let it rust under a stone and be lost. Lay up your treasure according to the commandments of the Most High, and it will profit you more than gold." What is at stake here is not the virtue of being a generous lender who offers the borrower the most generous of terms. The demand is far more radical: Ben Sira exhorts his students to *lose* their money on behalf of the poor. No pretense is made that the funds will be returned.

But if this is the case, the question posed at the beginning of our discussion returns with a vengeance: why categorize this sort of activity as a loan? If lending means anything, it means the hope for the eventual return of one's funds. One answer to that question is to preserve the dignity of the recipient. In the ancient world it would have been humiliating to receive money purely as a gift, as though one were incapable of making restitution. Judaism has long revered the idea of calling such gifts loans, even when the chance of repayment is almost nil, so that the beneficiary can save face. But there is another answer as well that is provided in the very next verse: "Lay up your treasure [in heaven . . .] and it will *profit* you more than gold." Paradoxically what constitutes an almost certain loss of wealth in earthly terms becomes the privileged means of securing it in heaven. Ben Sira introduces an idea that will emerge as a key theme in the preaching of Jesus—the treasury in heaven. Though Ben Sira does not provide any details as to how this works, one must presume that the poor person serves as a sort of conduit through which one can convey goods from earth to heaven. But the conduit must be of a very special nature because both the donor and the recipient stand to profit from this transaction. The money expended as charity returns to the donor as a credit to a heavenly bank account. It is also striking that Ben Sira says that the *silver* that was given away as alms ("Lose your silver . . . ") becomes a deposit that is worth more than *gold* ("it will profit you more than gold"). In antiquity as in the modern era, gold was a far more precious metal than silver. In giving away something of lesser value one attained something far greater.

As anyone knows, one of the best strategies for dealing with the uncertainties that the future might offer is the accumulation of at least a modest nest egg. In our day, this would mean minimally funding a retirement account so that when one enters one's dotage and can no longer work, there will be funds available to cover living expenses. In Ben Sira's mind, the surest way to deal with such worries about what Lady Fortune might have on offer was to fund a heavenly treasury. For God Almighty himself has promised that these "monies" will rescue one from any and all affliction. "Store up almsgiving in your treasury," Ben Sira concludes, "and it will rescue you from every disaster; better than a stout shield and a sturdy spear, it will fight for you against the enemy."

Before closing, I would like to return to Ben Sira's presumption that generosity to the poor fulfills a demand of the Torah (29:1, cf. v. 9). As we observed, there is no single commandment in the five books of Moses to which we can turn as a source for this idea. The nearest equivalent—and the one most often cited by scholars—is Deuteronomy 15:1–11. The context is the Sabbatical year of remission (*shemittah*), during which all creditors must waive their rights to collect what is due to them. Obviously, such a demand would cause most reasonable persons to think twice about making a loan when the year of remission drew near. The Sabbatical year would render null and void all the rights of creditors. Best to do your lending well in advance of this particular year if you hope to recover your money. But Moses, the author of Deuteronomy informs us, took a dim view of such economic calculations.

> If there is among you anyone in need, a member of your community in any of your towns within the land that the LORD your God is giving you, do not be hard-hearted or tight-fisted toward your needy neighbor. You should rather open your hand, willingly lending enough to meet the need, whatever it may be. Be careful that you do not entertain a mean thought, thinking, "The seventh year, the year of remission, is near," and therefore view your needy neighbor with hostility and give nothing; your neighbor might cry to the LORD against you, and you would incur guilt. Give liberally and be ungrudging when you do so, for on this account the LORD your God will bless you in all your work and in all that you undertake. Since there will never cease to be some in need on the earth, I therefore command you, "Open your hand to the poor and needy neighbor in your land." (Deut 15:7–11)

What is to be carefully noted in this passage is the *supernatural* dimension of showing monetary kindness to others. By issuing a loan into the head-winds of the upcoming year of remission—an "irrational" act if there ever was one—the pious Israelite demonstrates his faith that God will reward in like manner. "Give liberally," Moses exhorts, *"for on this account* the LORD your God will bless you."* This theological claim, I would suggest, is hardly different from what we find in Ben Sira.

I claimed in the previous chapter that almsgiving became a central pillar of Second Temple Judaism because it was considered to be *avodah,* that is, a means of directly addressing and serving the God of Israel. In conjunction with this, I argued that its particular role in Israel's liturgical service was that of a loan one made to God. For many persons with whom I have shared this idea, the reaction has been that of considerable perplexity. Not only is it unseemly to imagine God as someone in need of a loan, but the very idea itself calls to mind the nefarious practices of selfish creditors exploiting their vulnerable clients. The natural default position would seem to be well rendered by the following story about the assistance the prophet Elisha provides for a widow who is about to lose her very children to a heartless creditor.

Now the wife of a member of the company of prophets cried to Elisha, "Your servant my husband is dead; and you know that your servant feared the LORD, but a creditor has come to take my two children as slaves." Elisha said to her, "What shall I do for you? Tell me, what do you have in the house?" She answered, "Your servant has nothing in the house, except a jar of oil." He said, "Go outside, borrow vessels from all your neighbors, empty vessels and not just a few. Then go in, and shut the door behind you and your children, and start pouring into all these vessels; when each is full, set it aside." So she left him and shut the door behind her and her children; they kept bringing vessels to her, and she kept pouring. When the vessels were full, she said to her son, "Bring me another vessel." But he said to her, "There are no more." Then the oil stopped flowing. She came and told the man of God, and he said, "Go sell the oil and pay your debts, and you and your children can live on the rest." (2 Kings 4:1–7)

Though the story touchingly renders the service Elisha provides for this young widow, it also reveals the terrible quandary into which she was placed by her creditor.

Yet I have contended that this particular picture is not the only way in which the Bible depicts the relationship of creditor to debtor. Creditors could also be seen as generous persons who fulfilled an important role in the "welfare" system of antiquity. To appreciate this we must bear in mind that non-interest-bearing loans were an essential part of the economic "safety net" that ancient Israelite culture provided for what was basically a subsistence agricultural economy. Should a farmer find himself without money to purchase seed during the planting season, his kinsmen or neighbors were the most likely persons to turn to for help. As Seeligmann has argued, loans were a moral obligation of the tribal unit to help the poor. On this view the creditor was seen as one who was performing a charitable deed. This picture appears several times in the Psalms:

> The wicked borrow, and do not pay back,
>   but the righteous are generous and keep giving. (37:21)
> [The righteous] are ever giving liberally and lending,
>   and their children become a blessing. (37:26)
> It is well with those who deal generously and lend,
>   who conduct their affairs with justice. (112:5)

and is repeated in the book of Proverbs:

> Those who oppress the poor insult their Maker,
>   but those who are kind to the needy honor him. (14:31)

> Whoever is kind to the poor lends to the LORD,
>   and will be repaid in full. (19:17)

The most surprising of all these texts is certainly the last, Proverbs 19:17. It makes the point crystal clear that the one who assists the poor with a loan is actually doing business with God. Indeed, this text provides the deep structure that stands behind Ben Sira's own teaching. As we have seen, though Ben Sira understood a loan to a neighbor to be a divine obligation, he was also realistic enough to know that the recipients of such largesse might not be able to reciprocate. Though the borrower would act deferential in order to secure the loan, when the time came to repay, he would seek numerous delays. In the end, the creditor would be lucky to get back half of what he loaned. What was surprising, however, was Ben Sira's insistence that none of these pragmatic concerns need worry the one who loans to the truly indigent. Here the money that appears to be lost is confidently restored. Because the guarantor of these funds was God, they accumulate beside him in a heavenly treasury where they can be disbursed as necessity requires ("it will rescue you from every danger").

What Ben Sira does not explicitly say, though it can be clearly inferred, is that his teaching can be trusted only to the degree that one has faith in God. As we have noted, a creditor is an aptly named individual—in order to make a loan he must believe that he has a reasonably good chance of seeing his money returned. On the face of it a divine treasury might seem to be the safest place to store one's wealth. But its true value is directly proportional to the faith one has in the divine being who underwrites the deposits. Or to put it another way, the safety of the divine treasury is a dependable notion only for those who have a deep faith in God. If it were otherwise, everyone would be in a race to share their goods with the poor. Almsgiving, it turns out, becomes an extraordinary index of the faith (Glaube) of the believer (Gläubige) through his financial generosity as a creditor (Gläubiger).

CHAPTER FOUR

Material Wealth and Its Deceptions

Do not trust in wealth that lies,
for it provides no benefit on a day of wrath.

—Sirach 5:8

"Make for yourselves friends from the mammon of unrighteousness" (Luke 16:9).
They are called "mammon of unrighteousness" in the sense of faithless and deceptive, for they are not to be depended upon, but often desert one man and
pass on to another.

—Cornelius à Lapide (1567–1637)

The concept of the treasury in heaven originates in a fundamental
economic concern: how to prepare for the uncertainties of the
future. One time-tested solution to this challenge is to accumulate a "rainy-day" fund that will tide one over during difficult times. Ben
Sira clearly has this strategy in mind but inverts it radically when he
teaches:

> Store up almsgiving in your treasury,
> and it will rescue you from every disaster;
> Better than a stout shield and a sturdy spear,
> it will fight for you against the enemy. (29:12–13)

In these verses, it is not the storing of goods in earthly treasuries that will
protect one in the future, but the distribution of those goods to the poor!
Paradoxically, the money one donates is not lost for good but rather

accumulates in a (heavenly) treasury with the specific purpose of insuring oneself against the uncertainties of the future. Almsgiving provides a far better form of security than could be gained from earthly wealth; it has the power to rescue one from any and every type of disaster. In this chapter, I want to show that Ben Sira's bold proclamation issues from a careful reading of Proverbs 10:2 (and its near relation, 11:4) and that the interpretation of this text shaped Second Temple Jewish and Christian thought about almsgiving.

A Treasury of Wickedness

There can be no question that this promise regarding the future was inspired by two closely related sayings found in the book of Proverbs:

> The treasuries of wickedness provide no benefit,
> but almsgiving [*tsedaqa*] delivers from death. (10:2)
> Riches provide no benefit on the day of wrath,
> but almsgiving [*tsedaqa*] delivers from death. (11:4)[1]

It is important to notice that while our latter proverb simply says that riches are of little value, the former speaks about *treasuries (otserot)*, a noun that derives from a root meaning "to lay or store up goods." Consider its usage in 2 Kings 20:16–17: "Then Isaiah said to Hezekiah, 'Hear the word of the LORD: Days are coming when all that is in your house, and that which your ancestors *have stored up* until this day, shall be carried to Babylon; nothing shall be left, says the LORD.'" Equally illuminating is the usage in Isaiah 23:18 regarding the punishment that was to befall the great mercantile center of Phoenicia, the city of Tyre. Rather than being able to benefit from its financial profits, the city would end up supplying them to those it had exploited: "Her profits *will not be stored* [same root as the word *treasury*] or hoarded, but her merchandise will supply abundant food and fine clothing for those who live in the presence of the LORD." What both of these texts bring to the foreground is the age-old practice of storing goods that one does not need in the present in order to provide for the contingencies of the future. The accumulation of capital over time (otserot) will not provide the protection that one had anticipated.

It is also important to note the structure of the poetic couplet, "The treasuries of *wickedness* [resha] provide no benefit; but *almsgiving* [tsedaqa] delivers from death." The nouns used to mark wickedness and generosity, *resha* and *tsedaqa,* are natural opposites in biblical Hebrew.[2] As such, it should be expected that a translation of the proverb will bring out the nature of the implied contrast. As is often the case in poetry, the B line frequently leaves the subject mentioned in the A line unexpressed, the presumption being that the reader will carry that idea forward. Thus in the couplet: "The Lord is great in Zion; he is exalted over all the peoples" (Ps 99:2), we presume that the second line has filled out the implications of the first. To express the idea more prosaically: the Lord's greatness in Zion is made manifest in his exaltation *there* over all the peoples. In other words, the idea of the Lord's residence in Zion is to be carried over from the first to the second line. One should argue accordingly for our proverb. If *resha* and *tsedaqa* are natural opposites, then it would be logical to suppose that though "treasuries of wickedness" (otserot resha) provide no benefit, *"treasuries* of generosity" (otserot tsedaqa) will deliver from death. Ben Sira, I would contend, presumes such an interpretation when he writes: "Store up almsgiving *in your treasury,* and it will rescue you from every disaster" (29:12). The logic is as simple as it is elegant—the wicked store their goods in earthly treasuries mistakenly thinking that this will provide a hedge against the future, while the righteous give away their goods to the poor and in so doing fund a heavenly treasury that will be a trustworthy bulwark against any perilous contingency. Thus the concept of a "treasury in heaven" is born.

It is worth making one final observation about Ben Sira's paraphrase of Proverbs 10:2 before moving on. Though the first clause of this couplet was crucial for generating the idea of a treasury in the second, he has ignored it in his own teaching. In his paraphrase, he attends solely to the second half of the proverb: "Store up almsgiving in your treasury, and it will rescue you from every disaster; / Better than a stout shield and a sturdy spear it will fight for you against the enemy." He has no interest in declaring that the "treasuries of wickedness" (or "riches") provide no benefit for the future. This omission is easily explained by the rhetorical context. Ben Sira's concern in this chapter is with the Torah's injunction to provide loans for the poor (29:1). In order to bring out the surprising role that God plays in this process he contrasts ordinary, garden-variety loans made to a friend or neighbor (vv. 1–7) with those made to the indigent (vv. 8–13). In the interest of this particular contrast, any reference to the improper accumulation of money will be an unnecessary distraction. From Proverbs 10:2, he derives one lesson alone—that almsgiving puts one in touch with the *divine* realm; it funds a treasury in *heaven.* In order to bring out the supernatural aspect of this divine treasury, he digresses for a moment to fill out in greater detail the sort of benefits it will provide: "it will rescue you from *every* disaster; better than a stout shield and a sturdy spear, it will fight for you against the enemy."[3]

Sirach 5 and 31

Though Sirach 29 was not terribly interested in the first half of our two proverbs, in chapter 5 the author weaves together what appear to be two very different themes: the unreliability of wealth and the inability of the human agent to discern how God has blended mercy and wrath. Let us begin by laying out the two different themes.[4] The first concerns the unreliability of wealth:

> 1a. Do not lean on your wealth,
>   nor say, "I can do as I wish."
> 1b. Do not lean on your own power,
>   pursuing whatever your soul desires.
> 2. Do not follow the path of your heart and eyes,
>   pursuing improper appetites.
> 3. Do not say: "who can prevail [over me]?"
>   For the LORD will seek redress for the oppressed.

The second theme is the relationship between mercy and wrath:

> 4a. Do not say: "I have sinned,
>   yet what has happened to me?"
>   Truly God is slow to anger.
> 4b. Do not say: "The LORD is merciful,
>   He will blot out all my sins."
> 5. Do not put so much trust in [God's] forgiveness
>   that you add sin to sin.
> 6a. Do not say:[5] "His mercies are innumerable;
>   He will forgive my many sins."
> 6b. For he is both merciful and wrathful
>   and his rage will fall upon the wicked.

What unites these first two units is the sin of presumption about the future. In the opening unit, wealth tempts one to think that all is within one's power ("Do not lean on your wealth, nor say, 'I can do as I wish'"). Wealth, or more specifically the power it provides, makes one feel invincible. The clause "who can prevail over me?" recalls by way of contrast one of the benefits of almsgiving: "Better than a stout shield and a sturdy spear, it will fight for you against the enemy" (29:13). But a person who puts such trust in wealth and power will forget the special favor God has for the poor and his intention to seek redress from anyone who would harm them (v. 3b). In the second unit we see that a misplaced confidence in God's mercy is also dangerous because it leads to moral complacency. Why be concerned about stepping on the toes of others while climbing the ladder of personal ambition? "God's mercies are innumerable," this fool will reason, and "He will forgive my many sins."[6]

In the last section of this instruction, Ben Sira brings the two teachings about wealth and forgiveness into direct conversation:

> 7a. Do not delay in turning to him,
>   nor put it off from one day to the next.
> 7b. For his anger can go forth at any time,
>   and in the day of vengeance you will be swept away.
> 8. Do not trust in wealth that lies,
>   for it provides no benefit on a day of wrath.

He begins with the dangers of presuming on God's forgiveness and urges his readers to turn to God right away (v. 7a). Because one cannot know the moment of judgment (v. 7b), Ben Sira advises, it is never wise to presume on divine mercy. But then he brings his teaching to a close with an abrupt return to the theme of wealth: "Don't trust in wealth that lies, / *for it provides no benefit on a day of wrath.*" The second half of this verse is virtually a word-for-word repetition of Proverbs 11:4 ("Riches *provide no benefit on the day of wrath*"), while the first half, I will contend, recalls Prov 10:2 (*"the treasuries of wickedness provide no benefit"*).

It might seem that Sirach 5:8a ("Do not trust in wealth that lies") has little relation to Proverbs 10:2. "Wealth that lies" and "treasuries of wickedness" appear to be quite different in meaning. In order to see the relationship between the two, we must look at Proverbs 10:2 more closely. Most translations have understood the phrase "treasuries of wickedness" as "ill-gotten treasures," as though the wickedness in question pertained to the illicit means by which they were acquired. Though this is possible, it is not without its problems. Most notably, it is not exactly clear why the ill-gotten treasuries of the A line would be set in contrast with financial generosity in the B line. A more natural contrast would be that of hoarding and generosity. And the very usage of the noun *otsar,* "treasury" or, perhaps better, "storehouse," suggests as much. As Bruce Waltke argues, the contrast of a storehouse with generosity suggests the accumulation of wealth for personal use as opposed to giving it away to those in need. "Paradoxically," Waltke writes, "the wicked . . . store up physical assets for themselves and lose their lives, and the righteous use their resources to serve others and store up life for themselves."[7] It seems to me that Waltke has anticipated how Ben Sira has understood this line. Ben Sira's paraphrase makes the matter quite clear: "Do not trust in wealth that lies (nikse-sheqer)," in other words, wealth that cannot deliver on its promises. And what might those promises be? Let us recall what Ben Sira said just a few verses earlier: "Don't lean on your wealth, nor say, 'I can do as I wish.' . . . Do not say, 'Who can prevail [over me]?'" This matches Waltke's understanding that Proverbs 10:2 also speaks to the deceptive power of money. If Waltke is correct, then Ben Sira's paraphrase has simply exposed that subtle teaching to the light of day.

There is one more text in Sirach that bears directly on our theme. In 31:1–11, Ben Sira takes up again the challenge that wealth provides for the believer. "The rich person toils to amass a fortune," he writes, but "when he rests he fills himself with dainties" (v. 3). The exact opposite, however, characterizes the dilemma of the needy: "The poor person toils to make a meager living, and if ever he rests, he becomes needy" (v. 4). In this comparison the benefits of accumulating wealth are clearly in view—a tidy bank account allows one the leisure to enjoy the fruits of one's labors. Those who live from hand to mouth, in contrast, rue a day of rest. For without any spare capital at hand, the cupboard is quickly emptied.

Yet lest one think that money is an unqualified good, Ben Sira then deftly documents its downsides:

> 5. One who pursues gold will not be justified (yinnaqeh);
>   one who loves profits will be led astray by it.
> 6a. Many have been entrapped by gold
>   as have those who trusted in precious gems.
> 6b. [They cannot be saved from evil
>   nor delivered on a day of wrath.]
> 7. It is a stumbling block for the foolish;
>   the simple-minded are taken captive by it.

I have put the line "They cannot be saved from evil . . . " in italics because it was probably inserted by a later copyist.[8] But like many such additions, it is not without value. As I shall note below, it focuses the reader's eye on the central theme of the poem. For now it will suffice to note the dark side of money. It cannot justify; indeed, far worse, it leads one astray.

One might conclude from what we have seen that, though money has limits, it is far better than being poor and living from one day to the next without hope of any rest. After all, as long as one is not a fool, one can be reasonably confident that these dangerous shoals can be safely navigated. But Ben Sira will allow no such comfort. His concluding words of praise for the righteous man who is also rich leads one to wonder whether such a fellow could ever be found,

> 8. Happy is the rich person who is found blameless,
>   and who does not go after gold [*mammon*].
> 9. *Who* is he, that we may praise him?
>   For he has acted wondrously among his people.
> 10a. *Who* has been tested by it and found perfect?
>   Let it be for him a ground for boasting.
> 10b. *Who* has had the power to transgress and did not transgress,
>   and to do evil and did not do it?
> 11. His prosperity will be established,
>   and the assembly proclaims his acts of charity [Hebrew: praise].

Ben Sira does not believe that money is necessarily evil. As Bradley Gregory observes, what is morally significant is how one values it. But at the same time money is not an inert substance, indifferent to the one who possesses it.[9] Rather, wealth exerts an almost eerie power over its possessor such that it is nearly impossible not be possessed by it. Roland Murphy catches the tone of this section when he writes that Ben Sira "manifests a certain awe, almost of disbelief, that the rich person has survived the dangers stemming from his own riches. The real sin of the rich person is to fail in trust, to have put one's trust in mammon."[10]

The last verse of our poem is certainly the key to the entire unit. The one who stands up to such a powerful temptation "will be established, and the assembly proclaims his acts of charity." Now the full story is in view—having money is tantamount to a spiritual ordeal whose outcome is determined by whether one has the courage to give it away. It is this particular point, I would claim, that has generated the secondary addition we noted above: "[Those entrapped by gold] cannot be saved from evil nor delivered on a day of wrath." Not by accident, this addition recalls Proverbs 11:4 ("riches provide no benefit in a day of wrath") and sets up the contrast that becomes clear at the end, "the assembly proclaims his *acts of charity* [*tsedaqa*]." Charitable deeds, as we know by now, really do provide deliverance.

The key point to be learned from the passage is the considerable spiritual danger that resides in money. "Who has been tested by it and found perfect?" Ben Sira asks. Almost no one, he implies; only those who made their wealth a resource for others. Ben Sira 31:1–11 can be read as an extension of Proverbs 10:2. Hoarding wealth not only "does not benefit," it tempts one to ignore a reliance on God.

Tobit

The influence of Prov 10:2 and 11:4 can also be found in two different places in the book of Tobit. In the first instance, Tobit is giving what he believes is his last instruction in Torah to his son Tobias. In the middle of that address he says:

> Do not turn your face away from anyone who is poor, and the face of God will not be turned away from you. If you have many possessions, make your gift from them in proportion; if few, do not be afraid to give according to the little you have. *So you will be laying up a good treasure for yourself against the day of necessity. For almsgiving delivers from death and keeps you from going into the Darkness.* (Tobit 4:7b–10)

I have italicized the key passage. Like Ben Sira 29:11, Tobit has deduced from Proverbs 10:2 that the contrast between "treasuries of wickedness" and "almsgiving" serves to underscore two different economies. On the one hand, we have the economy of this world, where the hoarding of goods leads to a foolish optimism about the future ("treasuries of wickedness"). On the other hand is the divine economy in which the unstinting distribution of goods to the poor (tsedaqa, "almsgiving") funds the only dependable treasury—a treasury that will deliver one even from the powers of death. Just as in Ben Sira (5:8), Tobit has combined the diction of both Proverbs 10:2 and 11:4. From 10:2 he gets the idea of a "treasury," while in 11:4 he finds the theme of "a day of wrath" ("necessity" [*anagkē*] in the Greek of Tobit is a good translation). He then further glosses the laconic phrase "delivers from death" as "*keeps you from going into the Darkness.*" The glossing of death as a descent into darkness will not surprise the careful reader of this tale. God tests the faith of Tobit by rendering him blind—a state that he will characterize as being bereft of light.

In one other location in this book we find an instruction to give alms, and that comes from the lips of the angel Raphael. This occurs near the end of the book, just after Tobit has greeted his son Tobias, who has returned home with his new bride and has healed his father of his blindness. Raphael exhorts Tobit to tell all Israel about the wonderful things that God has done for him and to continue to give instruction about the power of almsgiving. "Do good," Raphael exhorts,

> and evil will not overtake you. Prayer with fasting is good, but better than both is almsgiving with righteousness. A little with righteousness is better than wealth with wrongdoing. *It is better to give alms than to lay up gold. For almsgiving saves from death and purges away every sin.* (Tobit 12:7–9)

Again, I have put the key lines in italics. Like Ben Sira and Tobit himself, Raphael contrasts giving alms with laying up gold. He also believes that almsgiving delivers from death, but he adds another detail: it cleanses one from sin.[11] Just as almsgiving brought Tobit from darkness to light, so it will deliver Israel from the penalty of exile under which it is laboring. In the case of Israel, sinfulness has accounted for its present condition—unlike Tobit, who was struck blind as part of a divine test—and it will not escape its deathlike state until it has been redeemed from its sins.[12] Almsgiving will be the key instrument to make that happen.

The Parables of Enoch

Let me add one other Jewish text from the turn of the Common Era that has drunk deeply from the well of Proverbs 10:2 and 11:4, the book known as 1 Enoch.[13] In a portion of the work known as The Book of Parables (chapters 37–71), our writer speaks of the moment of the last judgment when the wicked kings will get their comeuppance. As the kings are brought forward to face what awaits them, they acknowledge their errant ways. "Would that we might be given respite," they lament,

> that we might glorify and praise and make confession in the presence of your glory. And now we desire a little respite and do not find it, we pursue it and do not lay hold of it. And light has vanished from our presence, and darkness is our dwelling forever and ever. (1 Enoch 63:5–6)

Like the figure of Dives in Luke's Gospel (16:19–31), these kings have learned that the period for penance has lapsed and their final judgment has been sealed. They have left the light of earth for the darkness of Sheol. They go on to confess their failure to glorify the name of God: "Our hope was on the scepter of our kingdom and the throne of our glory," they declare, "but on the day of our affliction and tribulation, it does not save" (1 Enoch 63:7b–8a).

This confession is similar to Proverbs 11:4, "Riches provide no benefit on the day of wrath." And, as if to put an exclamation point on the lesson of this wisdom trope, our contrite kings add: "Our lives are full of *ill-gotten wealth,* but it does not prevent us from descending into the flame of the torture of Sheol" (63:10). It is worth noting that the Ethiopic original liter- ally reads "wealth of wickedness."[14] Though the standard translation of this genitival relationship ("ill-gotten wealth") is possible, it is not ideal. What is at issue in this passage is not economic exploitation (though that may have occurred as well) but rather the hubristic presumption that wealth will provide deliverance on a day of wrath. It recalls Ben Sira's warning not to be lulled into complacency by wealth. For that reason, I would recall Lapide's suggestion in the epigraph and gloss the phrase: "wealth that cannot be depended upon." The wickedness in question is not so much the manner by which the money was acquired in the first place as it is the false hopes that were subsequently attached to it. These kings of flesh and blood preferred to glory in their own power and might rather than acknowledge their total and unqualified dependence on the King of Kings.

Luke 12

The faulty estimation of what the accumulation of wealth can produce is also clearly reflected in the parable of the Rich Fool in Luke (12:16–21). In this particular example, I cannot demonstrate that Luke is directly dependent on our proverb. Rather, what I hope to establish is that the theological issues raised by that proverb—especially the hopes that are to be put in heavenly treasuries—are fundamental to the structure of the Lucan parable. In a word, the proverb has exerted indirect pressure on the story Luke will tell.

Luke's Gospel relates this parable within a larger literary unit that consists of four parts. It begins with (A) a conversation in which Jesus is accosted by a man who feels he has been cheated out of a portion of his inheritance (vv. 13–15). Jesus reprimands the man for worrying about the accumula- tion of wealth. The purpose of life, Jesus teaches, does not consist in accumulating possessions. This succinct teaching provides the occasion for (B) the parable itself and (C) a lengthier teaching directed to his disciples alone about God's providential care. The unit concludes with (D) a statement regarding the treasury in heaven. Let us begin with the parable (B):

> Then he told them a parable: "The land of a rich man produced abundantly. And he thought to himself, 'What should I do, for I have no place to store my crops?' Then he said, 'I will do this: I will pull down my barns and build larger ones, and there I will store all my grain and my goods. And I will say to my soul, "Soul, you have ample goods laid up for many years; relax, eat, drink, be merry."' But God said to him, 'You Fool! This very night your life is being demanded of you. And the things you have prepared, whose will they be?' So it is with those who store up treasures for themselves but are not rich toward God." (Luke 12:16–21)

> (C) He said to his disciples, "Therefore I tell you, do not worry about your life, what you will eat, or about your body, what you will wear. For life is more than food, and the body more than clothing. Consider the ravens: they neither sow nor reap, they have neither storehouse nor barn, and yet God feeds them. Of how much more value are you than the birds! And can any of you by worrying add a single hour to your span of life? If then you are not able to do so small a thing as that, why do you worry about the rest? Consider the lilies, how they grow: they neither toil nor spin; yet I tell you, even Solomon in all his glory was not clothed like one of these. But if God so clothes the grass of the field, which is alive today and tomorrow is thrown into the oven, how much more will he clothe you—you of little faith! And do not keep striving for what you are to eat and what you are to drink, and do not keep worrying. For it is the nations of the world that strive after all these things, and your Father knows that you need them. Instead, strive for his kingdom, and these things will be given to you as well." (vv. 22–31)

> (D) "Do not be afraid, little flock, for it is your Father's good pleasure to give you the kingdom. Sell your possessions, and give alms. Make purses for yourselves that do not wear out, an unfailing treasure in heaven, where no thief comes near and no moth destroys. For where your treasure is, there your heart will be also." (vv. 32–34)

To interpret the parable of the Rich Fool properly it is important to see how it fits into its larger literary context. Jesus gives two important teachings in this section: first, he addresses the gathered crowd with a parable about the Rich Fool (unit B) who hoarded his money, and then he turns to his disciples and exhorts them not to worry about what they will eat or wear (C). Though these two units are different in focus, Jesus brings them together in his conclusion (D).

He begins his concluding remarks (D) by explaining why there is no reason for worry about food or clothing: "it is your Father's good pleasure to give you the kingdom" (v. 32). This statement clearly refers back to the immediately preceding teaching (C) on worldly anxiety: "For it is the nations of the world that strive after all these things, and your Father knows that you need them. Instead, strive for his kingdom, and these things [food and clothing] will be given to you as well" (v. 31). But the next two sentences ("Sell your possessions and give alms . . . ") point further back to the parable of the Rich Fool. For at the end of that parable, Jesus made a contrast between those who "store up treasures for themselves" and those who are "rich toward God." The term that is used to describe the destination of one's alms in our summary statement, "[unfailing] treasure" (*thesauros*, v. 33), is the same word that describes the fool's hoarding of his resources, "who store up treasure for themselves" (*thesaurizo*, v. 21). Because being "rich toward God" is the opposite of laying up treasures for oneself, it must refer to the act of distributing goods to the poor. Moreover, the contrast between storing treasure for oneself as opposed to God recalls the antimony that was so basic to the way in which Proverbs 10:2 was read in both Ben Sira and Tobit.

What unites the parable (B) and the exhortation (C) is the lesson they provide about how to contemplate the future. The parable is introduced by a reprimand that Jesus gives to a young man who is worried about securing his portion of the family inheritance. The true meaning of life, Jesus told him, does not consist of possessions, even when they exist in abundance (v. 15). The temptation for the wealthy is to think that because they have abundant resources, the future will be bereft of worries. A vast store of money, they believe, can be relied upon to save them from the uncertainties that the future might hold.[15] And so the teaching of Proverbs 10:2 is stood on its head: an ample treasury—in this case enormous barns— can provide a secure hedge against the ravages that may lurk in the future. Our Rich Fool believes that his freedom from anxiety will allow him to enjoy the fruits of his labor. "Soul," he reasons, "you have ample goods laid up for many years." *What harm could the future hold that would not be covered by your wealth?* "Relax, eat, drink, be merry!" (v. 19). The Rich Fool has ascribed a power to human wealth that Ben Sira had explicitly warned against (cf. 5:1–3 and 8).[16] Only through generosity to the poor can one make adequate preparation for the future.

The second address, given to the disciples alone, goes a little bit deeper. Since they have given up *everything* to follow Jesus (unlike the individuals in the crowd, whose attachment to Jesus is not so all-consuming), they have ample reason to worry about the future. It is one thing to put false hopes in accumulated wealth, quite another to give it all away and greet the future without a penny to your name. Jesus assuages the disciples' fears by returning to the imagery of the storehouse. (At this point, it is worth pointing out that the term in Hebrew for treasury in Proverbs 10:2 literally means "storehouse." It is a place where any sort of material good, not just money, can be laid up.) "Consider the ravens," Jesus urges, "they neither sow nor reap, *they have neither storehouse nor barn,* and yet God feeds them. Of how much more value are you than birds!" (v. 24). And because you are of such value to God, he will certainly provide for you just as he does for the ravens. So give your possessions away as alms and "strive for his kingdom." God knows what you need and "these things will be given to you as well."

By focusing on the false security that money provides, Jesus provides a teaching that draws deeply on the way Proverbs 10:2 was read by Ben Sira, Tobit, and the author of 1 Enoch 37–71. Ben Sira 31 may be the most apposite example, for it states that wealth can be the means by which God will test the mettle of his servants ("It is a stumbling block for the foolish; the simple minded are taken captive by it"). A fully stocked storehouse may appear to offer security for whatever Lady Fortune has up her sleeve, but such security is deceptive (*nikse-sheqer*).[17]

We have seen that Proverbs 10:2 and its near relative 11:4 exerted a strong influence on Second Temple sources, each source using the proverb for its own purposes. What they all agree on, however, is the important role alms-giving plays as a *diagnostic* of faith. It is natural to place hope in accumu-lated wealth. Yet the sources we have considered have strongly qualified those hopes. Material wealth is not to be shunned—neither Ben Sira nor Tobit was an ascetic—but neither is one to put undue confidence in it. Ultimately, only God is worthy of such confidence, and the commandment to give alms depends on a profound faith in that fact—you become more secure by giving your money away.

We saw in Sirach 29 a focus on the second half of the proverb—the power of almsgiving to save the generous soul from any imaginable danger that might confront him in this world. "Store up almsgiving in your trea-sury, and it will rescue you from every disaster." The figure of Tobit followed a similar strategy. But rather than providing us with several metaphors for rendering the idea of being "delivered from death," he gave us just one—almsgiving delivers from death and "keeps you from going into the Darkness." The function of this particular gloss is transparent; because Tobit had been struck with blindness as his "reward" for being virtuous, it was particularly apt that almsgiving have the power specifically to deliver one from such darkness. Raphael's instruction included a different variation, emphasizing that almsgiving cleanses one's account of the debt caused by sin. This is a fitting image for his speech because he is concerned to address the ongoing problem of the exile. The hoped-for return of the nation to its land can be accomplished only once the debt has been paid.

Sirach 5 and 1 Enoch 63 take the first half of the proverb as their point of departure. I have noted the ambiguity of the phrase "treasuries of wickedness." Though almost all modern translators have rendered this genitival clause as "ill-gotten wealth," we have seen that this did not really work well with the parallelism of almsgiving. A far more natural antinomy would be avarice and generosity. And this is precisely what we find. For Ben Sira and 1 Enoch the problem with wealth is that it gives one a deceptive confidence about the future. Money has a power that might seem to be able to obviate all difficulties, but experience shows that this is not the case.

The most complex of all these texts is Luke 12:13–34. The pericope ends with an instruction to fund a treasury in heaven, where neither moth nor rust would destroy, and thieves could not break in (vv. 33–34). This teaching points back both to the story about the Rich Fool (vv. 16–21), who had thought well-stocked barns would guarantee a carefree future, and to the anxiety of the disciples about having given up earthly wealth to follow Jesus (vv. 22–32). The rich man has made precisely the error our proverb warns about—he has concluded that his storehouses will grant true security ("Soul, you have ample goods laid up for many years"). But he has forgotten to ponder the world to come. What value will wealth have for him there? Better to be rich toward God through charity than to have "stored up" (*thesaurizo*) many goods for oneself.

Reprise: Is Charity a Selfish Act?

I would like to address a question that has been hanging over our heads through the first several chapters. It has been my thesis that almsgiving became such an important part of Second Temple Judaism (and by extension the early church and synagogue) because it was not just a human transaction but a sacrifice made to God himself. Chrysostom captures this sensibility quite well in the fourth century when he urges his congregants after the celebration of the Mass to go out into the streets and to continue encountering Christ at the "many altars" they will find at every street corner. We can profitably compare this to the habit of Jewish beggars addressing their potential patrons with the words: *zeki bi*—"acquire a merit in heaven through a gift to me." As the purpose of the altar was to convey goods from heaven to earth, the poor were imagined, in both Judaism and Christianity, as direct conduits to the Holy One (Blessed be He!). Just as God actually eats, in the "realistic" world of the Temple cult, so in the realistic world of the almsgiving cult, God actually borrows money. (And so the candid words of Rabbi Yohanan: "Had it not been written in scripture, it would have been impossible to say it."[18] The Peshitta [Syriac Bible] does Rabbi Yohanan one better by translating the verse in such a way that the loan metaphor disappears! The realistic language of the cult is always a scandal.) For this reason, Proverbs 10:2 and 19:17 became the defining markers of this new form of spirituality: Almsgiving delivers from death and almsgiving is a loan to God that he will surely repay.

This image has always been a stumbling block for Protestants. It confirms their biggest worries about the nature of religious piety in both Judaism and Catholicism: they are religions in which the believer dictates to God the terms of his salvation. Gunther Bornkamm summarizes this "inferior" form of piety as follows:

> In late Judaism, the doctrine of rewards receives its final destructive turn. The reward ceases to be God's free promise and becomes a form of financial capital which individual observers of the law acquire for themselves in heaven and whose payout they can await with certainty. The religious see themselves in the position of a person who is about to emigrate and has invested funds in a bank within the country to which he will soon arrive. God has given the law to these religious persons so that they can create this assurance for themselves and acquire this capital.[19]

In this oft cited work, Bornkamm makes it clear that this financial model of exchange began in the synagogue but was later adopted by the Roman Catholic Church.[20] Indeed, on the very first page, he declares that just as Martin Luther freed us from this religious error through his doctrine of salvation by grace alone, so Immanuel Kant (not by accident, a fellow

Lutheran) freed us from the moral error of eudaimonism with his doctrine of duty.[21] No act could be moral, Kant argued, if it was prompted by self-interest.

In spite of these anti-Catholic and -Jewish prejudices, there is a point to be made here. I think most would agree that an act rises in moral stature to the degree that it is not governed by self-interest. But the severity of the Kantian perspective is often overlooked by those who brandish this weapon against the early Jewish construal of charity to the poor. Let me offer two reasons why we should temper our enthusiasm for Kant in these matters.

Pope Benedict XVI, in his encyclical letter on love (*Deus caritas est*), has expressed serious reservations about an ethics that would completely separate unmerited love for the other (*agape*) from love that benefits the self (*eros*). "Were this antithesis (between *agape* and *eros*) to be taken to extremes," Benedict argues, "the essence of Christianity would be detached from the vital relations fundamental to human existence, and would become a world apart, admirable perhaps, but decisively cut off from the complex fabric of human life. . . . Man cannot live by oblative, descending love (*agape*) alone. He cannot always give, he must also receive."[22] Benedict is arguing for an important principle of Catholic theology: grace heals and elevates nature; it does not obliterate it. Any account of our moral life must begin with who we are as *embodied* beings. In this respect we must confess that built into our very DNA is the aspiration for self-preservation and self-fulfillment; human beings are no more able to detach themselves from these desires than they are able to stop breathing on their own. (Even were one successful in the latter, the result would be fainting, at which point the body would begin breathing again on its own. Even the suicide requires a noose.) The genius of the treasury in heaven is that it takes the primal fears we all share about what the future may bring and converts them into actions in service to others. It is a paradoxical economy of exchange that this idea sets in motion. Becoming wealthy requires distributing one's goods to the poor.

But the deeper problem with the Kantian perspective is the decision to focus solely on the moral agent. If we are going to judge the theological value of the "treasury in heaven" through this lens alone, there is little question that a considerable challenge lies ahead. It is hard to argue with Antigonus of Socho: "Be not like servants who serve their master on condition of receiving a gift." But it is important, for this very reason, to pay close attention to the issue on the table in Proverbs 10:2, the exegetical source for the concept itself. This text's primary concern is not moral but metaphysical. By this I mean that it is intended to help us set our gaze beyond the mere appearances of this world toward its ultimate God-given nature.

This proverb presents the careful reader with a construal of the world that is dramatically at variance with that of the jaded realist. Though it may appear that a good supply of stocks and bonds is the best assurance for a prosperous future, scripture presents a different portrait of the nature of the reality. The believer recognizes himself in a world that rewards charity because it was founded upon charity. The point is subtle but worth restating: when I fund a treasury in heaven, I make a statement about the *nature* of the world God has made. There is something profoundly evangelical (*eu* + *angelizo*—"to spread the good news") about this. Funding a treasury becomes a rational act for the believer because by acting this way she is actually swimming with the current that God has fixed in the created order. This is why the one who gives away her money becomes the most effective saver for the future. The emphasis is not on my own self-interest but on unlocking a secret about the structure of the universe.

Let us return for a moment to the mishna of Antigonus: "Be not like servants who serve their master on condition of receiving a gift." It's hard to dispute the wisdom of this saying, but if we gaze behind the veil, wouldn't we want to contend that servants—over the long run—can serve a master in this selfless fashion only if they believe in his beneficence? To Kant's horror there is an implied metaphysics to the execution of duty.[23] Doubling back to Pope Benedict, maybe one must first affirm the reality of the treasury in heaven in order to serve the Master of that Treasury upon condition of no reward. A paradox to be sure. But a paradox that honors our *human* nature which grace—however powerful it may be—must work with, not against. The book of Tobit, sketched in clear deference to the book of Job, makes precisely that point, and to this book we now turn.

CHAPTER FIVE

Deliverance from Death

Consider and answer me, O LORD my God!
  Give light to my eyes, or I will sleep the sleep of death.
—Psalm 13:3

What joy is left for me any more? I am a man without eyesight; I cannot see the
light of heaven, but I lie in darkness like the dead who no longer see the light.
—Tobit 5:10

In our previous chapter we examined the way in which the proverbial
saying "almsgiving delivers from death" was understood in Ben Sira,
Tobit, Enoch, and the Gospel of Luke. But we did not have the opportunity to ask precisely what deliverance from death might mean. For most
Bible readers, the only possible understanding of this verse is the one that
we saw in the parable of the rich fool (Luke 12:16–21). To be saved from
death means to be saved from everlasting damnation and to enjoy the
benefits of the resurrection of the body in the coming Kingdom of God.

But to the surprise of many, that is not what the authors of Proverbs,
Tobit, or Ben Sira intended to teach. When these books were written, the
Jewish expectation of a bodily resurrection was not yet widespread. If
almsgiving was to provide deliverance from death, it had to do so within
the temporal frame of this world. For these writers, to be delivered from
death meant to be saved from what appeared to be a devastating tragedy—
terrible illness, the death of one's children, or exile to a hostile nation. A
moment, to be sure, that encroached upon the domain of physical death

70

but in the end did not enter that dark door. The best place to see how this could be understood is in the book of Tobit.[1]

The Trials of Tobit

This book is set during the first few decades after the Assyrian invasion of the northern kingdom of Israel (to be distinguished from its southern counterpart, the kingdom of Judah, whose capital was Jerusalem) in 721 BCE and the forced exile of many of its leading citizens to Nineveh, the capital city of Assyria. As soon as Tobit arrives in Assyria, he begins to distribute alms to his needy compatriots. In this particular book, alms include the provision of food for the hungry, clothes for the naked, and burial for the dead. Initially, Tobit is greatly rewarded for his piety; he is appointed to a high-level post in the administration of the Assyrian king Shalmaneser. Once, while traveling on official business in the East in the realm of Media (an ancient Iranian kingdom), he decides to leave some of his earnings on deposit with a kinsman whom he trusts:

> Because I was mindful of God with all my heart, the Most High gave me favor and good standing with Shalmaneser, and I used to buy everything he needed. Until his death I used to go into Media and buy for him there. While in the country of Media I left bags of silver worth ten talents in trust with Gabael, the brother of Gabri. But when Shalmaneser died, and his son Sennacherib reigned in his place, the highways into Media became unsafe and I could no longer go there. (1:12–15)

Presumably he does this in order to diversify the considerable wealth with which he had been blessed.[2] Though Tobit was renowned for his generosity, he was no fool when it came to managing his own finances: should his funds in Nineveh dry up, he could be assured of the safety of these additional monies. At this point in the story, Tobit has been amply rewarded for his piety. Through his generosity he has become exceedingly rich.

But things take a terrible turn for the worse when Sennacherib comes to the throne. After being thwarted in his attempt to capture the city of Jerusalem and thus bring the entire province of Judah to its knees, he retreats in shame to Nineveh. Upon his return Sennacherib vents his rage upon the exiles from northern Israel who reside in Nineveh. He has a number of them put to death and then, to add insult to injury, he leaves their bodies unburied—the most ignominious thing one can do to an enemy in the ancient Near East. In spite of the great danger, Tobit assumes upon himself the obligation to bury the unattended corpse (known in Jewish law as *met mitsva*). Tragically, the king gets wind of what he is doing and puts a price on his life. Tobit, in great fear and haste, leaves Nineveh to seek asylum in the countryside. All of his belongings are expropriated; he is left penniless and, much worse, family-less.

Yet Tobit's fortunes quickly change. Shortly after Sennacherib returns to Nineveh, he is assassinated. His son, Esarhaddon, comes to power and, as luck (or better, Providence) would have it, he appoints Ahikar, Tobit's nephew, to a high post in his royal office. Ahikar uses this newfound power to intercede on behalf of his uncle, and in short order Tobit is allowed to return to Nineveh and rejoin his family. So in spite of a brief moment of despair, almsgiving appears to be an activity that God conscientiously rewards.

When Tobit returns to his family, it is late spring and we see Tobit and his family celebrating the feast of Pentecost. Tobit's virtues are again on display:

> At our festival of Pentecost, which is the sacred festival of weeks, a good dinner was prepared for me and I reclined to eat. When the table was set for me, and an abundance of food placed before me, I said to my son Tobias, "Go, my child, and bring whatever poor person you may find of our people among the exiles in Nineveh, who is wholeheartedly mindful of God, and he shall eat together with me. I will wait for you, until you come back." So Tobias went to look for some poor person of our people. When he had returned, he said, "Father!" And I replied, "Here I am, my child."[3] Then he went on to say, "Look, father, one of our own people has been murdered and thrown into the market place, and now he lies there strangled." Then I sprang up, left the dinner before even tasting it, and removed the body from the square and I laid it in one of the rooms until sunset when I might bury it. When I returned, I washed myself and ate my food in sorrow. (2:1b–5)

The alacrity with which Tobit takes up his charitable responsibilities is striking. As biblical scholars have long noted, the Bible rarely indicates a person's desire to perform a commandment or fulfill a responsibility by describing his personal feelings. Rather, it is the habit of biblical writers to indicate personal dispositions by describing the *actions* of the moral agent. We learn, for example, that Abraham is zealous to fulfill the commandment of sacrificing Isaac from the fact that he rises early in the morning and saddles his own donkey (rather than allowing his servants to do it).[4] Similarly, we learn of Tobit's zeal for the law by the fact that he has left his dinner untouched in his haste to tend to the exposed corpse. His extraordinary zeal, as we will shortly see, does not go unnoticed by the heavenly host; indeed, it becomes the cause of his deliverance at the end of the book.

After he has buried the corpses and returned to his home, Tobit washes himself and then lies down beside a wall in his courtyard to fall asleep.[5] Unbeknownst to Tobit, there are sparrows perched upon that wall, and "their fresh droppings fell into [his] eyes and produced white films." He visits several different physicians, but they only make matters worse. "The more they treated me with ointments," Tobit reports, "the more my vision was obscured by the white films, until I became completely blind" (2:10). For two years, he is cared for by his nephew Ahikar. But then Ahikar relocates to Elymais, a kingdom far south of Nineveh, at the head of the Persian Gulf, and Tobit's life takes yet another bad turn: for two subsequent years he becomes dependent on the care of Anna, his wife.[6]

In despair over his plight, Tobit turns in prayer to God and pleads that he take his life. God, as the reader learns at the close of this prayer, has heard Tobit's earnest words and has been stirred to rectify what has gone awry. Ironically, Tobit has a sense that his prayer has been heard but believes that God intends to take his life and so spare him from any further dishonor. Confident that his life is near its end, he does what fathers often do in the Bible—he calls his son to his bedside for one last moment of instruction.[7]

The occasion for the instruction is Tobit's sudden recollection of the funds that he had left on deposit in Media. Though the roads to Media had become unsafe shortly after he left, evidently things have improved enough to make the journey imaginable. Yet it should be emphasized that the way to Media was never completely safe, and the lessons of the past, as we will see, were not lost on Tobit's wife Anna. While getting ready to provide Tobias with instructions as to how the money could be retrieved, Tobit opens what he believes is his last will and testament by instructing Tobias to abide by three essential commandments: (1) To maintain, honor, and eventually bury his mother after Tobit has passed away; (2) to give alms generously to all the deserving poor; and (3) to seek out a wife from the descendants of his ancestors and not from a foreign people.

Upon hearing his father's wishes, Tobias immediately gives his consent. But before sending him on his way, Tobit exhorts his son to seek out a trustworthy man to guide him on the journey—an obvious nod to the dangers involved in making this trip and an attempt to mitigate them. As it turns out, the man that Tobias hires for the job is none other than the angel Raphael. Providence is clearly on the side of this family.

During the first stop, at the Tigris River, Tobias goes to wash his feet and is attacked by an enormous fish. Raphael instructs him to grab the fish, bring it ashore, and remove its gall, heart, and liver. The heart and liver will prove valuable when Tobias reaches the city of Ecbatana in Media. There he will meet Sarah, an only child who is destined to be his wife. There is a slight challenge, however, for it seems that Sarah has been engaged to seven men, each of whom has mysteriously died on the night of their wedding. Tobias is obviously apprehensive about his potential bride, but Raphael assures him that all will be fine provided that he and Sarah turn to God in prayer and that he roast the heart and liver taken from the fish within his wedding chamber so as to drive away the wicked demon Asmodeus, who had slain the previous seven suitors. The tactic works. Tobias is able to consummate the marriage and—to the surprise of all— greet the following morning.

Tobias sends Raphael ahead to secure the money left on deposit while he remains in Ecbatana for the fourteen days allotted for the celebration of the wedding. Raguel and Edna, the parents of Sarah, provide Tobias with half of their estate and promise him the remainder when they die. With that, Tobias, Sarah, and Raphael depart, taking with them numerous household servants as well as the extraordinary wealth that Tobias has stumbled into. It must have been a formidable sight to see this caravan make its way along those ancient roads. Upon his return to Nineveh, Tobias first greets his mother, who has been anxiously awaiting his return at the roadside, then meets his father just outside the door of the home. When he applies an ointment made from the gall of the fish to his father's eyes, the white film which had blinded Tobit falls to the ground, and Tobit can again see his son and all the goods that he has brought back to Nineveh.[8]

Give Light to My Eyes

It is not by accident that our author has chosen blindness as the particular motif with which to test the faith of Tobit. To be blind in the Bible is to be equated with the dying or the dead. Consider, for example, the states of Isaac, Jacob, and Eli at the ends of their lives.[9] All suffer from poor vision. Isaac, for example, is fooled by his son Jacob as a result of his impaired eyesight (Gen 27). Though he has intended to pass on the patriarchal blessing to his firstborn, Esau, his second born, Jacob, dresses himself up so as to resemble his brother and in this fashion exploits his father's blindness to acquire the blessing for himself. Jacob appears to be set up for the same sort of trickery at the hand of his son Joseph. Although Joseph has wanted his father to provide the highest form of blessing for his first-born son, Manasseh, the nearly blind Jacob is perceptive enough to see through this tactic and give the preferential blessing to Ephraim, the second born (Gen 48:17–20). Eli's dim vision overlaps (1 Sam 3:2) his inability to supervise his sons' priestly activity in a proper fashion.

Elsewhere in the Bible, darkness is the defining feature of Sheol, the place where many of Israel's dead are consigned. Consider this example from the book of Job: "Before I go, never to return, to the land of gloom and deep darkness, the land of gloom and chaos, where light is like darkness" (10:21–22). Similarly, a person on the way to death could be described as one whose lamp has gone out. Consider the words of Bildad, a friend of Job as well as an ardent believer in the notion that God punishes evil wherever it may appear: "Surely the light of the wicked is put out, and the flame of their fire does not shine. The light is dark in their tent, and the lamp above them is put out. . . . They are thrust from light into darkness, and driven out of the world" (18:5–6, 18).

Correlatively, we read in the book of Psalms about those who believe their time on earth is near its end. They implore God to take note of their plight:

Consider and answer me, O LORD my God! Give *light to my eyes,* or I will sleep the sleep of death. (13:3)

My heart throbs, my strength fails me; as for the *light of my eyes*—it also has gone from me. (38:10)

In all of these poetic texts, whether from Job or Psalms, it is presumed that God is the one who illumines the eyes: "It is you who light my lamp; the LORD, my God, lights up my darkness (Ps 18:28). As Patrick Miller astutely notes, "light is an image for life."[10]

What is more, the figure of Tobit affirms this very truth in his own words. When his son Tobias introduces him to Raphael for the first time, they exchange initial pleasantries as all well-mannered individuals do. But when Raphael, in all innocence, goes on to say: "Joyous greetings to you!" Tobit is cut to the quick. No longer able to keep his composure, he lets despair get the best of him: "What joy is left for me any more? I am a man without eyesight; I cannot see the light of heaven, but I lie in darkness like the dead who no longer see the light. Although still alive, I am among the dead. I hear people but I cannot see them" (5:10). Similarly near the end of the book the image of light returns. After Tobias has applied ointment to Tobit's eyes and the white film falls away, we are told that he "saw his son and threw his arms around him and wept and said to him, "I see you, my son, the light of my eyes!" Then he addresses his God with words of thanksgiving:

> Blessed be God
>> and blessed be his great name,
>> and blessed be all his holy angels.
> May his holy name be blessed
>> throughout all the ages.
> Though he has afflicted me,
>> he has had mercy upon me.
>> Now I see my son Tobias! (Tobit 11:14–15a)

The key phrase for our purposes is Tobit's affirmation that though God has "afflicted [him], he has [now] shown mercy" on him by allowing him to "see [his] son Tobias." Just a couple of chapters later, Tobit will offer a song of thanksgiving for the larger Israelite community. In that version he will recycle this line and modify its form slightly yet significantly:

> Blessed be God who lives forever;
>> because his kingdom lasts throughout all ages.
> For he afflicts, and he shows mercy;
>> he leads down to Hades in the lowest regions of the earth,
>> and he brings up from the great abyss,
>> and there is nothing that can escape his hand. (13:1–2)

Whereas earlier Tobit stated that the God who had once afflicted him had now shown mercy, now he provides a further gloss on this act of redemption: God "afflicts and he shows mercy; *he leads down to Hades . . . and . . . brings up from the great abyss.*"

What must be emphasized is the fact that Tobit connects his blindness with entering the realm of death itself. This sort of language can sometimes puzzle the modern reader, for the temptation is to reduce extravagant claims such as these to "mere" metaphor. But for biblical writers that would not be accurate, for death in their minds was a more flexible concept.[11] It encompassed not just the moment of drawing one's last breath but also those tragic moments when one's very life was at risk: terrible illness, blindness, and exile. Jon Levenson has expressed this insight quite well:

Whereas we think of a person who is gravely ill, under lethal assault, or sentenced to capital punishment as still alive, the Israelites were quite capable of seeing such an individual as dead. Or, to be more precise, they could do so in their poetic literature without, it seems to me, implying that in a more prosaic genre (like historiography or religious law) they would make the same categorization. In other words, for us death is radically discontinuous with life, a quantum leap, as it were, lying between the two. For the psalmists, by contrast, the discontinuity lay between a healthy and successful life and one marked by adversity, in physical health or otherwise. . . . We are predisposed to think that ancient Israelites conceived of death as involving two stages, one characterized by intense affliction but capable of reversal and another permanent and irreversible, like death as modern secular thought conceives it. In fact, they saw illness as continuous with death and thought of the reversal of illness as so miraculous as to be in the nature of a resurrection.[12]

Time and again in the psalter, the psalmist prays to be pulled out of Sheol, thus asking of God a dramatic intervention that will reverse what appears to be an inevitable plunge into darkness. It is this powerful combination of a dreaded inevitability with a dramatic and unexpected reversal that leads the biblical author to describe such an experience as a resurrection from the dead. Taking this biblical language into account, one can see why the author of Tobit describes the restoration of Tobit's sight as a resurrection from the dead. For he had thought himself to be consigned to an unhappy end—blind and bereft of grandchildren—yet at the end of the day he lives twice as long as he had expected and with his restored vision is able to enjoy the return of his son and the birth of his grandchildren. By the time we reach the denouement of our tale, we can see that the promised reward for one who gives alms—deliverance from death—has been fulfilled.

The same sort of imagery is found at the very end of the book when Tobit provides Tobias with his last instruction in Torah. As to be expected, Tobit puts special emphasis on the command to give alms. It will save you from death, Tobit declares, and then he adds the example of what had happened to his nephew Ahikar. We should recall that Ahikar supported Tobit for the first two years after he became blind, an act of mercy that was amply rewarded:

See my son, what Nadab did to Ahikar who had reared him. Was he not, while still alive, brought down into the earth? For God repaid him to his face for this shameful treatment. Ahikar came out into the light, but Nadab went into the eternal darkness, because he tried to kill Ahikar. Because he gave alms, Ahikar escaped the fatal trap that Nadab had set for him, but Nadab fell into it himself, and was destroyed. So now, my children, see what almsgiving accomplishes, and what injustice does—it brings death! (14:10b–11)

Commentators have occasionally puzzled over what exactly it was that Nadab did to Ahikar and what happened to him.[13] Some have claimed that Nadab actually dies as a result of his wickedness ("Nadab went into the eternal darkness"). But on the basis of how resurrection language works in this book, that is not a necessary conclusion. The reason for the confusion among scholars, however, is important to clarify. The fact that our author is so beholden to the imagery of light and darkness makes it difficult to discern to what particular circumstances it refers. The fact that our text contrasts the fate of Ahikar and Nadab as either coming into the light or entering darkness leads me to believe that we are talking about a more mundane (to our sensibility) situation. Nadab had threatened Ahikar with death, perhaps in the form of imprisonment or exile, but in the end fell into the trap he had laid. Tobit's formulation of that ancient proverb had proven accurate: almsgiving does deliver one from death and *going into darkness*. The lack of historical detail in this tale about Nadab and Ahikar is significant—its intent is to focus our attention on the truthfulness of Tobit's earlier instruction.

The Return of the Beloved Son

Though the author of Tobit clearly puts a great deal of emphasis on the healing of his blindness, it would not be fair to the overall narrative to limit our discussion of Tobit's resurrection to the moment when Tobias anoints his eyes with the salve made from the gall of the fish. There is another aspect of the book that plays into this theme as well. When Tobit decides to send Tobias on the trip to Media, just before he thinks he will die, he assumes an enormous risk upon himself and his family. Tobias is an only child and unmarried to boot. Should he fail to return, he would leave his parents childless. There would be no one to support Anna or to preserve Tobit's name after his death (cf. 6:14–15).[14] These are among the gravest calamities that could strike a person in the ancient world, a state that would also be akin to death. This tragic condition is well reflected in any number of biblical narratives, including the book of Ruth and the second half of Isaiah.[15]

But the best parallel to the risk Tobit assumes (and the reward he will reap) when he sends Tobias on that fateful journey is found in the Joseph story. Both narratives turn on the decision of a father to send his beloved son on a dangerous journey. And in both of these stories the restoration of the beloved son is understood as a moment of resurrection. It is my contention that one cannot understand the book of Tobit without paying careful attention to the way in which it draws upon the book of Genesis. But in order to establish this thesis we must pause briefly to review Joseph's story.

The narrative begins with the elevation of Joseph as the beloved of his father, the anger this occasions among the other siblings, and the fateful decision of Jacob to send Joseph on a journey that ends with what his father is led to believe has been a horrible death at the hands of a wild animal. When Jacob learns of the death, he painfully laments the loss of the firstborn son of his beloved wife, Rachel. His other sons urge him to abandon his mourning attire once the period appointed for such a rite has passed, but Jacob refuses. "No," he declares, "I shall go down to Sheol to my son, mourning" (Gen 37:35). Several chapters later, Jacob finds himself in a similar situation. With the famine intensifying in the land of Canaan, he commands his sons to descend to Egypt to purchase more grain. But Judah informs his father that the man in charge of grain in Egypt had told them not to return without their youngest sibling, Benjamin. By this time in the story, Jacob has learned that sending his sons off on such a journey is fraught with danger. In despair over the prospect of losing the second of his two sons from Rachel he declares: "My son shall not go down with you, for his brother is dead, and he alone is left. If harm should come to him on the journey that you are to make, you would bring down my gray hairs with sorrow to Sheol" (42:38).

But eventually the circumstances of the famine forces Jacob to relent and release his son. Yet strikingly, it is this "sacrifice" on the part of Jacob that brings the whole set of tragic events that had befallen this family to closure. By agreeing to send Benjamin on this risky venture, Jacob not only secures food for himself and his family but also receives back Simeon and even Joseph, the son who he had thought was dead.

> So they went up out of Egypt and came to their father Jacob in the land of Canaan. And they told him, "Joseph is still alive! He is even ruler over all the land of Egypt." He was stunned; he could not believe them. But when they told him all the words of Joseph that he had said to them, and when he saw the wagons that Joseph had sent to carry him, the spirit of their father Jacob revived. Israel said, "Enough! My son Joseph is still alive. I must go and see him before I die." (Gen 45: 25–28)

One should observe that our text says "the spirit of [Jacob] revived" (literally "came back to life") when he heard the news about Joseph. This certainly is a link back to his plaintive cry at the beginning of our tale when he learned of Joseph's death: "I shall go down to Sheol to my son, mourning." It is also significant that Jacob says, "Enough! My son Joseph is still alive. I must go and see him before I die." But he does not say "Enough! My son Joseph is still alive. I must go and see him before I die *and go down to Sheol to be with my ancestors.*" As Jon Levenson has shown, it is striking that the book of Genesis (or the larger narrative complex from Genesis to 2 Kings) never refers to a hero of the faith descending to Sheol.[16] *Sheol,* as scholars are slowly coming to realize, is not a prosaic word referring to the domain where *all* the dead dwell as in the rest of the ancient Near East. Rather, Sheol refers to that place where *those who have lived incomplete lives reside.* This includes those like Jacob who lose their children. That is why Jacob referred to the danger of his entering Sheol when he (1) learned of the death of Joseph and (2) worried about the impending threat to Benjamin. It was not his own death that troubled Jacob, but the possibility of dying without any of the children his beloved wife Rachel had borne him.

Jacob's life, however, becomes complete again with the return of Joseph and the opportunity to see and bless him (48:15–16) as well as his grandchildren (48:20) at the end of his life. Though it is perhaps a slight exaggeration, I am inclined to call a scene such as this the beatific vision in its Hebrew Bible inflection. Jacob himself gives splendid testimony to this when he says to Joseph: "I did not expect to see your face; and here God has let me see your children also" (48:11). It is precisely the enjoyment of a moment like this that enables the author of the book of Genesis to dispense with the grim imagery of Sheol in describing the eternal fate of our worthy hero. True enough, there is no postmortem experience of divine blessing. But strikingly, there is no reference to a descent into Sheol. What is put front and center is the biblical hero living to a ripe old age and having the good fortune to see and bless his sons and grandsons.

The parallels to Tobit are quite remarkable. He too is put in the position of having to send his only and beloved son on a life-threatening journey. The risks posed by that trip are hinted at by Tobit himself and subsequently acknowledged openly by Tobit's wife, Anna. Tobit alerts us to the dangers involved in the short prayer he says just before his son's departure: "May God in heaven bring you safely there and return you in good health to me; and may his angel, my son, accompany you both for your safety" (5:17a).

Of course, all interpreters have noted the irony of Tobit's invocation of an angelic accompaniment, given that Raphael stands at the ready to depart with the boy. But Tobit himself knows nothing of such irony—Raphael was a human being in his eyes—and for that reason he calls upon God to show special favor to his son for the journey he is about to undertake. Anna, however, is much less circumspect in giving voice to risks at hand. Our narrator informs us that, just before the journey,

> [Tobias] kissed his father and mother. Tobit then said to him, "Have a safe journey." But his mother began to weep, and said to Tobit, "Why is it that you have sent my child away? Is he not the staff of our hand as he goes in and out before us? Do not heap money upon money, but let it be a ransom for our child. For the life that is given to us by the Lord is enough for us" (5:17b–20).

Yet it is precisely the *risk* that Tobit takes that leads not only to the return of the money he had left on deposit but to the restoration of his sight, the marriage of his son, the acquisition of an enormous inheritance, and eventually the birth of seven grandchildren. Just as Jacob in the book of Genesis is greatly rewarded for his decision to part with Benjamin, so Tobit becomes the recipient of blessings he could never have dreamed of when he sent Tobias to Media.

Modern readers have overlooked the fact that our author understood the restoration of Tobias as a moment of resurrection proper. In order to drive home this point, let us note that our author takes special care to tie the theme of the son's return to that of the healing of Tobit's blindness. Both are understood in terms of a movement from darkness to life, death to resurrection. Consider, for example, Anna's cry of anguish when she figures out that Tobias has not returned on the day he was expected: "'My child has perished and is no longer among the living.' And she began to weep and mourn for her son, saying, 'Woe to me, my child, *the light of my eyes,* that I let you make the journey'" (10:4–5). Similarly, when Tobit's sight is restored, it is not merely the return of his vision that prompts his blessing of God but the chance to *see* his son: "Then Tobit saw his son and threw his arms around him, and he wept and said to him, 'I see you, my son, *the light of my eyes!'*" (11:13b–14a). The motif of the light of one's eyes, which earlier had referred to the onset of blindness, is now extended to include the loss (and eventual restoration) of the sight of the beloved son. In short, to be deprived of the beloved son is to be in the darkness of Sheol; to have him restored is to be bathed in the light of life.

Let me add one final motif to anchor more firmly the links between the figures of Tobias and Joseph. Just before the return of Tobias, we learn that his mother, Anna, has been anxiously awaiting the return of her son day by day at the road leading into Nineveh. It's a heartbreaking scene to imagine. But when Tobias does eventually appear on the horizon, Anna races out to embrace him and exclaims: "Now that I have seen you, my child, I am ready to die" (11:9). These words recall those of Jacob when he had learned from the messengers that Joseph was still alive: "Enough! My son Joseph is still alive. I must go and see him before I die" (Gen 45:28), and his words of greeting upon seeing Joseph: "I can die now, having seen for myself that you are still alive" (46:30).[17]

Of course, Jacob does not die immediately upon seeing Joseph. He is granted the privilege of many more years of life. At the end of his long life, he is granted the beatific moment of being able to see his son and grandsons and to give his paternal blessing to them all (Gen 48:8–21). And so it is for Tobit as well: a man who thought he was preparing for a tragic, premature death at the age of sixty-two, blind, poor, and utterly dependent on the mercy of others, ends up living twice as long, regaining his eyesight, having his wealth restored and multiplied beyond his wildest dreams, and being blessed with seven grandchildren (14:2–3). With complete honesty, Tobit can instruct his family members to be diligent in their almsgiving, never counting the odds regarding the rewards of generosity, for obedience to this command will truly deliver one from death.

CHAPTER SIX

Is Charity Always Rewarded?

Tobit was blind, yet he taught his son the way of God. You know this is true, because Tobit advised his son, *Give alms, my son, for almsdeeds save you from departing into darkness* (Tob 4:7, 11); yet the speaker was in darkness himself. Do you see from this that it is a different light that rises for a just person, and good cheer for those of straightforward heart? Tobit had no eyesight, yet he told his son, *Give alms, my son, for almsdeeds save you from departing into darkness.*

He had no fear that his son might say in his heart, "Did you not give alms yourself? Why, then, are you talking to me out of your blindness? Darkness is where almsgiving has evidently led you, so how can you advise me that *almsdeeds save you from departing into darkness?*"

How could Tobit give that advice with such confidence? Only because he habitually saw another light. The son held his father's hand to help him walk, but the father taught his son the way, that he might live.

—St. Augustine, Homily on Psalm 96

A common assessment of Tobit is that the book reflects what biblical scholars have come to call the "Deuteronomic" retribution theology. What is meant by this is the penchant of the book of Deuteronomy to attribute a life of blessing to obedience to the Torah and a life of suffering to the reverse. At first glance, this characterization of the theology of Tobit seems accurate. For the last chapter of the book makes it clear that if you do good (that is, give alms), you will see the light of day; if you do evil, deepest darkness lies in waiting.[1]

Yet it would be a terrible oversimplification to reduce the message of Tobit to a narrative rehearsal of a wooden deed-consequence theology. For this would be to overlook the central moment in the entire narrative, the divine testing of Tobit. When Tobit prepares to send his son on a fateful journey, he is well aware of the great risk he is taking. Life has not offered him reasons to remain confident in the promises of God. Though scripture had promised that "almsgiving delivers from death," it seemed for Tobit that the reverse was true: works of charity brought one to the threshold of death itself. Augustine, in the epigraph to this chapter, captures this sense well when he notes that Tobit, while he himself is totally blind, teaches his son that almsgiving "saves [one] from departing into darkness." Surely Tobias could have retorted: "[Yet] darkness is where almsgiving has clearly led you, so how can you advise me that almsdeeds save you from departing into darkness?"

The figure of Tobit has been patterned on another man whose faith was sorely tried, Job.[2] A close reading of the book of Tobit requires a careful comparison of these two books. The outer prose frame of the book of Job (chapters 1–2, 42) has a comic structure. It opens with God praising his faithful servant's piety before the heavenly assembly: "Have you considered my servant Job? There is no one like him on the earth, a blameless and upright man who fears God and turns away from evil" (1:8). But a certain heavenly adversary (sometimes translated "Satan") is not persuaded. Job, he contends, is pious simply because of the good life he has lived. In order to clear his faithful servant from this calumnious charge, God allows the adversary to afflict Job. Job survives the test and, in the end, his wealth is restored twofold. He lives to the age of one hundred and forty and to see "his children, and his children's children, four generations" (42:16). The inner poetic dialogues (3–40), on the other hand, consist of a heated theological debate as to whether God can be depended on to reward the works of the just. In these chapters the reliability of divine Providence is put to the test.

In order to understand the plight of Job, one must lend a sensitive ear to his painful complaints in the book's central chapters. This requires a momentary bracketing of how the book ends. Though the reader knows that Job will eventually be rewarded, this is by no means clear to Job or his friends in the midst of their theological debates. Job must make painful decisions about the life of faith in view of a God who appears utterly indifferent to his plight.

The reader of the book of Tobit must possess a similar attentiveness to its structure. Like the book of Job, the book of Tobit possesses a comic outer frame. After God has tested Tobit's faith, he is rewarded with riches beyond counting (chapter 14). But the central moment of Tobit's life (chapters 2–4) consists of a trial that puts the heart of his religion to a painful test. Tobit loses nearly everything he holds dear, and God remains utterly indifferent to his suffering. As with the book of Job, the key to a proper reading of this book is to avoid letting its end overdetermine the trial that stands at its center.

Testing Tobit's Faith

The book of Proverbs teaches that almsgiving will deliver one from all adversity. As we saw in the previous chapter, this formula, at first, works like a charm for Tobit. But after Sennacherib suffers a defeat in Judah, he unleashes his rage on Tobit's kinsmen in Assyria. Tobit's stubborn display of piety puts his very life in danger. Eventually he loses all his property and is driven into exile (1:19–20).

A new king comes to power and allows Tobit to return. But as soon as he comes home, Tobit sends his son into the streets to find a poor person with whom they can share a meal during the feast of Pentecost. When his son ventures forth, he discovers the body of a fellow Jew who was murdered and left to rot in the marketplace. Tobit immediately springs from his chair and hastens to retrieve the body. While burying the corpse, he is mocked by his neighbors: "Is he still not afraid?" they ask. "He has already been hunted down to be put to death for doing this, and he ran away; yet here he is again burying the dead!" (2:8).

That night Tobit falls asleep in a courtyard; the droppings of sparrows that are perched in the wall fall in his eyes, and he becomes blind. Though this tragic event seems to be a moment of terrible bad luck, we learn later in the tale that the whole set of circumstances has been providentially arranged. Near the end of the book, after Tobit has been healed from his blindness, the angel Raphael says: "I will now declare the whole truth to you and will conceal nothing from you. . . . That time when you did not hesitate to get up and leave your dinner to go and bury the dead, *I was sent to you to test you*" (12:11a, 13–14a).

Commentators have puzzled, however, over the exact parameters of the test.[3] And this confusion is understandable because unlike the book of Job, where God and the heavenly adversary discuss both the reason and the means of the test before anything happens, we learn about the test of Tobit's faith only retrospectively.

The task of solving this mystery is left to the reader. It is clear that Tobit's blindness has provided the occasion, but what exactly is the test, and what does God expect from Tobit as a sign that he has passed it?

Tobit as a Joban Figure

To understand this better, let us return to the book of Job. As we have noted, the books of Job and Tobit have numerous structural parallels and a careful reading of Job will cast much light on how we should approach the text of Tobit. In the book of Job the issue on the table is whether Job would serve God for naught (1:9). The test comes in two stages. It begins with a conversation between God and Satan. God asks the angelic adversary whether he has given any thought to his servant Job, a man whose reverence for God is without peer. Satan is not impressed and answers: "Does Job fear God for nothing?" Job's piety, Satan reasons, is hardly exemplary; it is rather simply the result of being favored by God. "But stretch out your hand now, and touch all that he has," Satan suggests, "and he will curse you to your face" (1:9–11).

After Job's children and possessions are taken away, he is understandably disconsolate and gives voice to his grief: "Naked I came from my mother's womb, and naked shall I return there; the LORD gave, and the LORD has taken away; blessed be the name of the LORD" (1:21). Nevertheless, Job remains devout in his faith. "In all this," the narrator concludes, "Job did not sin or charge God with wrongdoing" (1:21–22).

Once Job has passed this first test, the groundwork is laid for a second. God addresses the adversary with words of praise for Job's perseverance. "Have you considered my servant Job?" God inquires. "There is no one like him on the earth, a blameless and upright man who fears God and turns away from evil. He still persists in his integrity, although you incited me against him, to destroy him for no reason" (2:3). But the adversary remains unpersuaded. "Skin for skin! All that people have they will give to save their lives," he responds. "But stretch out your hand now and touch his bone and his flesh, and he will curse you to your face" (2:4–5). God accepts this challenge, and Job is tested a second time, now with a hideous skin disease that repels his neighbors and brings him to the point of death.

The contours of the Joban narrative are picked up nicely in Tobit.[4] Let us recall that Tobit is also subjected to two different trials. In the first trial,

King Sennacherib murders various Israelites in Nineveh and leaves their corpses unburied. Tobit perseveres in his works of mercy by continuing to bury the dead even when it violates an edict of the king. Tobit pays a high price for his integrity; he loses all he owned. Yet through it all, Tobit remains steadfast in his faithfulness. As soon as he returns home, he resumes his generous ways, even though he has to suffer the taunts of his neighbors—a trial that will be repeated shortly through the recriminations of his wife, Anna. But this first test, like that of Job, is limited to the loss of possessions. What if God went further and touched his very person? "Skin for skin," the adversary in Job has argued, "all that people have they will give to save their lives." So God permits a testing of Job that involves his very person. And something very similar happens to Tobit. Though at first the reader believes that Tobit became blind due to the unhappy accident of having sparrow droppings fall in his eyes, at the end of the book we learn that there was nothing accidental about it. For just before he departs for heaven, Raphael reveals that the blindness has been part of a divine test (12:13–14).[5]

But as close as these parallels to Job and Tobit are, they do not tell us the subject of Tobit's test. Though the author of the book of Job is quite explicit about the subject of the test—will Job serve God for naught?—no overt declaration of this sort is made in the book of Tobit. Because we learn about such a test only retrospectively at the end of the tale, the task of discerning its exact contours is left to the reader. I will contend that the answer to this puzzle can be found in the way in which Tobit's wife Anna functions, to a considerable degree, as a literary parallel to Job's wife.

Anna and Job's Wife

In the book of Job, the initial challenge to Job's faith is posed by his wife. While Job wallows in his sad condition, scraping the festering sores on his body with a potsherd, his wife approaches and says, "Do you still persist in your integrity? Curse God, and die." Job, however, is curt in his reply: "You speak as any foolish woman would speak. Shall we receive the good at the hand of God, and not receive the bad?" (2:9–10). In the case of Tobit, a similar challenge is raised by Anna. His blindness had made Tobit dependent on his wife's income as a weaver. Though the contemporary reader will not blink an eye at such a detail, given the familiar role of women in the workforce, the situation was quite different in antiquity. "There is wrath and impudence and great disgrace," Ben Sira teaches, "when a wife supports her husband" (25:22). And to drive home the disgrace of being dependent on another, he adds:

> My child, do not lead the life of a beggar;
> *It is better to die than to beg.*
> When one looks to the table of another,
> One's way of life cannot be considered a life. (40:28–29)

One day, while Tobit is languishing in his ignominy, Anna receives a goat from her employers as a bonus. Tobit, in despair, interprets it as an act of thievery.[6] Insulted by Tobit's persistent charge that she stole the animal and her patience at a breaking point, Anna erupts: "Where are your acts of charity? Where are your righteous deeds? These things are known about you" (2:14b). Though Anna comes off far better than Job's wife—for the pointed barb she aims his way is, in part, a legitimate riposte to the way Tobit had badgered her about the animal she received as a gift—she remains, like Job's wife, skeptical about the fruits of his piety. Rather than asking Tobit to curse God and die, she adroitly highlights the dissonance between what scripture has promised, "almsgiving delivers from death," and Tobit's present condition: "Where are your acts of charity?"

The question that she puts to Tobit (and the reader) is a Joban one. If almsgiving is the very summit of Torah observance, and if the reason for that devotion lies in the promises God has made, then *where* are the good results that are your due? According to the logic of the book, they should have been securely stored in a "heavenly treasury," from which they could be "withdrawn" in a time of trial. But as Anna's question implies, Tobit's heavenly treasury seems to have suffered the fate of earthly wealth; it has failed in a time of crisis ("the treasuries of the wickedness provide no benefit"). His good deeds have been cast into the void, where they are no longer noticed by God. Put this way, Anna's question is not as innocent as it might appear. To be sure, she does not exhort Tobit to curse God as Job's wife does, but she does imply that the very heart of his religion—trust in the precepts of God—is worthy of reevaluation, and perhaps repudiation. The subject of the test has finally come into focus: How committed is Tobit to the commandment of almsgiving? Will he continue to follow this commandment even though it not only has not provided the expected reward but, far worse, seems to have led to his personal demise?

The Journey of Tobias

Tobit's response to this test comes in two stages. First, immediately after his wife has declared that his acts of charity have produced no visible results, and God's abandonment of him has become public knowledge, Tobit turns to God in prayer and declares his belief in God's trustworthiness, a habit that will become known in rabbinic prayer as "declaring the justice of the divine decree" (*tsidduq ha-din*):

> You are righteous, O Lord,
> And all your deeds are just;
> All your ways are mercy and truth;
> You judge the world. (3:2)

The striking thing about this declaration of God's righteousness is that it provides a succinct reply to the theological challenge of his wife just two verses earlier. Her question had been: "Where are your acts of charity (*eleēmosunai*)? Where are your righteous deeds? (*dikaiosunai*)," while his response to God is an unwavering declaration that "you are righteous (*dikaios*) . . . and all your deeds are just (*dikaia*)." In the underlying Hebrew or Aramaic, the juxtaposition would also have been striking as three of the four Greek words I have noted derive from a single Semitic root: *ts-d-q*.[7]

Yet however impressive Tobit's emphatic declaration of God's righteousness may be, it hardly answers Anna's question. Indeed, he would seem to concede the higher ground to Anna when he prays that God take his life (3:6). At this point in the story, the reader has every right to conclude that a life of almsgiving has led to nothing; Tobit's "heavenly treasury" has gone bankrupt. But Tobit's response to Anna is not finished. In the second and far more important stage, Tobit remembers the money that he had left on deposit with Gabael at Rages in Media earlier in the book. Calling to mind his request for death just a moment earlier, he asks "Why do I not call my son Tobias and explain to him about the money before I die?" (4:2). But to the surprise of the reader, it takes Tobit quite some time before he gets to the subject of the money. After he calls Tobias, he provides him with a lengthy instruction regarding the Torah (4:3–19) before returning, at the very end of the chapter (4:20–21), to the subject of the money left on deposit. In the middle of that instruction a strong emphasis is put on the need to give alms. As we have seen, Tobit grounds the reason for this in words that recall Proverbs 10:2, "So you will be laying up a good treasure for yourself against the day of necessity. For almsgiving delivers from death and keeps you from going into Darkness" (4:9–10). Though it has been plausibly suggested that the Torah instruction was a secondary addition—that the chapter originally would have begun with Tobit's proposal to send his son to retrieve the money (4:1–2) and his subsequent departure (4:20 ff.)—this cannot be true.[8] The sending of Tobias and the instruction to give alms constitute the very center-piece of the book. Given the poverty in which Tobit now finds himself, the only way for his son to assume the role of an almsgiver (and avoid the ignominy of the alms receiver) is to come upon a substantial sum of money.[9]

The sending of Tobias provides an ingenious answer to Anna's implied question: Will Tobit persevere in his obedience to this commandment?[10] By instructing his son to continue his practice of charity and then sending him to retrieve the money that will make that possible, Tobit provides an affirmative answer to that question. For it is those funds which will allow Tobias to escape the terrible penury from which the family currently suffers and emerge as a devoted almsgiver himself.[11] The promises attached to the command to give alms are deemed trustworthy in spite of the fact that they have not been realized in Tobit's own lifetime.

Additionally, the sending of the son demonstrates the tremendous risk that Tobit is willing to take to substantiate his belief in the truth of the divine promise. For should Tobias not return, Tobit will have no one to care for his wife or remember him after he dies, a moment that he believes is just around the corner. His lineage and so any memory of him will come to an end. There is a reason why ancient Israelite culture took extraordinary measures to make sure that one not die childless.[12] For in the biblical world, as well as in the ancient Near East as a whole, children were the primary means of providing a legacy after one's death. It was their responsibility to honor their parents' names once they were deceased. Only when we understand the risk of losing an only begotten son can we see how this particular trial will answer the question whether Tobit will serve God for naught. Tobit's devotion to the Torah is so profound that he has put his very future—that there be a son to remember his name after his death—on the line in order to remain obedient to it.

The Sacrifice of Isaac

So far we have explored how closely Tobit tracks the storyline of Job. But the potential loss of an only son points to another intertextual link: the story of Abraham's near sacrifice of Isaac. In order to pursue this line of thought, let us briefly digress and consider the way in which Tobit's life has been shaped by elements in the book of Genesis.

In the previous chapter we examined the similarities between the story of Jacob's sending of Benjamin to Egypt and Tobit's sending of Tobias to Media. Besides the specific parallel between the words of Anna and those of Jacob when they learned that their sons have survived their respective ordeals, we saw that in both cases the dangerous journey that was undertaken resulted in gains that were unimagined by the fathers. Both stories end with restoration from Sheol and what I have called the beatific vision in its Old Testament inflection—the opportunity to bless their sons and grandchildren before they die.

Yet as Jon Levenson has shown, Jacob's sending of Benjamin on this dangerous journey to Egypt also bears a number of parallels with the journey of Abraham and Isaac to Mount Moriah. Each involves a father who must put his beloved son at terrible risk, yet each results in blessings the father could never have dreamed of.[13] In the story of the sacrifice of Isaac, the surprises include the provision of a substitute for the son, a new grounding of the divine promise in the obedience of Abraham, and the restoration of a son ready for marriage. Let us pause for a moment on the subject of marriage.

The theme of marriage is made evident in two ways: first, when Abraham is blessed by God after his ordeal, all the promises that are made are simply repetitions of what God had said earlier save one. Having saved him from the horrible act of sacrificing his son, the angel of the Lord calls to Abraham a second time and says:

> By myself I have sworn, says the LORD: Because you have done this, and have not withheld your son, your only son, I will indeed bless you, and I will make your offspring as numerous as the stars of heaven and as the sand that is on the seashore. And your offspring shall possess the gate of their enemies, and by your offspring shall all the nations of the earth gain blessing for themselves, because you have obeyed my voice. (Gen 22:16–18)

The blessing that Abraham receives in this passage has three parts: first, the promise of numerous offspring; second, power for those offspring over their enemies; and finally, the dissemination of blessing to the other nations of the earth. The first is simply a mild transformation of what had been stated earlier in 13:16 ("I will make your offspring like the dust of the earth") and 15:5 ("Look toward heaven and count the stars. . . . So shall your descendants be"), whereas the third and final part was mentioned already at the call of Abraham in 12:3 ("I will bless those who bless you . . . and in you shall all the families of the earth be blessed"). What is unprecedented is the piece in the middle, "And your offspring shall possess the gate of your enemies." This line points not backward but forward; it anticipates the blessing Isaac's future wife Rebecca will receive from her family just before her departure for the land of Canaan: "May you, our sister, become thousands of myriads; may your offspring gain possession of the gates of their foes" (24:60).

The story of the sacrifice of Isaac or, as it is known in Hebrew, the *aqedah*, ends with what seems to be a complete non sequitur—the genealogy of Nahor, brother of Abraham. One might have thought that this genealogy should have been introduced at the end of chapter 11, when the genealogy of Abraham's extended family was first given. It would have served an excellent literary function there: it would have emphasized the surprise of God's election of Abraham and Sarah, for in contrast to this couple that was unable to have children, Nahor's wife, Milcah, and concubine Reumah were able to bear twelve sons, a symbolic number that bespeaks completeness and divine blessing. Yet one item sticks out in this genealogy and explains why it appears here:

> Now after these things it was told Abraham, "Milcah also has borne children, to your brother Nahor; Uz the first born, Buz his brother, Kemuel the father of Aram, Chesed, Hazo, Pildash, Jidlaph, and Bethuel." *Bethuel became the father of Rebekah.* These eight Milcah bore to Nahor, Abraham's brother. Moreover, his concubine, whose name was Reumah, bore Tebah, Gaham, Tahash, and Maacah. (Gen 22:20–24)

The surprise in this text is the narrative aside in the middle, "Now Bethuel also became the father of Rebekah." This brief excursus ties the theme of Isaac's marriage to his survival of the ordeal of the aqedah. This linkage supports the suggestion of Hugh C. White that the sacrificial rite can be understood as marking Isaac's "passage into independence and manhood."[14] Whereas Isaac enters the story a mere adolescent, dependent on and obedient to the commands of his father, at its close he emerges as a man ready to marry and establish a household of his own.

It is striking that Ishmael also finds a woman suitable for marriage after he has survived a very similar life-threatening ordeal (Gen 21:12–21).[15] As scholars have noted, this tale has multiple parallels with the aqedah. It opens with the command that Abraham cast Hagar and her son out of his household and send them into the wilderness, a trek that portends death (v. 12). After the water Hagar has brought with them fails, she abandons Ishmael, not wishing to watch him die (vv. 15–16). At this point of ultimate despair, when all hope has been lost, an angel of God calls to Hagar from heaven just as an angel will call to Abraham (21:17; 22:11). Hagar's eyes are miraculously opened and she spots a well that will provide the water they need to survive (21:19) just as Abraham is shown the ram that is to be offered in place of his son (22:13). God promises to make a great nation of Ishmael (21:18) as he does for the offspring of Abraham (22:17), and the story comes to a close when Ishmael grows up and his mother secures a wife for him from the land of Egypt (21:21), just as the aqedah closes with two signs of the betrothal to Rebecca (22:17, 23). The fact that both of these narratives end with references to marriage must be underscored. In both cases the ordeals that these sons must undergo end with the beginning of a new family.

Another similarity between the trials that Ishmael and Isaac undergo is the fact that each takes place during a *journey*. As we have seen, Tobias's life is also put at risk through a journey. The danger of the trip itself is emphasized from the start, when Tobit commands him to find a companion for the trip who will know the way. As luck would have it, Tobias bumps into and then hires a man who goes by the name Azariah, but who in fact is the angel Raphael. Yet things take a far more ominous turn when Tobias learns that the house they will stay at in Ecbatana belongs to Raguel and Edna, the parents of Sarah. Raguel "has no male heir and no daughter except Sarah only," Raphael declares, "and you, as next of kin to her, have before all other men a hereditary claim on her.[16] Also it is right for you to inherit her father's possessions. Moreover, the girl is very sensible, brave, and very beautiful, and her father is a good man" (6:12). We might add that Raphael's words reinforce the command that Tobias had received from his father just before his departure: "First of all, marry a woman from among the descendants of your ancestors; do not marry a foreign woman, who is not of your father's tribe; for we are the descendants of the prophets" (4:12). The taking of Sarah's hand is, in part, an act of obedience to his father's will.

On the one hand, such obedience seems extraordinarily attractive. Who would not leap at the possibility of marrying a young woman who is wealthy, without siblings (no competitors for the inheritance), sensible, and beautiful to boot!? Yet as was the case for Ishmael and Isaac, Tobias will not secure his bride until he has undergone a dangerous trial. Sarah, it turns out, is not quite the lucky find that she first appears. Tobias, we learn, has heard about the deaths of all her previous suitors and responds with trepidation to Raphael's proposal,

> Brother Azariah, I have heard that she already has been married to seven husbands and they died in the bridal chamber. On the night when they went in to her, they would die. I have heard people saying that it was a demon that killed them. It does not harm her, but it kills anyone who desires to approach her. So now, since I am the only son my father has, I am afraid that I may die and bring my father's and mother's life down to their grave, grieving for me—and they have no other son to bury them. (6:14–15)

A link back to the Joseph story is established when Tobias remarks that he fears his death would "bring my father's and mother's life down to their grave, grieving for me," for such is the result Jacob fears when he is compelled to part with Benjamin, his beloved son (Gen 42:38, 44:29, cf. 37:35). But there is a link to the aqedah as well. Tobias is quick to emphasize that he is an *only* son; his parent's future rests totally on his fate.

There are still more linkages to the aqedah, as Tzvi Novick has shown.[17] Let's begin with the first day of the journey. By early evening, Tobias and Raphael reach the Tigris River and decide to set up camp (6:2). Tobias goes down to bathe his feet in the water and is suddenly attacked by an enormous fish. When he cries out in anguish, Raphael tells him to catch hold of it and bring it ashore. "Cut open the fish and take out its gall, heart, and liver," Raphael instructs. "Keep them with you, but throw away the intestines. For its gall, heart, and liver are useful as medicine" (6:5). Oddly, Tobias asks no questions about the purpose behind these peculiar instructions. Instead, he simply does what he has been told: "after cutting open the fish, the young man gathered together the gall, heart, and liver; then he roasted and ate some of the fish, and kept some to be salted" (6:6a). Only the next morning, when they are on the road again, does he pose the expected question:

> And the two continued on their way together until they were near Media. Then the young man questioned the angel and said to him, "Brother Azariah, what medicinal value is there in the fish's heart and liver, and in the gall?" (6b–7).

Raphael responds that if one burns the heart and liver, the resulting smoke can be used to drive away demons (6:17–18), a piece of advice that will become extraordinarily useful on Tobias's wedding night, when he fears that the demon Asmodeus will put him to death just as he had done to the previous seven suitors. Tobias recalls the sage advice of Raphael, finds the fish's liver and heart, and turns them into smoke. The odor of the fish "so repelled the demon that he fled to the remotest parts of Egypt" (8:3), and Tobias is saved from the fate that had befallen the other suitors.

As Novick notes, the peculiar deferral of Tobias's initial question about the purpose of the fish (6:6b–7) is paralleled in the story of the aqedah. There we learn that Abraham "rose early in the morning, saddled his donkey, and took two of his young men with him, and his son Isaac; he cut the wood for the burnt offering, and set out and went to the place in the distance that God had shown him." After Abraham spots the designated mountain for the sacrifice on the third day of the journey, he tells his servants: "'Stay here with the donkey; the boy and I will go over there; we will worship, and then we will come back to you.' Abraham took the wood of the burnt offering and laid it on his son Isaac, and he himself carried the fire and the knife" (22:3, 5–6a). Curiously, Isaac poses no question about the significance of this ominous act. Like Tobias, he simply does as his father bids him. Only later in the story, once they have begun to make their way to Mount Moriah, does he pose the question:

> And the two continued on their way together. Isaac said to his father Abraham, "Father!" And he said, "Here I am, my son." He said, "The fire and wood are here, but where is the lamb for a burnt offering?" (22:6b–7)[18]

But it is not just the structure of the two stories that is similar. There is also evidence of direct citation of Genesis 22 in the book of Tobit. Novick notes that the phrase "the two of them walked on together" is rare in the Bible; it occurs just three times, and two of them are found in Genesis 22.[19] It is certainly significant that the very same phrase is found in the book of Tobit: "*And the two walked on together* until they were near Media. Then the young man questioned the angel . . ." And just as in the aqedah, the phrase is used in the book of Tobit to introduce a question that would have been more appropriately voiced earlier in the tale.

I might add that in both the aqedah of Ishmael and that of Isaac, the apparent victim is asked to carry the items that signal the ordeal he will have to undergo.[20] For Ishmael, it is the skin of water that will give out and threaten a death of dehydration in the desert, whereas for Isaac it is the wood that is to be used for the pyre on which he is to be sacrificed. Tobias joins this grouping by being asked to carry the heart and liver of the fish that will be used on his wedding night with Sarah to drive away the demon Asmodeus (8:2–3). This moment of marital consummation is thought to be so dangerous that Raguel orders his household servants to dig a grave as soon as Tobias makes his way to his marital bed (8:9–11).

The Testing of Abraham

Let's pause for a moment and take stock of where we have come. I have claimed that the book of Tobit has been deeply shaped by two intertexts, the testing of Job and the near sacrifice of Isaac. The central scene in the entire book of Tobit—the journey of Tobias to retrieve the money left on deposit in Media—recalls the story of Isaac's journey to Mount Moriah. But at the same time, the willingness of Tobit to send Tobias on this journey constitutes Tobit's answer to Anna's Joban question: "*Where* are your acts of charity?" Tobit so deeply believes in the promises of God that he is ready to risk all that he has by sending his only begotten son on a perilous journey. The heart of the book of Tobit is the result of an intersection of Job and the patriarchs of Genesis.

A striking parallel to this particular combination can be found in the Book of Jubilees, a work that was written in roughly the same time period as was Tobit.[21] Like Tobit, the Book of Jubilees interprets the story of the aqedah through a Joban lens. The author of Jubilees was puzzled by the fact that an omniscient God needed to test Abraham to learn about his character. Working on the assumption that God's actions are consistent across the biblical canon, the author of the Book of Jubilees imports the story of Job into his retelling of the aqedah. He does this by dividing the first sentence of Genesis 22 into two parts and inserting a story based on the book of Job into the middle. God's test of Abraham, on this reading, is the result of Prince Mastema's (another name for Satan) worries about the integrity of the patriarch.

> During [this time] (= Gen 22:1a),
>> there were voices in heaven regarding Abraham, that he was faithful in every-thing that he had told him. . . . Then [Satan] came and said before God: "Abraham does indeed love his son Isaac and finds him more pleasing than anyone else. Tell him to offer him as a sacrifice on an altar. Then you will see whether he performs this order and will know whether he is faithful in every-thing through which you test him." Now the Lord was aware that Abraham was

faithful in every difficulty which he had told him. . . . In everything through
which he tested him he was found faithful. He himself did not grow impatient,
nor was he slow to act; for he was faithful and one who loved the Lord.
The Lord said to him: "Abraham, Abraham!" He replied: "Yes?" (= Gen 22:1b).[22]

The similarities between Tobit and Jubilees are striking. In the book of
Tobit, the near-fatal journey of Tobias to the east to secure his bride recalls
the dangerous ordeal that Isaac underwent at Mount Moriah. Both Tobias
and Isaac carried the elements of their potential death and deliverance. And
both were delivered by the help of an angel. And just as in the book of Tobit,
the journey itself answered a question about the nature of Tobit's obedience,
so Abraham's obedience in Jubilees constitutes an answer to question the
heavenly adversary (Prince Mastema) has made about his character.

Tobit's Ironic Instruction

We can strengthen this claim by tending to the words Tobit uses in what he
thinks is his last opportunity to instruct his son in the ways of Torah. As we
have noted, the central command of the Torah for Tobit and the author of
this book is the command to give alms, which is formulated in terms that
derive from the book of Proverbs: "[By giving alms] you will be laying up a
good treasure for yourself against the day of necessity. For almsgiving
delivers from death and keeps you from going into the Darkness" (4:9–10).
If we were to interpret this statement from the perspective of Tobit's last
words about almsgiving (14:8–11), its meaning would be clear. The one
who is generous will most assuredly prosper in the end. The book provides
us with a classic narrative embodiment of the central claim of the book of
Deuteronomy—those who obey the commands of the Torah will be
blessed. But if we bracket the conclusion of the book for a moment and
attend to Tobit's moment of Torah instruction just before the departure of
Tobias on the journey, it is anything but a simple recycling of Deuteronomy.
Tobit transmits what the book of Proverbs teaches about alms to his
son with the full knowledge that its truth has *not* been reflected in his
own life. The irony is breathtaking, and it is crucial to appreciate its full
depth.

In order to appreciate the immensity of this irony, let's compare what
Tobit says about almsgiving with what he says about his own life. In his
recycling of Proverbs 10:2, Tobit adds that almsgiving is a means of accumulating a heavenly treasury that will "deliver one from death" and "keep

you from going into the Darkness." Yet just one chapter later, when Tobit hears Raphael's friendly words, "Joyous greetings to you!" he responds most bitterly: "What joy is left for me any more? I am a man without eyesight: I cannot see the light of heaven, but lie in darkness like the dead who no longer see the light. Although still alive, I am among the dead. I hear people but I cannot see them" (5:10). The reader, like St. Augustine in the epigraph to this chapter, is arrested by the disparity. How can Tobit, a man who has lost his eyesight due to his generosity and now "lie[s] in darkness like the dead," teach his son that giving alms will deliver one from death and descending into darkness? Could Tobit not face the facts and admit that the truth was just the reverse?

But Tobit's instruction would be reasonable if he presumed that although this piece of wisdom did not hold true within the temporal constraints of his own life, it will be vindicated in the life of his son. The wisdom tradition held that only the elderly can truly be sages; you need the long view to put the events of life in their proper perspective. Sometimes even the span of an entire human life is insufficient. Evidence of God's providence often requires a couple of generations to pass. This is nicely illustrated in the book of Sirach. In 11:26–28, Ben Sira discusses the very problem that concerns us: how to account for the delay in a reward for good behavior. His solution is that one must take the longest view possible. Sometimes one must wait until one's dying day to see the enactment of divine justice. But in other cases, not even this is sufficient to confirm God's justice. One must await the next generation: "Call no one happy before his death; *through his posterity* (literally, "his end") a person becomes known" (v. 28).[23] Because the Old Testament imagines the fundamental identity of the person to continue in the life of their offspring, it is hardly surprising that Tobit would consider the eventual prosperity of his son to be a fitting reward for the obedience he demonstrated.[24]

In addition to this example one should also compare another teaching of Ben Sira:

> The charity (*eleēmosunē*) done by a father will not be forgotten,
>   It will be credited to you against sins.
> In a day of affliction it will be remembered to your benefit;
>   As fair weather upon frost, so will your sins be dissolved.[25] (3:14–15)

Here the main concern is that the merciful deeds done by the father collect in heaven and do not disappear with his death. Though the father may not have benefited, the funds are still retrievable and can rescue the son "in a day of affliction," a phrase that recalls Proverbs 10:2 and 11:4. From these two portions of Ben Sira we learn that the identity of the father is not to be understood in the restrictive modern sense as being limited to the constraints of his earthly life. His identity is not fixed until the moment of "his end" (Ben Sira 11:28), which means both the day of his death and the extension of himself in the lives of his offspring. In such a worldview, the transferability of one's heavenly treasury to a child is to be expected.

If we presume that Tobit understands his son's life to be inextricably bound to his own, then he can convey the teaching of Proverbs 10:2 in good conscience. Almsgiving might not have preserved the father from an early demise, but that does not mean its effects cannot filter down to his son. God has preserved the stored-up capital of Tobit's treasury. But how will Tobias be able to continue fulfilling this commandment if he remains in penury? The only conceivable answer is to send him to Media to collect the money left on deposit.

Yet this is a radical act, for sending his son on such a journey as this is fraught with great risk. Anna appears to have sized up the situation in a far more rational manner. When Raphael and Tobias are about to embark on their journey, Tobit wishes them well, but Anna begins to weep and cries out,

> Why is it that you have sent our child away? Is he not the staff of our hand as he goes in and out before us? Do not heap money upon money, but let it be a ransom for our child. For the life that is given to us by the Lord is enough for us. (5:18–19)

Rather than putting their only child at risk, Anna is willing to forgo a vocation of charity, exchanging both the privileges and responsibilities of wealth for the life of her son.

Anna's Reservations

In making such a proposal, Anna shows herself to be a prudent woman. In the ordinary course of human affairs, it would be difficult to find fault with her reasoning. The health of an only child would seem to trump the demands of this commandment. But risks such as the one that Tobit has proposed are what differentiate the heroes of faith from ordinary individuals. Consider for a moment the two Moabite women Orpah and Ruth.

Each had been married to a son of the Judahite Naomi. Tragically, Naomi's husband and her two sons die, leaving all three women childless. For Naomi there is little point in remarrying because she is near the end of her childbearing years. Since agricultural conditions have improved in Judah, Naomi decides to return home. The two Moabite women are now in a quandary. What should they do in order to maximize their chances of finding a new husband? At first both decide to follow Naomi on her trek back to Bethlehem. But Naomi finds this decision ill advised. "Go back," she urges, "each of you to your mother's house. . . . The LORD grant that you may find security, each of you in the house of your husband" (Ruth 1:8–9). But both daughters are unmoved by this plea and remain steadfast in their desire to migrate to Judah. Naomi must redouble her rhetorical efforts. "Turn back my daughters," she exclaims,

> Go your way, for I am too old to have a husband. Even if I thought there was hope for me, even if I should have a husband tonight and bear sons, would you then wait until they were grown? Would you then refrain from marrying? No, my daughters, it has been far more bitter for me than for you, because the hand of the LORD has turned against me. (1:12–13)

After this second intervention, Orpah decides to return home, while Ruth perseveres in her desire to accompany Naomi. As commentators have long noted, Orpah's decision is quite prudent. In the ancient world the chances of finding a spouse would be immeasurably greater at home, where parents and family members could assist in securing a mate. Naomi is altruistic in the very best sense of the word when she urges her daughters-in-law to remain in Moab. (Conversion, we must remember, was hardly imaginable at this time, given the tribal nature of religious affiliation.) And there is not just the impediment of these societal variables to consider, for as Naomi notes, her own God has abandoned her ("the hand of the LORD has turned against me"). Why would Orpah or Ruth want to leave the comforts of their homeland in order to take a chance on a deity who has so heartlessly spurned Naomi?

The author of the book of Ruth has set the situation up this way in order to accentuate the *supernatural* dimension of Ruth's decision to enter the land of Israel. By painting Orpah's choice to remain in Moab as eminently reasonable, the author sets in bold relief the audacity of Ruth's decision to go up to the land of Israel. Boaz acknowledges this fact when he meets Ruth for the first time. After Ruth has expressed her surprise that such a notable citizen as Boaz would take an interest in a lowly maiden such as herself, Boaz declares:

> All that you have done for your mother-in-law since the death of your husband has been fully told me, and how you left your father and mother and your native land and came to a people that you did not know before. May the LORD reward you for your deeds, and may you have a full reward from the LORD, the God of Israel, under whose wings you have come for refuge! (2:11–12)

These words recycle what God said to Abraham back in Genesis 12. For he too left his parents and native land to set out for an unknown destination. In return for this great risk, Abraham was promised extraordinary things. And just so for Ruth. Though Boaz's words do not promise great things to come—after all, he is not God and has no such power—they do ask God to reward his courageous servant. Ruth will find refuge under the wings of Boaz (3:9, cf. 2:12) and will bear a son who will be part of the lineage of David himself (4:18–22).

Particularly striking about the portrait of Ruth are the Joban undertones.[26] For as we have seen, Naomi makes it clear that the God of Israel has made her life very bitter. Indeed, at the close of the first chapter, Naomi is utterly despondent. Yet it is to this Joban God that Ruth wishes to attach herself. The reward that she will eventually receive is completely unexpected and not the result of some self-serving calculation that the God of Israel is uniquely able to reward the virtuous. On the contrary, Ruth attaches herself to Naomi and her God in full cognition of all that has befallen her mother-in-law. It is this selfless act that Boaz acknowledges and that God will, in the end, reward in a prodigal fashion.

If we return to the book of Tobit with this in mind, we can grasp more fully the nature of Anna's fears about parting with her son. Like Orpah she takes the reasonable position. Her maternal worries hardly condemn her. Quite the reverse, they win our admiration. But her worries are the necessary barometer by which we can measure the faith of Tobit, a faith that answers the test that Raphael has been charged with putting in motion and that is mediated by the remonstration of Anna herself: What are the results of your charity and righteousness? The fact that you have failed has become well known within the village. Had Tobit been satisfied with the logic of Anna's argument against sending Tobias to Media, not only would he have died a blind manx, but his son would have been deprived of his marriage to Sarah and the many children and extraordinary wealth that came with it.

■

At issue when we began was the question of whether Tobit should be classified as a novella that inscribes within its story form a theology of simple retributive justice: give alms and you will be rewarded. At one level the answer has to be yes. Tobit cleaves to the commandments, and by the end of the tale the payoff is enormous. But the danger of attending to this aspect of the book alone is that one will fail to appreciate the significance of the most important event in the entire story: Tobit's decision to send Tobias on a journey to Media to retrieve the money that was left on deposit there. The central claim of this chapter has been that this decision is fraught with terrible risk, and it is precisely this risk that reveals the supreme faith Tobit has in the power of the commandments God has bequeathed to Israel. Tobit has come to see that his obedience to Torah is not going to be rewarded within the context of his own life, a point driven home by the biting question his wife Anna poses after he has been struck blind by God: "Where are the fruits of your charitable deeds?" Though Tobit's despair is made clear in his acerbic response to Raphael's greeting ("What joy is left for me anymore? I am a man without eyesight"), his persistent obedience in the face of such a trial is demonstrated in the instruction he has given his son Tobias just a moment earlier: "Almsgiving delivers from death and keeps you from going into the Darkness." This contradiction, I have noted, creates a gap in our story that appears nearly unbridgeable. How could a man suffering in darkness as a "reward" for his charity continue to hold fast to the scriptural promise?

I have suggested that the only way to make sense of the disparity is to presume that Tobit believes that though the commandment has not worked out in the course of his own life, this piece of divine teaching will be vindicated in the life of his son. And so Tobit passes the terrible Joban test to which he has been subjected. He will continue to serve his God for naught, that is, without hope for a reward in the context of his own life. But it is precisely his faith in the eventual fulfillment of the divine promise that not only proves the mettle of his own devotion to the God of Israel but also enables the reward for that faith to take shape. Though the sending of Tobias on this journey would be considered foolhardy according to any sort of rational accounting (so Anna and by extension Orpah), in light of the divine promise there are supernatural reasons to believe it is the logical course to follow. Like Abraham and Ruth before him, Tobit makes a decision whose wisdom, in the moment of its being made, can be appreciated only in retrospect. The difference between a madman and a saint is narrow indeed, as the tradition has always taught. It is the appreciation of the aqedah-like character of the fateful fourth chapter of this book that allows us to see how Tobit passes the Job-like test he must endure and why the labeling of this book as a Deuteronomic novella so badly misses the mark.

CHAPTER SEVEN

Charity and the Goodness of Creation

God saw everything that he had made, and indeed, it was very good.

—Genesis 1:31

It is different for people who see creation through your Spirit, for you are seeing it through their eyes. Thus when such people see that these things are good, you are seeing that they are good; whatever created things please them for your sake, it is you who are arousing their delight in these things; and anything that gives us joy through your Spirit gives you joy in us.

—Augustine, *Confessions,* 13.31.46

Before venturing into the second half of my book, I would like to step back for a moment and take stock of where we have come. This chapter will function as a conclusion and a summary synthesis of the first part of my argument and return to an issue that is frequently a source of great controversy: What do we make of charitable deeds that are, at least in part, motivated by self-interest?

I began this book with a consideration of the unique role that charity to the poor played in the development of Judaism and Christianity in their formative days. The importance of charity was deeply inscribed in the book of Tobit where it served as the central focus of three different summaries of the Torah: first, during Tobit's initial "deathbed" instruction (4:5–11); second, during Raphael's final remarks before his departure (12:6–10); and finally, when Tobit really is at the point of death (14:8–9). But the prominence of charity as a religious practice was also reflected in everyday speech. One need not have read the book of Tobit to know its importance; casual conversation would have done the job. I have noted that Hebrew and Aramaic speakers in rabbinic times could use the word *commandment* in one of two ways: either to speak to one of the 613 commandments that Moses received at Mount Sinai or to highlight the significance of the most important of all commandments—almsgiving. Charity was, to cite the idiom of the day, *the* commandment.

But alongside the legal stands the sacramental. I have argued that one of the reasons that charity gained such extraordinary significance is that it was understood as more than a horizontal action involving a donor and recipient; it also had a vertical dimension. To give alms was to perform an act of worship of God (*avodah*). The Greek translation of Hosea 6:6 captured this perfectly: "I desire mercy [toward your neighbor] not [just] sacrificial service." Just as service at the sacrificial hearth provided food for God (as though he suffered from hunger), so donation of goods to the poor is considered a loan to God (as though he has fallen on hard times).

This perspective, I have noted, has not been well received in modern times. If charity is simply a form of exchange, and God becomes the guarantor of my generosity, then what remains of value to the moral act itself? Doesn't concern for the poor become a means of pursuing naked self-interest?

I have suggested that one answer to that problem can be found in Sirach 29. Issuing a loan, our wise sage teaches, is an inherently *risky* endeavor. And that is the reason that Ben Sira sandwiches his treatment of almsgiving between a discussion of conventional loans and going surety. The outer frame of this text is important to bear in mind. Lending one's money to anyone under any circumstances can be a perilous affair. There is ample reason to be circumspect about this form of assistance for one's neighbor. Yet Ben Sira does not believe that any of these worries holds when one is approached by the truly down and out. "*Lose* your silver for the sake of a friend," he admonishes, "do not let it rust under a stone and be lost." What Ben Sira is contrasting in this verse are two means of saving one's money— the more conventional means of hiding the funds where they cannot be stolen (see the parable of the talents in Matthew 25:14–30), and the extraordinary strategy of donating those funds to those in need. To be sure, Ben Sira informs his students that by implementing this strategy they will fund a treasury in heaven that will provide more profit than gold, but can one really argue that this is done purely out of self-interest?

In my first chapter I asked the reader to imagine herself seated at a table listening to the advice of a seasoned financial adviser and a renowned holy man. The former would propose purchasing an impressive list of stocks and bonds; the latter would direct your attention to the poor on the street. If the goal is to secure a safe and secure retirement, what is the truly prudent way of proceeding? It seems to me that the person who follows the advice of the holy man is not acting out of a simple *material* calculation. The reason Ben Sira has sandwiched his discussion of alms between an exposition about the dangers of issuing loans and going surety is to give expression to the *extraordinary faith* that is required to loan to the poor. To give a loan to the truly down and out, I have claimed, makes a statement about the trustworthiness of God. By giving God a loan, one becomes his creditor—that is, his believer.

That this sort of concern is central to these early sources is evident from the way in which they describe the temptation to hoard one's money. Accumulating wealth in Ben Sira, Tobit, and the Gospels is not bad in and of itself; the danger lies in thinking that the funds one has saved will secure one against the onslaughts of Lady Fortune. The Rich Fool in Luke's Gospel errs in putting his faith in the ability of Mammon to save him on the day of wrath ("Soul, you have ample goods laid up for many years; relax, eat, drink, be merry!"). What Ben Sira, Tobit, and Jesus demand of their hearers is a faith in the power of generosity to provide deliverance in the future. And they always situate that faith against the background of what the world would esteem as a more sensible strategy. Earthly treasuries appear to offer far more security than their heavenly counterparts. At the heart of this system lies an enormous paradox: in order to gain eternal wealth, one must put one's earthly goods at considerable risk. To gain one's life one must first lose it. If we take the narrative setting of the heavenly treasury seriously, it's hard to imagine how one could reduce this particular concept of generosity to simple self-interest.

The book of Tobit provides us with another way of coming at the problem of self-interested giving. As any lexicographer can testify, words can take on very different meanings depending on the type of sentence in which they are found. In a similar fashion, religious teachings often vary in meaning depending on the context in which they are deployed. The lives of the saints, for example, have allowed the faithful the means to see how the teachings of the Gospel can be embodied in concrete human lives. My favorite example of how a biblical verse can be turned on its head depending on the context of a human life comes from Gregory of Nyssa's commentary on the psalm titles. Psalm 58 is one of those problematic imprecatory psalms, in which the supplicant is filled with a terrible hunger for vengeance. In verse 10, we read: "The righteous will rejoice when they see vengeance done; they will bathe their feet in the blood of the wicked." For many modern readers this verse would be better suited to a terrorist pamphlet than to Holy Scripture. But Gregory of Nyssa notes two things: first, that the book of Psalms is the prayer book of David; and, second, that the title of this particular psalm begins with the words "do not destroy." It just so happens that David speaks these very words in 1 Samuel 26:9. In that chapter, David is being relentlessly pursued by his mortal adversary Saul. When by dint of luck or providence David finds himself in front of a helpless, sleeping Saul, his right-hand man exhorts him to make a quick end of his enemy. "God has given your enemy into your hand today," Abishai observes; "now therefore let me pin him to the ground with one stroke of the spear; I will not strike him twice." But David refuses to give in to temptation. "Do not destroy him," he commands, "for who can raise his hand against the Lord's anointed, and be guiltless?" If we read the psalm in the fashion that Gregory has proposed, then the cry for vengeance is nothing other than a *fallible*, yet understandably *human* desire of David, which is overcome by the power of the Holy Spirit. For this reason the psalm itself has come to be called an "inscription" (or perhaps better, "public monument") in the superscription, for it has come to be seen as a witness to the power of God to snuff out the seemingly unquenchable rage of his servant.[1]

Similarly, in Chapters 5 and 6, we have had the opportunity to see how the lived experience of a biblical figure can provide considerable depth and nuance to the exposition of proverbial wisdom. The book of Tobit takes as its central theme the practice of giving alms to the poor. In many senses one could argue that Tobit embodies in narrative form the rabbinic dictum that almsgiving is the sum of all the commandments. This is evident not only from the ubiquity of the practice but also from the fact that on three different occasions when the reader is treated to an instruction in Torah, almsgiving takes center stage (4:7–11, 12:8–10, and 14:11). Indeed, in the last two examples, almsgiving is practically the only item on the table. We have also seen that the scriptural explanation for the importance of this commandment comes from the book of Proverbs: "So you will be laying up a good treasure for yourself against the day of necessity. For almsgiving delivers from death and keeps you from going into Darkness" (Tob 4:10; cf. Prov 10:2).

And now the question returns: What does this proverb that is so central to the book mean? On a simple reading, one could argue (and many have!) that it is simply another variant on the theme of retributive justice. "If you do good, you will prosper" becomes "If you are generous, you will acquire a handsome endowment." Indeed, some commentators on the book are happy to point the reader back to its scriptural source and leave the matter at that. The book is through and through "Deuteronomic" in tone.

To be sure, the outer frame of the book of Tobit would seem to confirm our worries about a theology built on the structure of a simple exchange. Give alms, the book of Proverbs teaches, and the treasury that accumulates in heaven will deliver you in the end. Yet the heart of the story itself conveys a very different picture. Tobit is a figure who not only does not profit from his good works but whose good works become the very source of his suffering. The question posed by the book is whether Tobit (and by extension, the implied reader) will persevere in the commandment even though the promised reward has been deferred. In other words, does generosity remain valuable even if I cannot profit from it? I have always been struck by the fact that as soon as the idea of a treasury in heaven comes into view, so does its Joban critique and eventually its deeper affirmation by a chastened Tobit. The lesson is clear: Ben Sira and Tobit must be read in concert as the canon demands.

As we saw, in the midst of his terrible trial Tobit answers the question put to him affirmatively. As a result of his selfless pursuit of what the Torah teaches, he becomes the recipient of a reward he could never imagine. But the point is not a simple theology of "do good and you will prosper" but rather one of "persevere in goodness no matter what the present historical circumstances may seem to indicate."

I have argued along two different tracks that the concept of the treasury in heaven retains its theological integrity. Through these chapters I claimed that the reason that scripture attaches a reward to charity is not simply to appeal to self-interest (though an element of that remains) but to make a statement about the nature of the world. What kind of stuff is it made out of and how might I profit from the way in which it has been constructed? The concept of a treasury in heaven is about metaphysics more than morality.

All analogies limp, but let me try one more. My wife was once in charge of a swimming class for adults that included a number of individuals who had had near-drowning experiences in their younger years. This naturally led to an extraordinary fear of the water. Now, anyone who has done a proper investigation of the physics of water knows that the human body is buoyant enough to float quite naturally on its surface. But in order to exploit this fact, you have to be *relaxed,* and, in turn, must *trust* the capacity of water to hold your body afloat. The more you fear the water, the more you tense up. And the more you tense up, the more you thrash about. The result? It's nearly impossible to come up for air. Because the students my wife taught had been conditioned to fear the water, they could not trust its natural capacity for buoyancy. They could grasp the physics of the situation on land without any problem, but entering the water brought a whole host of demons to the fore. Knowing something and acting on that knowledge are often two quite different things.

And so we might say for the concept of a treasury in heaven. What stands behind this idea, I have tried to argue, is a claim about the *nature* of the world. To the casual observer, the world, like the middle of Lake Michigan, can be a frightening and unstable place. There is a reason that the Greeks and Romans revered the goddesses Tyche and Fortuna. There is no hard evidence that charity will consistently be rewarded. In the short run, an astute financial adviser will always look better than the holy man. But the memory and fame of the holy man will certainly outlast the reputation of even the best investor. That is why readers relish narratives like the book of Tobit. There is almost an instinctive desire to believe that the world was formed out of love.

Anna's worries and the scorn of Tobit's peers, however, will always seem to be the more sober view: "Is he still not afraid? He has already been hunted down to be put to death for doing this, and he ran away; yet here he is again burying the dead." For the cultured despisers of the treasury in heaven, the only suitable response to this critique would be an even more adamant declaration of the desire to give, irrespective of any reward. That would be an altruistic act in its purest form.

But I have suggested that the theology of generosity in Ben Sira and Tobit goes in a different direction. Their focus is not so much on the moral agent (and the question about his "purity of heart") as on a claim about the *nature* of the world God has created. It is for this reason that I picked the text from Augustine as the epigraph of this chapter. In his mind it is not obvious that the world is good as God declares at the end of Genesis 1, just as it was not obvious to Voltaire in the wake of the Lisbon earthquake or to many living on the Asian Rim after the onslaught of the great Tsunami of 2004. In the face of human tragedy it is difficult, if not impossible, for human eyes to affirm the goodness of the created order. One can affirm such a truth only by seeing it through God's eyes. That is the position of the writer of the book of Tobit.

Tobit continues to give alms not because of a pure altruism but because he believes in the goodness of God. On this basis he presumes that the promised reward has not been canceled but has been delayed a generation. God does reward charity, Tobit instructs his son (4:7–11), but sometimes the timeline is longer than a single human life. The reward does not erase the value of the moral act; rather it tells us something about the nature of the world and the God who created it. Belief in the treasury in heaven is, by extension, belief in the goodness of the world God has made, and in the goodness of the God who made it. Belief of this nature requires the aid of supernatural grace, and this is why we laud his trust in the treasury in heaven.

PART TWO

Charitable Deeds as Storable Commodities

CHAPTER EIGHT

Can Merits Be Transferred?

Happy are the righteous! Not only do they acquire merit for themselves, but they also acquire merit for their children and their children's children to the end of all generations.

—Babylonian Talmud, Yoma 87a

I n the first part of this book, we treated the treasury in heaven in light of its opposite, the treasuries of wickedness, or, as Ben Sira puts the matter, deceptive treasuries. Our chief goal was to contrast the behavior of hoarding in order to secure one's future with that of generosity. One theme we did not consider at any length was the treasury in heaven as a place where good deeds could be stored and later drawn upon to deliver one from death.

The Anxiety About Purgatory

As soon as we begin to make our way down this path we find ourselves entering a dense thicket of theological debates that arose during the Reformation. For there can be no question that the biblical image of the treasury in heaven eventually gave rise to the Roman Catholic Church's infamous *thesaurus meritorum* ("treasury of merits"), which in turn played an enormous role in the emergence of the doctrine of purgatory and the practice of selling and purchasing indulgences. One illustration is worth a thousand words. In a Middle English collection of devotions one finds a

poem entitled "The Relief of Souls in Purgatory," which contains a trian-
gular drawing on the right side of the page (figure 3). At the top of the
triangle sit Christ and the saints in the midst of heaven. At the lower right-
hand side is a group of persons seated in a large tub who are being lifted
out of purgatory. On the lower left a priest is celebrating Mass, and below
him a layman is offering alms to two paupers, one of whom has an artificial
leg. The three spheres are linked by a rope that is fastened to a pulley at
the top. The celebration of the Mass and the giving of alms exert a force
that "pulls" the souls from their torment in purgatory and "lifts" them
safely into heaven. The almsgiving of a son or daughter, this image teaches,
can deliver parents from the throes of death.

According to the theology of the Catholic Church, there are two stages
to the forgiveness of sins. The first follows from a proper confession of the
deeds in question by the penitent and the words of absolution spoken by
the confessor. Though the guilt of the sin is itself forgiven, it is not the case
that the consequences for that sin simply disappear.[1] The effects of the
wrongful deed must still be borne. If an individual dies in a state of grace,
he is marked for heaven; that is the promised destination. But if there are
penalties for sins that have not been paid, then a stop in purgatory is
required in order to "purge" oneself of these ill effects. One way to pay
back the debts that one owes God for the sins that one has committed is
through almsgiving. As the prophet Daniel had advised the penitent king
of Babylon: "Redeem yourself from the debt of your sins by alms, and your
iniquities by generosity to the poor" (4:27).[2]

The logic of the text from Daniel is quite straightforward. If sins are
imagined as debts that accrue in heaven, then the most sensible way to pay
them back would be to deposit funds in a heavenly treasury. And this is
precisely the logic followed by the angel Raphael when he informs Tobit
and Tobias that not only does almsgiving save from death but it "purges
away every sin" (12:9). Indulgences follow naturally from this worldview. If
the heavenly treasuries have been superabundantly endowed by the sacrifice of Christ and the charity of the saints who have been given the grace
to participate in Christ's all-sufficient merit, then it is altogether reasonable to conclude that laypersons should be able to benefit from the largesse
of their gracious benefactors. What the church does when it promulgates
indulgences is simply put its seal of approval on specific acts of charity for
the poor. One is not buying one's salvation—that is solely a matter of God's
grace. One is decreasing the time required to pay off the debts on

Figure 3   From a Middle English poem titled "Of the relefyng of saules in purgatory," showing the souls of the righteous dead being "drawne up oute of purgatory by prayer & almosdede" (British Library. © The British Library Board. MS Additional 37049, fol. 24v.)

unresolved sins. Or, in an important variation on that theme, as an act of love and solidarity, one can also pay down the debt owed by family members.

The notion that the treasury in heaven is governed by such economic metaphors and that it could, in turn, generate the notion of indulgences has made the entire topic something of a third rail in New Testament exegesis. New Testament scholars have noted the deep similarities between the treasury in heaven and the concepts of sin and virtue in rabbinic writings.[3] This has provided New Testament scholars with a considerable challenge because this Jewish theology of sin not only has an extraordinary overlap with later Catholic thinking but it also seems to be part of Jesus' own preaching. For this reason the highly esteemed Lutheran scholar Günther Bornkamm took pen in hand and wrote a short monograph on the theme of meritorious action in the Gospels, trying to show that Jesus' own preaching was quite different from that of his Jewish contemporaries, even though there are a considerable number of parallels at the level of terminology.[4]

On the Transferability of Merits

For most of these Protestant scholars, the mercantile metaphors of Second Temple and rabbinic Judaism were the classic telltale signs of a failed religion. By imagining sins as debts and virtuous actions as merits, the Jews of Jesus' day imagined salvation as something that could be purchased by human works. In 1977 E. P. Sanders wrote a landmark book, *Paul and Palestinian Judaism,* that addressed this anti-Jewish prejudice head-on. He made the important distinction between soteriology, "how one became a Jew," and sanctification, "how one progressed in the religious life after salvation." In Sanders's view, the former was the result of God's grace, while the latter was subject to human works. Jews did not buy their way into heaven; they were "elected," that is, chosen to this privileged status by the grace of God. But election did not mean resting on one's laurels. One kept the commandments in order to grow in grace, and in return for this obedience one could count on a reward.

So far, so good for Sanders. When we turn to the issue of merit making proper, however, Sanders stumbles on the issue of purgatory. In his consideration of the Hebrew root *zakah,* from which we get the noun *zekut,* "merit," he fails to see that the term arises from a financial background and as a result underplays the role of merit making in rabbinic thought. Time and again he tries to argue for a nonfinancial understanding of the key terms, *zekut* and *hov*, credit and debt. Needless to say, these arguments are not successful.

Furthermore, it is striking how he begins his consideration of the merits of the fathers (*zekut avot*) in rabbinic thought. His discussion is governed by the fear that the concept might support the notion that such merits could be transferred to a third party at the final judgment. Sanders begins his discussion by acknowledging that obedience to the commandments is understood as a meritorious action in rabbinic thought. What concerns Sanders is the idea that "merits can be compiled and *transferred at the judgment so as to counterbalance demerits.*" Such a view would imply that meritorious deeds did have salvific effects. "Many scholars," Sanders continues, "have seen in the phrase *zekut avot*, 'merits of the fathers,' a view analogous to the supposed Roman Catholic view of the *thesaurus meritorum*, treasury of merits, which are compiled by the works of supererogation and innocent suffering of the saints."[5] This fear over a transfer of merits is certainly grounded in Protestant polemics against the practice of indulgences. As oftentimes happens in polemical contexts, the position of the offending party is exaggerated to make the point more forcefully. But such exaggerations can come at the cost of truth. It should be noted that no Catholic theologian ever said that indulgences could be used to free a sinner from perdition. If one is damned for one's sins, indulgences have no soteriological value whatsoever. The same is true for Judaism.[6] To be fair to Sanders, it is not the case that he is imputing this view to Catholicism (note well his diction: "the *supposed* Roman Catholic view"), but he unconsciously allows this polemic to govern his discussion of the Jewish sources. So afraid is he of finding this notion in rabbinic texts that he underplays the role of merits in rabbinic thought.

In the discussion that follows these opening remarks, Sanders is concerned to show that, though the deeds of the fathers were rewarded, "they did not establish a treasury of *transferrable* merits," and, most emphatically, there is no evidence that these merits could be transferred at the final judgment.[7] He closes his discussion by conceding, however, that there is a "sense of solidarity of benefit" in rabbinic literature.

> The deeds of the fathers obviously benefit their descendants, for they cause God to remember the covenant, to do good deeds for Israel, and to suspend punishment for transgression. The existence of righteous contemporaries

benefits all, for it is for their sake that God does not inflict the punishment which the world deserves. Further, a man's good deeds are of benefit to himself, since God is faithful to reward obedience. None of this, however, amounts to a transfer of merits, to a view that merits offset demerits, or, in fact, to anything which is properly called a "doctrine of merits." The only "doctrine" is that God is faithful to reward and punish. We now see a further nuance, that descendants may be rewarded for their father's good deeds. But transgressions are atoned for or are punished, not offset; and men are rewarded for their good deeds, they do not *achieve* the world to come by piling up a "treasury of merits," nor by drawing on one stored up by someone else. In short, the Tannaitic [early rabbinic] discussions of *zekut* do not accord it any place in "Rabbinic Soteriology."[8]

Though there is much to commend in this summary, especially the emphasis on the fact that heaven cannot be won simply by human merits, there is also room for correction. Sanders goes too far when he writes that there is no such thing as a "transfer of merits" or "a view that merits offset demerits."

Merit Making in Second Temple Judaism

A far better assessment of the issue can be found in a more recent article by Menahem Kister.[9] Kister takes issue with Sanders's sweeping judgment against a doctrine of merits in rabbinic thought. He begins his case with a citation from the Babylonian Talmud (Yoma 87a). The text opens with the terse exclamation, "Happy are the righteous!" and then provides an explanation—"Not only do they acquire merit for themselves, but they also acquire merit for their children and their children's children to the end of all generations"—and finally a proof drawn from the Bible: "For Aaron had several sons who deserved to be burnt like Nadab and Abihu (Leviticus 10) . . . but the merit of their father helped them." The righteous are then compared to the wicked. Again, our text begins with an exclamation, "Woe to the wicked!" and then provides an explanation that is followed by a historical example: "Not only do they acquire condemnation for themselves, but they also acquire condemnation for their children and their children's children to the end of all generations. Many sons did Canaan have who were worthy to be ordained like Tabi, the slave of Rabban Gamaliel, but the guilt of their ancestor caused them (to lose the chance)."

This text clearly expresses the idea that the deeds of the ancestors have a decisive influence on the fate of their descendants. The righteous bequeath their merits to their offspring, and the wicked similarly pass on their debts. But the notion that the sins of the fathers could affect the sons has an older pedigree than the Babylonian Talmud; it is inscribed in the Ten Commandments themselves. There it is said that God "visits the iniquity of the fathers upon their children to the third and fourth generations" (Exod 20:5).[10] But perhaps the best place to see the embodiment of this idea in the Bible is in the story of Elijah's rebuke of King Ahab. After his wife, Jezebel, has arranged for the murder of Naboth so that the royal house can lay claim to this man's property, the prophet Elijah appears and condemns the action in the strongest terms possible. Speaking in God's name Elijah says:

> I will bring disaster on you; I will consume you, and will cut off from Ahab every male, bond or free, in Israel; and I will make your house like the house of Jeroboam son of Nebat, and like the house of Baasha son of Ahijah, because you have provoked me to anger and have caused Israel to sin. Also concerning Jezebel the Lord said, "The dogs shall eat Jezebel within the bounds of Jezreel." Anyone belonging to Ahab who dies in the city the dogs shall eat; and anyone of his who dies in the open country the birds of the air shall eat. (I Kings 21:21–24)

Immediately upon hearing this dire proclamation, Ahab is cut to the quick. He tears his clothes, puts on sackcloth, and fasts. Elijah appears a second time to modify the punishment: "Because [Ahab] has humbled himself before me, I will not bring the disaster in his days; *but in his son's days I will bring the disaster on his house*" (v. 29, italics mine). It is crucial to note that the act of wrongdoing has put in motion consequences that not even contrition can wholly undo. God's response to Ahab's repentance is to modify the terms of what is coming but not to overturn it completely. The connection between deed and consequence is part of the natural order of creation, and God's free choice to make a world in which consequences follow necessarily upon certain deeds cannot be overturned completely.[11]

The Bible is not silent on the influence of good deeds either, though we lack colorful stories like that of Ahab and Elijah on the subject. The book of Deuteronomy makes clear the transgenerational effects of obedience: "Be careful to obey all these words that I command you today, so that it may go well with you *and with your children after you* forever, because you will be doing what is good and right in the sight of the LORD your God" (12:28; italics mine). And the ideal is also attested in Psalms:

> I have been young, and now am old,
>> yet I have not seen the righteous forsaken
>> or *their children* begging bread. (37:25; italics mine)

What we see in rabbinic literature is the use of a financial metaphor to account for this biblical phenomenon.

But the use of commercial terminology is not original to rabbinic Judaism. It is part of the patrimony of Second Temple Judaism as a whole. Kister shows that the very same logic can be found already in the book of Ben Sira. At the end of that book there is a long and quite well-known paean to Israel's righteous ancestors in which he lists many of the most famous figures of the Bible, beginning with Enoch and concluding with Nehemiah (44:16–49:16). Before turning to those illustrious ancestors proper, Ben Sira prefixes some words of introduction. He remarks that a few of Israel's righteous men "have left behind a name, so that others may declare their praise." But for many, many others, "there is no memory, they have perished as though they had never existed" (44:8–9). In spite of that fact, all hope is not lost. For "these were also men of charity [*hesed*]," Ben Sira observes, "whose righteous deeds have not been forgotten; their goodness will remain with their descendants, and their inheritance with their children's children. . . . The *memory* [from the root *zakar*] of their deeds shall abide forever, their charitable deeds [*tsedaqa*] shall never be wiped out [root *maḥah*]" (44:10–11, 13).[12]

As Kister notes, the parallelism between being remembered (*zakar*) and not being wiped out (*maḥah*) is probably modeled inversely on Psalm 109:14, a text that concerns the legacy of iniquity:

> May the iniquity of his father *be remembered* [*zakar*] before the LORD,
> and do not let the sin of his mother be blotted out [*maḥah*].

This psalm presumes a situation exactly the opposite of Ben Sira 44. In this case the punishment for someone who is unkind to the poor (v. 16) is that both his sins and those of his parents will be indelibly etched in God's mind (v. 14), never to be blotted out. These two texts provide us with excellent testimony as to the long-term consequences of good and evil deeds. Such actions are registered as a perpetual memorial before God, where their requisite effects redound across the generations.

Kister closes his consideration of Ben Sira's teaching on this point with a brilliant suggestion as to how another text might be read. In chapter 3, we find Ben Sira's well-known teaching on the respect one owes a parent.

He begins by declaring that acting charitably toward one's father and mother is profitable:

> Those who honor their father atone for sins,
>   and those who respect their mother are like those who lay up treasure.
> (3:3–4)

The parallelism of these lines is remarkable: honoring the father is matched by respecting one's mother, while atoning for sin is comparable to laying up wealth in a treasury. The only way to make sense of the latter is to presume that sins are debts that can be repaid by charitable deeds that have been stored in a heavenly treasury.

Ben Sira brings his teaching to a close with lines that presage 44:13 and recall Psalms 109:14: "The charitable deeds [*tsedaqa*] of [your] father will not be wiped out [*mahah*] . . . in a day of trouble it *will be remembered* [*zakar*] to you [by God] to cancel your sins as heat melts ice" (3:14–15). Many have understood the phrase "charitable deeds of your father" as an objective genitive: "charitable deeds done *toward* your father," that is, providing material support of the father during his old age.[13] Yet the parallelism of "being remembered" (*zakar*) and "not being wiped out" (*mahah*) is exactly the same as Sirach 44:13 and suggests a subjective genitive which would be rendered: "the charitable deeds *that belong to* your father will not be wiped out." On this view, it is the charity done by the father, preserved in a heavenly treasury, that God will take note of in the future in order to forgive the sins of the son.

Kister concludes his discussion of the text with these remarks:

> [Sirach 3:14] is clearly a reversal of the biblical verse, "May the sin of his fathers be remembered before God, and the iniquity of his mother not be wiped out" (Ps. 109:14), and an early form of the well-known rabbinic conception of *zekut 'avot*, "merit of the ancestors." Indeed, it is one of the earliest formulations of the concept of the "treasure of merits" (explicitly mentioned in Sir 3:4), of the view that "merits offset demerits" (see especially Sir 3:3, 15), and probably also of the notion of "transfer of merits" from ancestors to their descendants. These ideas also occur in rabbinic literature (*pace* E. P. Sanders, *Paul and Palestinian Judaism*).[14]

Ben Sira gives us clear evidence that acts of charity can be *stored* in heaven (3:4) and used to offset demerits (3:3). If Kister is correct in his reading of the phrase "charitable acts of your fathers" in 3:14, then Ben Sira also testifies to the idea that merits can be transferred to one's descendants—the first clear sighting of what will become the rabbinic doctrine of *zekut avot*.

In my next four chapters I will take up the theme of merit making in Second Temple Judaism and the New Testament with the particular intent of showing the fundamental importance of the concept of the treasury in heaven. It is true that merit making has its place in the Hebrew Bible as well, but everything looks completely different when we come to the early postbiblical period. Part of the reason for that is the fact that when the dominant metaphor for sin becomes that of a financial debt, it is altogether logical that merits are conceived of as credits. And just as debts can be transferred from one generation to the next, so also credits. E. P. Sanders was certainly correct to worry about scholars attributing a soteriological function to merit making in rabbinic religion (a red herring that was spawned by the polemics of the Reformation), but he went too far when he downplayed its financial aspect and denied that merits could be transferred.

CHAPTER NINE

Storing Good Works in Heaven

But the virtue [of almsgiving] is so important that though the other virtues exist without it, they can be of no avail. For although a person be full of faith, and chaste and sober, and adorned with other still greater decorations, yet if he is not merciful, he cannot deserve mercy. For the Lord says "blessed are the merciful, for God shall have mercy upon them" (Matt 5:7).

—Leo the Great, Sermon 10

"When I was hungry you fed me. . . ." Observe here that Christ puts one sort of good works, by which the Saints will merit the eternal glory decreed to them by Christ in the judgment, instead of every kind of good works. . . . As St. Augustine says, they are most profitable for obtaining the grace of God.

—Cornelius à Lapide, on Matthew 25:35

There are two principal places where the Gospel writers employ the concept of a treasury in heaven. The first is found in Matthew's Sermon on the Mount (6:19–21), with an important parallel in Luke that we have already discussed (12:34). The second is found in the story of the rich young man who approaches Jesus and asks him what good deed he must do to acquire eternal life. This narrative is attested in all three of the Synoptic Gospels (Matt 19:16–30, Mark 10:17–31, Luke 18:18–30). We will begin our discussion with the Sermon on the Mount and reserve the story of the rich young man for a subsequent chapter.

Matthew introduces the concept of a "treasury in heaven" (6:19–21) in the middle of the Sermon on the Mount (5:1–7:29). Though this concept is basic to the logic of chapter 6, it goes unexplained in the brief notice that

Jesus gives to it.[1] There is a clear presumption that the audience knows what the concept refers to and can link it to its larger literary context. In this chapter I would like to consider the problem of what Matthew's audience might have presumed about the nature of such a treasury.

The Structure of Matthew 6

The sixth chapter of Matthew divides into two sections. The first half is an account of how the traditional pious virtues of almsgiving, fasting, and prayer should be practiced (vv. 1–18), while the second concerns the relationship between service to God and worry about earthly possessions (vv. 22–34). The teaching on the treasury in heaven sits between the two (vv. 19–21).

The opening discourse on almsgiving, fasting, and prayer (6:1–18) begins with a warning that sums up the major theme of this entire unit: "Beware of practicing your piety [literally "doing righteousness"] before others in order to be seen by them; for then you have no wage beside your father in heaven" (6:1).[2] This is followed by three paragraphs that treat the three traditional forms of religious behavior. The first is almsgiving:

> So whenever you give alms, do not sound a trumpet before you, as the hypocrites do in the synagogues and in the streets, so that they may be praised by others. Truly I tell you they have received their wage. But when you give alms, do not let your left hand know what your right hand is doing, so that your alms may be done in secret; and your Father who sees in secret will pay your wage. (6:2–4)

This paragraph makes four points: (1) don't call attention to your almsgiving as the hypocrites do, for (2) they receive their wage in the form of adulation from their peers. Rather, (3) give alms in secret so that (4) your heavenly Father can bestow the wage you have earned. It is to be underscored that the worldly fame that the hypocrites receive in this life constitutes their *full* payment. The authentic disciple, however, can expect something far greater from God.

The next two paragraphs on prayer (vv. 5–15) and fasting (vv. 16–18) follow the same form and contrast the vanity of parading one's virtues in public to a more discrete enactment of them in private. Regarding prayer Jesus tells his disciples not "to stand and pray in the synagogues and at the street corners, so that they may be seen by others" (v. 5); while those who fast should not "disfigure their faces so as to show others that they are fasting" (v. 16). Jesus warns his audience that those who practice these pious virtues in such a way as to call attention to themselves will "have received their wage" (vv. 5 and 16). Each of the respective paragraphs closes with a brief word on how true piety is to be practiced: the one who prays should do so behind closed doors (v. 6), and the one who fasts should put on oil and wash his face so as not to be noticed by others (vv. 17–18). For only then will "your Father who sees in secret" pay you the wage you deserve (vv. 6, 18).

As W. D. Davies and Dale Allison have observed, the phrase Matthew repeats three times to express the receipt of a wage ("Truly I tell you, they have received their wage," vv. 2, 5, 16) is a technical expression and pertains to the drawing up of a receipt in a business transaction.[3] The presumption is that those who display their piety publically receive full compensation for their deed through the praise of other men. God, at the end of days, will owe them nothing more.

Having completed the teaching on the proper way to give alms, pray, and fast (6:1–18), Jesus concludes the chapter with a teaching about wealth (6:19–34). This unit begins with a brief instruction about the treasury in heaven:

> Do not store up for yourselves treasures on earth, where moth and rust consume and where thieves break in and steal; but store up for yourselves treasure in heaven, where neither moth nor rust consumes and where thieves do not break in and steal. For where your treasure is, there your heart will be also. (vv. 19–21)

It continues with a reference to the virtue of generosity (vv. 22–23),[4] and concludes with an injunction to put aside worldly concerns,

> Therefore I tell you, do not worry about your life, what you will eat or what you will drink, or about your body, what you will wear. Is not life more than food, and the body more than clothing? Look at the birds of the air; they neither sow nor reap nor gather into barns, and yet your heavenly Father feeds them. Are you not of more value than they? . . . And why do you worry about clothing? Consider the lilies of the field, how they grow; they neither toil nor spin, yet I tell you, even Solomon in all his glory was not clothed like one of these. But if God so clothes the grass of the field, which is alive today and tomorrow is thrown into the oven, will he not much more clothe you—you of little faith? Therefore do not worry, saying "What will we wear?" For it is the Gentiles who strive for all these things; and indeed your heavenly Father knows that you need all these things. But strive first for the kingdom of God and his righteousness, and all these things will be given to you as well. (25–33)[5]

The description of the treasury in heaven (vv. 19–21) can be read as either the conclusion of the first unit (vv. 1–21) or the opening of the second (21–34). It functions like a hinge binding the two halves of the chapter. What has not been properly appreciated is the way in which verses 1 and 19 also function as an *inclusio*, binding together all that comes in between. The reason for this is that most scholars mistranslate the first verse as: "Beware of practicing your piety before others in order to be seen by them; for then you have no wage *from* [*para*] your father in heaven." The rendering of the Greek proposition *para* (followed by a noun in the dative case) as "from" is odd; normally the preposition has that meaning only when it is followed by a noun in the genitive. *Para* plus the dative almost always means "with" or "in the presence of," emphasizing that a particular item is in the near vicinity of someone or something.[6] The dative marks a spatial rather than a possessive or originary usage like the genitive. Accordingly, the clause should be rendered "for then you have no wage *beside* your father in heaven." Given that the wages accrued by almsgiving are stored *in heaven*, the reference to their being in the presence of God is hardly surprising. Read this way, Matt 6:1 anticipates the concluding exhortation of 6:19 to store one's wealth in a heavenly treasury and compels us to see the practices of prayer, fasting, and almsgiving (vv. 2–18) as the specific means of doing so.

The Treasury in Rabbinic Writings

We have noted that Jesus presumes his audience is familiar with the concept of a heavenly treasury. But where does the modern reader turn to discover what these ancient readers presumed? Perhaps, as many have argued, the key appears in a set of rabbinic traditions that understood the concept in explicitly financial terms. One frequently cited text comes from Mishna *Peah*, "Regarding the following matters, a man may enjoy their fruit in this world and his principal will remain for him in the next: honoring father and mother, charitable deeds, establishing peace between a man and his friend; Torah-study is equal to all of them" (1:1). This mishna is usually glossed: "The good deeds that you do are convertible into a heavenly currency, the interest of which yields blessings for you in this life while the principal will remain untouched for your enjoyment in the world to come."[7] And so, many scholars have assumed, for the treasury of which Jesus speaks: the metaphor refers to good deeds which are converted into financial currency and stored in a heavenly bank.

Part of the reason why this particular mishnaic image has proven so popular among scholars is that the word *treasury* in English or *Schatz* in German calls to mind a place where money is stored. But it is worth recalling that the Greek word that Matthew uses, *thesauros,* or even more, the Hebrew (or Aramaic) term that underlies it, *otsar (otsara),* need not be financial at all. It can refer to a room for storing valuable or precious items.[8] Consider, for example, a well-known tradition about King Munbaz, a man from Adiabene who converted to Judaism and happened to be a rough contemporary of Jesus. During a terrible famine, he distributed a good portion of his wealth to those in need. According to a rabbinic tradition, he explained himself thus:

> My [non-Jewish] fathers gathered treasures for themselves down below, but I have gathered treasure up above. My fathers have gathered treasures in a place over which the human hand has power, but I have gathered treasures in a place where no human hand has power.[9]

Unlike Mishna *Peah,* the formidable "treasure" that Munbaz has gathered is not financial. In all likelihood, Munbaz is referring to the enormous grain stores of his ancestors that he emptied on behalf of the poor. But whether we understand the treasury in explicitly financial terms as in Mishna *Peah* or in agricultural terms as with Munbaz, the important feature to note is that good deeds are thought to possess a physical character that allows them to be "stored" in heaven.

In spite of the aptness of the story about King Munbaz, there are problems with the usage of rabbinic texts in explicating the historical background of the imagery found in the Gospels. Chief among them is the fact that rabbinic literature significantly postdates the New Testament. Some scholars have worried that these parallels from rabbinic literature are not suitable evidence for the interpretation of the New Testament because they are not attested in written form until the beginning of the third century CE. But this by no means excludes the possibility that they circulated orally long beforehand. In any case, there are a number of other Jewish texts that speak of storing up one's deeds in a heavenly treasury that are much closer in time to the New Testament. These texts, some have argued, provide us with a better set of sources with which to compare the Gospel traditions.

Evidence from the Second Temple Period

One excellent place to turn is a Jewish noncanonical text dating from around the turn of the Common Era, the Psalms of Solomon. In chapter 9, our author provides a brief account of Israel's exile at the hands of the Babylonians in 587 BCE. The main point of emphasis is the justice of God in punishing Israel. The text in question reads:

> Our works are in the choosing and power of our soul,
>   and in your righteousness you visit human beings.
> The one who practices righteousness *stores up* life for himself with the Lord,
>   and the one who practices injustice is responsible for the destruction of his soul,
>   for the judgments of the Lord are in righteousness for each man and house-
>   hold.[10] (9:4–5)

The key clause for us is the observation that the one who acts justly "stores up life for himself." The verb used for "stores up" (*thesaurizei*) is cognate to the noun we saw in Matthew (*thesauros*). For the author of this Psalm there is nothing necessarily financial about the heavenly treasury. One could understand the act of storage here as the simple act of laying up one's deeds for the future. As in the example about King Munbaz, however, the author imagines that good deeds have generated some sort of concrete substance. Only by imagining their "thing-ness" (*Dinghaft* in German) can we appreciate how they could be stored in heaven and generate their own reward.

A number of excellent examples could also be drawn from apocalyptic works including 1 Enoch, 2 Baruch, and 4 Ezra.[11] For our purposes, an example from 2 Baruch and 4 Ezra will suffice. Second Baruch dates from after the destruction of the Second Temple in 70 CE. Though the complete text survives only in Syriac, it depends on a Greek version that may have been a translation from a Hebrew or Aramaic original. As in many other apocalypses of this genre (4 Ezra is a close analogy), the author uses the catastrophe of 587 BCE as a means of reflecting on the events of 70 CE.

The section that concerns us begins with a searching question about justice. In dismay over the fact that righteous men and sinners have been punished equally, our author asks, "What have they profited who have knowledge before you and who did not walk in vanity like the rest of the nations, who did not say to the dead: 'Give life to us,' but always feared you, and did not leave Your ways?" (14:5).[12] Aware that there is no simple answer to this pressing question, our author declares that the problem is, in part, epistemological. How can a finite human mind understand the nature of divine action: "O Lord, my Lord, who can understand your judgment? Or who can explore the depth of your way? . . . For we have all been made like a breath. For as breath ascends without human control and vanishes, so it is with the nature of men, who do not go away according to their own will, and who do not know what will happen to them in the end" (vv. 8, 10–11). Ultimately, the only way to make sense of the problem of evil is to have faith that the righteous will be rewarded in the world to come. "For the righteous," our author concludes, "justly have good hope for the end, and go away from this habitation without fear, because they possess with you *a store of good works which is preserved in treasuries.* Therefore they leave this world without fear, and are confident of the world which you have promised to them with an expectation of joy" (v. 12).

It is striking to note how differently the author of this work characterizes good and bad deeds. At the moment of the final judgment, we read regarding the unjust that "the *books* will be opened in which are written the sins of all who have sinned." But for the just we learn that "the *treasuries* in which are stored [their] righteous deeds" shall be revealed (24:1). The deeds of the just are not simple entries in an accounting book that God consults. Rather they are storable substances that are capable of generating their respective reward. God is bound by his promises to honor the deeds that have accumulated in these treasuries and to pay out the wage that is due them.

Fourth Ezra provides us with a slightly different picture of the final judgment. For when "the Most High shall be revealed upon the seat of judgment," then "recompense shall follow, and the reward shall be manifested; righteous deeds shall awake and unrighteous deeds shall not sleep" (7:33, 35).[13] One should observe that the righteous deeds are imagined as persons who can be awakened in the night. And the reward they generate is "thing-like and spacious. It had separated itself from the moral agent a long time ago and had been guarded beside the Most High. At the last day, it is made manifest."[14] God has chosen to organize the proceedings of the final judgment in such a way that the deeds done by human beings will play the leading role in how the just are rewarded. This does not, however, obviate the need for divine grace. In all three of these texts (1 Enoch, 2 Baruch, and 4 Ezra), the authors make it clear that it is God who provides the wisdom and strength by which the saints grow in their obedience and faith. It is a system not of works apart from faith but of faith perfected by works.

The Connection Between Deed and Consequence in the Bible

In an important article published in the 1950s, the German Old Testament professor Klaus Koch noted that this sort of thinking about the relationship between a human action and its consequence already existed in the Old Testament.[15] He used the German phrase *Tun-Ergehen Zusammenhang* (deed-consequence connection) as a shorthand means of identifying the phenomenon. This is an unwieldy phrase, but behind it stands a simple thesis. Koch noted that readers of the Bible assume that God *actively* administers justice in the world. When someone commits a sin or keeps a commandment, it is God who takes note of what has been done and the attendant circumstances: degree of intentionality, first or repeated offense, age of the offender, and so forth. Having weighed all the variables that were relevant to the deed, God sets in motion a reward or punishment to match the circumstances. Yet there are many texts in the Bible, principally in the books of Proverbs and Psalms, that present a picture similar to what we saw in the Psalms of Solomon, 2 Baruch, and 4 Ezra: the deed itself generates the appropriate consequence. Let me begin with a few examples from the book of Proverbs:

> Whoever digs a pit will fall into it,
>> and a stone will come back on the one who starts it rolling. (26:27)
> Those who mislead the upright into evil ways
>> will fall into pits of their own making,
>> but the blameless will have a goodly inheritance. (28:10)
> One who walks in integrity will be safe,
>> but whoever follows crooked ways will fall into the Pit. (28:18)

And one extended example from the book of Psalms:

> If one does not repent, God will whet his sword;
>> he has bent and strung his bow;
> he has prepared his deadly weapons,
>> making his arrows fiery shafts.
> See how they conceive evil,
>> and are pregnant with mischief,
>> and bring forth lies.
> They make a pit, digging it out,
>> and fall into the hole that they have made.
> Their mischief returns upon their own heads,
>> and on their own heads their violence descends. (7:12–16)

In all these texts it is the deed itself that sets in motion a chain of events that leads to either punishment or reward. In fact, deed and consequence are so organically bound together that the latter appears to unfold naturally from the former.

The unmediated connection between deed and consequence constitutes something like a natural law within the universe.[16] God, of course, is by no means excluded. It is he who set up the cosmos to work in this fashion. But precisely because consequences flow so naturally from deeds, the biblical writer does not need to highlight divine agency every time someone is rewarded or punished. The result (Ergehen) is built into the deed itself (Tun).

Consequences, however, do not always *immediately* follow upon execution of a deed. Sometimes there is a considerable delay. This is illustrated quite well in a proverb we have examined earlier, "Riches do not profit in the day of wrath, but charity delivers from death" (11:4). The presumption here is that the "day of wrath" could come long after the performance of the charitable deed. It is again worth noting that God need not intervene directly. The deed itself brings about the promised result: *charity* delivers from death.

Sometimes, as Tobit himself feared, the results of good deeds will not become visible within the horizon of a single human life. The cross-generational influence of good deeds is nicely depicted in this wisdom psalm:

> I have been young, and now am old,
>> yet I have not seen the righteous forsaken
>> or their children begging bread.
> They are ever giving liberally and lending,
>> and their children become a blessing. (37:25–26)

To be sure, the psalmist does not deny that the consequences of a good deed can be seen within the life of the agent him- or herself. But more to our point is the conscious emphasis on the *durative* power of such deeds—they guarantee the well-being of the generation to come. In the case of Tobit, the issue is slightly different. Though Anna has doubted the durative quality of such deeds (*"where* are your acts of charity?"), Tobit remains certain that they still rest safe in his heavenly treasury. Even though the rewards for generosity have apparently been denied to him, he believes that they can be drawn upon by his son.

Perhaps the strongest case that can be made for Koch's proposal comes from the Bible's treatment of the consequences of sin. As Koch emphasizes time and again, sin generates a result that has a "thing-like" character. Sinners find that their hands are stained or their backs are loaded down with weights that will eventually crush them:

> There is no soundness in my flesh because of your indignation;
>   There is no health in my bones because of my sin.
> For my iniquities have gone over my head;
>   They weigh like a burden too heavy for me. (Psalms 38:3–4)

In this example, like many others in the Bible, sin has generated its own consequence, which will continue to dog the offender until he has secured forgiveness. In this case it is as though the sin brought into being a weight that the offender is forced to carry.[17] If that weight is not attended to in the form of some act of contrition and penance, it will bear down more and more until it overwhelms the sinner. But it is not the case that God is completely uninvolved. When the system goes off the rails and sinners appear to prosper, the psalmist will exhort God to "attend" to the act of sin that was committed and allow its consequence to surface. It is as though (to follow the metaphoric vocabulary of the Bible) God has "turned his face" from the sinner and left the evil deeds uncorrected.

The Treasury as a Storehouse for Good Deeds

Let us return to the text from the Psalms of Solomon that we began with. The crucial line reads: "The one who practices righteousness *stores up* (*thesaurizei*) life for himself with the Lord, and the one who practices injustice is responsible for the destruction of his own soul, for the judgments of the Lord are in righteousness for each man and household" (9:5). This treasury is nothing other than a place where the substance generated by good deeds is stored. Because deed and consequence are inextricably linked, these "stored" deeds will eventually bear their fruit. Whereas in the Bible an *individual* deed created a "sphere" that enveloped the moral agent and determined his destiny, in the Second Temple period these deeds were thought to collect as a *group* in heaven.

The notion that good deeds slowly collect over time goes a long way to explain the image of the treasury found in the Psalms of Solomon, as well as 1 Enoch, 2 Baruch, and 4 Ezra. Yet the portrait that we observe in these books imagines every good deed as equal in stature. As a result, it varies considerably from the privileging of alms that we have been tracing. Tobit 4:9–10 and Ben Sira 29:10–11 declare that it is charity and charity *alone* that can fund a treasury in heaven. As we have demonstrated, these texts are nothing more than exegetical paraphrases of Proverbs 10:2 and 11:4. And in those particular proverbs, the chief concern is how best to save for the future in order to fend off the ravages of what fortune might bring. Earthly goods fund material treasuries, but charity funds heavenly treasuries, and only the latter can truly save.

It seems that our Second Temple sources have provided us with two different lenses through which to view the heavenly treasuries. At its origin, the image is financial and concerns the way charitable deeds can be stored over time. The idea develops in explicit contrast to the act of laying up earthly goods. But no sooner does this image of a heavenly bank appear than it becomes serviceable for describing virtuous deeds in general. In both cases, however, Koch's notion of a "deed-consequence connection" adds considerable value, for it is always the deed itself that generates the corresponding reward.

Evidence from the Talmud

One might think that once the imagery of the treasury is generalized in this fashion it would swallow up the role that charity played. But that is certainly not the case. The story of the rich young man in the Synoptic Gospels, a text that postdates the Psalms of Solomon and is a near contemporary to 4 Ezra and 2 Baruch, shows us otherwise. When the young man asks Jesus how he might attain eternal life, Jesus responds: "Go, sell what you own, and give the money to the poor, and you will have treasure in heaven" (Mark 10:21). This text clearly ascribes special powers to the act of giving money to the poor; it is precisely these expenditures that generate a treasury in heaven. The special status of almsgiving was also well recognized in the patristic tradition. This can be seen, for example, from an anonymous Syriac text that reads: "Heaven declared: 'from me come the rains that descend upon the earth'; Earth replied: 'from me come acts of charity that are stored in heaven.'"[18]

Talmudic texts from the fifth century CE also accord a special value to the act of charity. One can see this illustrated in the discussion of Mishna *Qiddushin* 1:10 that is found in the Babylonian Talmud (*Qiddushin* 39a). The literary unit begins by juxtaposing a citation of that mishna

itself [A] with the mishna we have encountered from the opening of
tractate *Peah* [B]:

> [A] He who performs one precept is well rewarded, his days are prolonged, and
> he inherits the land, but he who does not perform one precept, good is not done
> to him, his days are not prolonged, and he does not inherit the land.

> [B] Regarding the following matters, a man may enjoy its profit in this world
> and his principal will remain for him in the next: honoring father and mother,
> charitable deeds, hospitality to wayfarers, establishing peace between a man
> and his friend, Torah-study is equal to all of them.

The immediate problem posed by these two paragraphs is the different
ways they evaluate commandment-keeping. Mishna *Qiddushin* [A]
presumes no distinction between the commandments, while Mishna *Peah*
[B] believes that certain commandments—among them, charity—result in
a special sort of reward. The Talmudic commentary that follows attempts
to make sense of the two positions. Rav Judah opens by saying, "Let me
gloss Mishna *Qiddushin* this way—'He who performs one [additional]
precept, *when his credits [zekuyot] are equally balanced [with his debits]*,
is well rewarded.' It is as though he kept the whole Torah." Rav Judah
asserts that Mishna *Qiddushin* has presumed a situation in which a person's
sins are equal in value to his virtues. Were the day of judgment to fall
anytime soon, such a person would be at considerable risk; just a single
extra deed would determine his eternal destiny.

The Talmud presses Rav Judah's opinion farther by carrying over this
particular assumption of an evenly weighted set of scales to Mishna *Peah*.
Does the keeping of just one of those five special commandments result in
eternal life even if the credits are vastly outweighed by debits? To this
question Rav Shemayah answers: Here we must presume a situation in
which we have an equal number of debits and credits. In that case, one
might presume that the scales would be balanced. But because the credits
acquired through those five special commandments are overweighted, the
scales will incline in favor of the individual.

There can be no question that the Talmudic commentary constitutes an
artificial attempt to harmonize two different mishnaic traditions. But the
harmonization is in itself revealing because it, too, reflects the privilege
that attends the charitable deed. For the position of Rav Shemayah is that
almsgiving produces a merit that is considered "heavier" than that of the
other commandments. In my view the leveling tendencies of Mishna

Qiddushin reflect the worldview of the Psalms of Solomon, 2 Baruch, and 4 Ezra, whereas the privilege of charity in Mishna *Peah* stems from the types of thinking we saw in Ben Sira and Tobit.

It cannot be accidental that the New Testament concept, which tends to tack more closely to that of Ben Sira and Tobit, is similar to Mishna *Peah*. We might also point out that this logic can be found in Luke's parable of the rich man and Lazarus. In that story a rich and a poor man have both died. The former descends to Hades and is tormented, while the latter ascends to heaven and is comforted at Abraham's side. When the rich man asks Abraham to send Lazarus down to "dip the tip of his finger in water and cool my tongue." Abraham answers: "Child, remember that during your lifetime you received your good things, and Lazarus in like manner evil things; but now he is comforted here, and you are in agony" (16:24–25). This picture is quite close to the one Eliezer Diamond has traced in rabbinic thought: he who avails himself of the blessings of this world will use up his reward and nothing will be left for him in the world to come.[19] As the parable goes on to teach, had the rich man listened to Moses and the prophets and been kind to the poor, he could have enjoyed his life on earth and would have been spared the fires of hell.[20]

I began this chapter with the observation that the concept of the treasury in heaven found in the Gospels is dependent on earlier Jewish sources. These texts presume that good deeds generate some sort of "substance" that can be dislocated from the moral agent and "transferred" to heaven for storage. In the future those stored deeds will call forth their appropriate reward. Though some texts generalize this principle and teach that any good deed was storable in this treasury, other texts presume that only charity has that privilege. New Testament writings appear to side with Ben Sira and Tobit in granting pride of place to gifts for the poor.

One question, however, remains. If Matthew presumes that the treasury in heaven is reserved for acts of charity, why isn't the discussion of the treasury in heaven (6:19–21) directly joined to the teaching about alms (6:2–4)? Why has Matthew included the intervening material about fasting and prayer (6:5–18)? The overall structure of the chapter seems to presume that the accumulation of a treasury depends on the virtues of charity, fasting, and prayer. To this problem we must now turn.

CHAPTER TEN

Prayer, Fasting, and Almsgiving

The most effective prayer [during fast days] to make requests of God is that which is supported by works of mercy, since those who do not turn away their hearts from poverty quickly turn the Lord's ear to themselves, as the Lord says: "Be compassionate just as your Father is compassionate" (Luke 6:36), and "pardon and you will be pardoned" (Luke 6:38).

—St. Leo the Great, Homily on a Solemn Fast Day

We have seen that Matthew's teaching on the treasury in heaven (6:19–21) concludes a unit concerned with the virtuous practices of almsgiving, prayer, and fasting (vv. 1–18). The treasury in heaven, on this understanding, is the place where the rewards from these particular deeds are stored. But does this imply that the primacy of almsgiving that we saw in Tobit and Ben Sira no longer holds? To answer this question we must begin with the significance of almsgiving within this particular triad of virtuous deeds.

The Almsdeed as Petition

As we have already seen, there are three important moments in the book of Tobit when one of the characters offers a teaching on the commandment to give alms. First, when Tobit is about to send his son to collect the money left on deposit (4:7–11), second, just before Raphael reveals his identity as an angel (12:8–10), and, finally, when Tobit is on his deathbed

(14:8–10). Let us look more closely at the words of Raphael just before his departure for heaven. He tells Tobit and Tobias that

> *prayer* with *fasting* is good, but better than both is *almsgiving* with righteousness. A little with righteousness is better than wealth with wrongdoing. It is better to give alms than to lay up gold. For almsgiving saves from death and purges away every sin. Those who give alms will enjoy a full life, but those who commit sin and do wrong are their own worst enemies. (Tob 12:8–10)

This instruction looks very similar to what Tobit says earlier in the book. Both make a special point to emphasize that almsgiving funds a heavenly treasury, and both cite Proverbs 10:2 in support of this perspective: "almsgiving saves from death." But whereas Tobit glosses this proverb with the clause: "and keeps you from going into the Darkness," Raphael adds: "and purges away every sin." As we saw, Tobit's wording fits his situation; almsgiving will eventually restore his sight. In the case of Raphael, the specific piece of advice looks forward to the contents of Tobit's prayer in chapter 13, when he compares his own situation ("For [God] *afflicts*, and he *shows mercy;* he leads down to Hades . . . and he brings up from the great abyss [13:2]") to that of the nation Israel just a few verses later:

> He will *afflict* you for your iniquities,
>   but he will again *show mercy* on all of you.
> He will gather you from all the nations
>   among whom you have been scattered. (13:5)

The implication of the parallelism is clear—just as God *afflicted* Tobit and then *showed mercy* by raising him from the dead, so he can do for Israel. Israel's affliction is understood as its exile while the mercy it awaits is being gathered back to the land of Israel.

But Israel's situation is in one respect quite different. When Tobit was struck blind it was part of a divine test; he was innocent of any wrongdoing. Israel's affliction, on the other hand, is a result of its deep and persistent rebellion against God. In Israel's case divine deliverance requires a spiritual return to the deity it has spurned:

> [He will gather you from all the nations . . .]
> If you turn to him with all your heart and with all your soul,
>   to do what is true before him,
> then he will turn to you
>   and will no longer hide his face from you. (13:6)

And so Raphael's gloss ("For almsgiving saves from death *and purges away every sin*") is altogether apt and fits its placement in the book. Israel as a nation can learn from the life of Tobit about the capacity of God to save those in dire need. But in order to benefit from that power, Israel must become worthy. To accomplish that, it must give alms and, by so doing, "purge away" all its sins.

Let's pause for a second on the image of almsgiving as a means of purging away sin. The term *purge* (*apokatharizo* in Greek) comes from a Semitic original that meant "to cleanse" or, perhaps better, "clear" an account of any outstanding obligation—in other words, to pay off a debt.[1] Almsgiving is uniquely able to do this because it funds a treasury in heaven, something that neither prayer nor fasting can accomplish on its own. Because of this unique capacity, Raphael singles it out as the most significant action among the three.

But we should not overgeneralize this "monetary" role. Almsgiving also functions as a form of petition. This is clear from what Raphael goes on to say:

> I will now declare the whole truth to you and will conceal nothing from you. Already I have declared it to you when I said, "It is good to conceal the secret of a king, but to reveal with due honor the works of God." So now when you and Sarah prayed, it was I who brought and read the *memorial* (mnēmosunon) of your prayer before the glory of the Lord, and likewise whenever you would bury the dead. And that time when you did not hesitate to get up and leave your dinner to go and bury the dead, I was sent to you to test you. And at the same time God sent me to heal you and Sarah your daughter-in-law. I am Raphael, one of the seven angels who stand ready and enter before the glory of the Lord. (12:11–15)[2]

What is crucial to see in this text is Raphael's role in bringing both prayers and alms to the attention of God in heaven. Both types of piety establish a "memorial" that prompts God to recall the deed and stirs him to respond. The same dynamic can be seen in the book of Acts in the person of Cornelius, a Roman soldier who revered the God of Israel. We learn that he "gave alms generously to the [Jewish] people and prayed constantly to God" (10:2). One day he had a vision in which an angel told him, "Your prayers and your alms have ascended as a *memorial* (mnēmosunon) before God" (v. 4). Thereupon, Peter is commanded to pay him a visit and eventually to baptize him and his entire household (vv. 34–48), an enormous turning point in the book of Acts, since it marks the beginning of the incorporation of gentiles into the evolving cadre of folks who identify themselves as followers of Jesus. But what cannot be missed for our purposes is that the almsdeed is conceived of as a concrete, substantial thing that functions as an aide-mémoire in heaven. One day, when God's eyes alight upon this memorial, he will be prompted to bestow upon Cornelius the reward that is his due. In order to get a proper handle on how an almsdeed can function as prayer, we must make a brief detour and consider how the ritual of fasting functions in the Bible.

Fasting as Petition

Because of the linkage of fasting to moments of penitence—the Christian reader will naturally think of Ash Wednesday and the season of Lent—scholars have assumed that this ritual's primary function has to do with the forgiveness of sins. Support for this presumption can be gained from Second Temple and rabbinic texts which assert that acts of self-mortification can repay the debt owed by sin.[3] But in biblical times, as David Lambert has argued, the primary purpose of fasting was to call attention to one's plight. Given that fact, it is no surprise that fasting is regularly employed when mourning the dead, an action that has nothing to do with sin.

But even more central to his argument is the association of fasting with prayer. "Petitionary prayer in the Hebrew Bible," Lambert observes, "usually arises from a state of affliction or crisis. Voicing that affliction, prayer captures the attention of YHWH and rouses him, as a God of mercy, to pity and hence action. While prayer constitutes a verbal articulation of the distress, fasting provides an equally expressive—indeed, given the difficulty of rendering pain in words, perhaps an even more expressive—physical manifestation. It therefore shares in the dialogical nature of prayer."[4] The key insight here is the *expressive* nature of fasting, and that is certainly the central reason why fasting is so closely tied to prayer. One might draw an analogy between fasting in antiquity and the role of the hunger strike in the modern world. The person who protests a governmental policy by abstaining from food raises the urgency of his petition to a much higher level. The plea is no passing affectation on the part of the aggrieved; he is willing to undergo considerable inconveniences to advance the message. Often, an action such as this will garner the attention of public media and place considerable pressure on the perpetrators of a given injustice to explain themselves. Though the analogy is not perfect, the comparison, Lambert asserts, "emphasizes that the element of protest, rather than penitence, can motivate fasting. Its frequent association with the lament . . . does indeed suggest that fasting expresses an element of protest against a decree deemed unfair or simply unbearable."[5] In this highly anthropomorphic understanding, one hopes to attract God's attention and by so doing persuade him to show mercy.

To illustrate this let us look at the prayer of Jehoshaphat, king of Judah in the ninth century BCE. The context is that of a military invasion: the Ammonites and Moabites have joined forces, crossed the Jordan River, and penetrated to the very heartland of the country. In great fear King Jehoshaphat imposes a fast on all of Judah, including even the women and children (2 Chronicles 20:3–4, 13). When the people have assembled, Jehoshaphat steps forward and offers a prayer:

> O LORD, God of our ancestors, are you not God in heaven? Do you not rule over all the kingdoms of the nations? In your hand are power and might, so that no one is able to withstand you. Did you not, O our God, drive out the inhabitants of this land before your people Israel, and give it forever to the descendants of your friend Abraham? They have lived in it, and in it have built you a sanctuary for your name, saying, "If disaster comes upon us, the sword, judgment, or pestilence, or famine, we will stand before this house, and before you, for your name is in this house, and cry to you in our distress, and you will hear and save." (2 Chron 20:6–9)

Having finished his declaration regarding what God has promised, Jehoshaphat gets right to the point. He implores God to act in accordance with his deeds of the past.

> See now, the people of Ammon, Moab, and Mount Seir, whom you would not let Israel invade when they came from the land of Egypt, and whom they avoided and did not destroy—they reward us by coming to drive us out of your possession that you have given us to inherit. O our God, will you not execute judgment upon them? For we are powerless against this great multitude that is coming against us. We do not know what to do, but our eyes are on you. (II Chron 20:10–12)

The absence of any sign of contrition for sin is striking. Though military assaults frequently are a sign of divine punishment, that is decidedly not the case here. Moreover, it is striking that even the children are asked to participate (20:13). Clearly they are not called forward because of any form of culpability; the presence of these innocent persons must be for a different purpose altogether.

The prayer of Jehoshaphat recalls a similar prayer in the book of Joel. Here the context is also that of a terrible crop failure, caused by either marauding armies or a myriad of locusts:

> Blow the trumpet in Zion;
>   sanctify a fast;
> call a solemn assembly;
>   gather the people.
> Sanctify the congregation;
>   assemble the aged;
> gather the children,
>   even infants at the breast.
> Let the bridegroom leave his room,
>   and the bride her canopy.
> Between the vestibule and the altar
>   let the priests, the ministers of the Lord, weep.
> Let them say, "Spare your people, O Lord,
>   and do not make your heritage a mockery,
>   a byword among the nations.
> Why should it be said among the peoples,
>   'Where is their God?'" (2:15–17)

The fast that the prophet has called is total; even "infants at the breast" will be involved. As in the case of Jehoshaphat, the purpose of the fast is to assist the prayers of petition that are being made to God. This is emphasized quite nicely in the very last line of the petition: "Why should it be said among the peoples, 'Where is their God?'" This sort of accusation—put in the mouth of the adversary and addressed to one who suffers innocently—is a commonplace in the book of Psalms. The psalmist quotes an accusation such as this because he presumes that God has a reputation that he is anxious to preserve. It is as though the supplicant is saying: "Look, I understand that my present condition may not seem to be dire enough to warrant your immediate attention, but note carefully what others are making of it. The fact that I, a devoted and well-known servant of yours, am suffering is calling into question your capacity to deliver and rescue. So if my own complaints are not sufficient to push you to action, then at least take note of the terrible damage this will do to your reputation." In intercessory prayers like this, the explanation for the terrible state of affairs is not some unacknowledged sin but rather a moment of inattentiveness on God's part. What the person at prayer seeks is a means of bringing the situation and its potentially dire consequences to the attention of God.

The Biblical Triad of Prayer, Fasting, and Sacrifice

Because fasting is so closely associated with intercessory prayer, it would be expected that a critique of one would entail the other. The prophet Jeremiah confirms this nicely:

> The LORD said to me: "Do not pray for the welfare of this people. Although they fast, I do not hear their cry, and although they offer burnt offering and grain offering, I do not accept them; but by the sword, by famine, and by pestilence I consume them." (Jer 14:11–12)

Although the context is that of the grave sins of the people of Judah that will eventually result in the destruction of Jerusalem and the exile of its leading citizens, the fasting that is at issue in this prophetic oracle is not simply penitential but also supplicatory. Like the fasts of Jehoshaphat and Joel, its purpose is to grab the attention of God and spur him to mercy. In this case, however, the decree is irrevocable. Accordingly, God tells Jeremiah: "[even if] they fast, I [will] not hear their cry."

The very phrasing of this verse is striking: God will not *hear* the cry of a fast. It is as though the fast itself is nothing but a prayer ("their cry") that God can attend to or spurn. There is a certain element of theater here; through fasting, prayer has been given an embodied script. We not only hear the supplication, we see it.

It is also worth noting that Jeremiah denies the effectiveness of three distinct types of cultic acts: fasting, prayer, and sacrifice ("although they *fast* . . . I will not hear *their cry*, and although they offer *burnt offering and grain offering*, I do not accept them"). This triad of prayer, fasting, and sacrifice also appears in Judges 20 when the Israelite armies meet with defeat after attempting to subdue the tribe of Benjamin. In despair over their grave misfortune, the Israelite army returns to Bethel to give thought to their defeat and ponder a strategy for the future:

> Then all the Israelites, the whole army, went back to Bethel and wept, sitting there before the LORD; they *fasted* that day until evening. Then they offered *burnt offerings and sacrifices of well-being* before the LORD. And the Israelites *inquired of the* LORD (for the ark of the covenant of God was there in those days, and Phinehas son of Eleazar, son of Aaron, ministered before it in those days), saying, "Shall we go out once more to battle against our kinsfolk the Benjaminites, or shall we desist?" The LORD answered, "Go up, for tomorrow I will give them into your hand." (Judg 20:26–28)

As in the examples we have already considered, the act of fasting occurs with prayer as a means of invoking a favorable response from God. In this case, unlike the others we have surveyed (except for Jeremiah 14), sacrificial rites are added to the rituals of fasting and intercessory prayer. It is not difficult to see the logic of this. In biblical thought, sacrifices were thought to be a means of serving God. In the realistic world of the cult, God was offered food and drink as servants would have done for any great king in his palace. And just as a feast was a time when a king would be particularly receptive to an appeal from one of its citizens, so, the logic holds, for the divine king in his temple. It was for this reason that morning and evening prayer gained the prestige they did—they coincided with the morning and evening sacrifices. Just as God is said to be present everywhere in the world he has created, but most present in Jerusalem in the ritual sphere, so God can be said to be available at any time of the day but most available during the daily sacrifices. Sacrifice, like fasting, was a means of attracting the attention of God so that he might attend favorably to his supplicants.[6]

If we can accept the claim that prayer, fasting, and sacrifice are a traditional grouping in biblical religion and that, in the Second Temple period, almsgiving came to be seen as a suitable substitution for sacrifice, it would be expected that texts from this period might reflect this transformation by creating the triad of almsgiving, fasting, and prayer. And that expectation is met, as we have seen, in the book of Tobit. Near the end of the book, when Raphael is about to depart and return to heaven, he takes Tobit and Tobias aside in order to address them privately. He begins by telling them that they must declare to all people the deeds that God has done on their behalf. For though "it is good," Raphael concedes, "to conceal the secret of the king," one must be quick "to acknowledge and reveal the works of God" (12:7). Then he turns to address the question of what is essential for a life devoted to serving the God of Israel. "Prayer with fasting is good," he says, "but better than both is almsgiving with righteousness." Almsgiving is crucial, Raphael argues, because it alone "saves from death and purges one from every sin" (12:8–9). In this brief moment of instruction, Raphael transforms the biblical triad of *sacrifice*, fasting, and prayer to *alms*, fasting, and prayer. And as if to make the point that almsgiving is the replacement for sacrifice, Raphael asserts that almsgiving is superior to fasting and prayer just as sacrifice was the highest form of service to God while the temple was standing, and that almsgiving atones for sin, a function that it shares with sacrifice alone.

Charity as an Act of Mercy

Let me return for a moment to the similarity between charity and fasting. As I observed above, fasting was frequently joined to intercessory prayer because it functioned as a means of persuading God to attend to one's cause. As biblical law had taught, God has a special place in his heart for the poor—'ani in Hebrew—and is fervently committed to assist them. By afflicting oneself through fasting (le-'annot nephesh, a simple verbalization of the noun 'ani), one places oneself in a similar position before God and therefore increases the chance that one's prayer will get a favorable hearing. Almsgiving has a similar role to play in quickening God's affection and mercy toward a supplicant.

Mercy is evident from the practice itself: one gives money to a beggar because one is moved out of pity for his desperate straits. This is reflected linguistically in the way in which the Septuagint translates the two Hebrew words that come to mean charity to the poor. Both hesed and tsedaqa are often translated by the Greek term eleēmosunē (sometimes simply eleos), an act of mercy. This led to some rather startling results. For example, the famous saying of the prophet Hosea, "I desire steadfast love [hesed] [toward God] not [just] sacrifice" (6:6) originally meant that God preferred loyalty ("steadfast love") to his covenantal norms over mere altar service. But when the Greek translator rendered the Hebrew term for loyalty with the word for mercy (eleos), the verse assumed an entirely different character. Whereas the Hebrew had privileged loyalty to God over sacrifice, the Greek translation said: "I desire mercy [toward the poor] not [just] sacrifice." In other words, a Hebrew term that had denoted a vertical relationship between man and God (specifically, the loyalty of Israel to the terms of the covenant) now had a horizontal set of referents (the merciful conduct of one man toward another).[7]

In Exodus 34, when Moses learns of the divine attributes, he is told that God is "abounding in steadfast love" (rab-hesed) toward Israel. Yet the Greek translation slightly alters the meaning so that the emphasis is no longer on loyalty but on mercy. This is not as great a shift as we saw in Hosea, perhaps, but it is significant nonetheless because we can see that human mercy is in a very real sense a miming of an essential and even definitive divine attribute. Almsgiving, it would stand to reason, became an effective petition when it was joined to prayer because it mirrored a defining characteristic of God. Stated more anthropomorphically, when a supplicant shows mercy to the poor, God is "impelled" to show a similar sort of mercy toward his pray-ers.

The logic of almsgiving that I have just intuited is confirmed in the rabbinic corpus. Let us consider a well-known story about Rabbi Tanhuma, a fourth-century figure, found in the midrashic collection *Genesis Rabbah*.[8] The occasion is a terrible drought that has struck the land of Israel. In accordance with biblical precedent and rabbinic teaching, Rabbi Tanhuma calls a fast. For one day, then a second, and finally a third, a fast is observed, but no rain falls. Aware that in this case Israel's sin must be sufficiently great that not even fasting can garner God's attention (recall Jeremiah 14: "although they fast I do not hear their cry"), Rabbi Tanhuma decides to take a different tack. He mounts his pulpit and proclaims to the people, "My sons, be filled with mercy upon each other, so that the Holy One (Blessed Be He!) will be filled with mercy upon you." The people immediately began to fan out into the streets to distribute charity to the poor. While doing so, a man is observed giving his estranged wife a few coins. Worried that this might constitute payment for illicit sexual favors, the people lodge a complaint with Rabbi Tanhuma: "How can we just sit here while this grave misdeed is committed?" The man is promptly summoned and interrogated about the payment. He explains himself thus: "Rabbi, I saw her in distress and was filled with compassion toward her." At that very moment, Rabbi Tanhuma lifts his face to the heavens and says: "O Lord of the universe, if this man, upon whom this woman has no legal claim for support, nevertheless took regard for her terrible plight and was filled with compassion for her, then what about You, about whom scripture says that you are gracious and compassionate?! We are the children of your beloved ones—the sons of Abraham, Isaac, and Jacob. How much more worthy are we that you would show compassion toward us." And with the completion of this urgent appeal to God, the heavens open, the rain falls, and the world enjoys relief from the terrible suffering wrought by the famine.

This story illustrates the effectiveness of almsgiving in turning God from a disposition of judgment to that of mercy. The biblical verse that was the occasion for this rabbinic story is Psalm 145:9, "The LORD is good to all, and his compassion is over all that he has made." But in biblical thought in general, it is never sufficient for a supplicant simply to voice an attribute of God ("the LORD is good") in order for that attribute to have its desired effect (mercy toward the supplicant); one must *enact* it through some sort of deed. Thus the logic of the Our Father: "forgive us our sins *as* we forgive those who have sinned against us." And similarly for the affirmation that God is compassionate toward his creation—in order to activate this truth, one must be compassionate to those in need. The angel Raphael had taught that fasting with prayer is good, but better than both is alms. This teaching is confirmed in the story of Rabbi Tanhuma: after the public fast had failed, almsgiving became the key that opened the door to God's heart.

The Durative Character of Charity

For many readers, the role of compassion in this rabbinic story will stand in considerable tension with the accounting metaphor that we have previously traced ("almsgiving purges—that is, cleanses—one's account of sin"). Yet I would like to contend that the two are not as far apart as one might imagine. As we saw in our last chapter, good and evil deeds have long-term consequences for their perpetrators. (This idea has not disappeared even in modern times. Consider the phrase—"that [act] will come back to haunt you!") But what deserves special emphasis is the fact that good deeds are not all the same in terms of the consequences they bring. The deed of compassion for the poor, unlike all other good works, does not garner simply a one-time reward. As the rabbis put the matter, it is a deed that yields a reward in the present while continuing to pay dividends in the future (Mishna *Peah* 1:1). In the financial terms we have been considering, almsgiving is the quintessential investment, for the payouts it produces never damage the underlying principal.

The *durative* quality of charity is best reflected in the way in which the deed is compared to offerings intended for the altar. When Raphael is about to depart for heaven, he informs Tobit that when he prayed and attended to the unburied dead, a *memorial* of that prayer or deed was brought before the throne of God (Tob 12:12). The term *memorial* was not chosen at random; it refers to the portion of a sacrifice that was thought to reside before the very presence of God. It is often an element that is stressed in Ben Sira's own teaching on sacrifice. At one point he remarks that "the offering of the righteous enriches the altar, and its pleasing odor rises before the Most High. The sacrifice of the righteous is acceptable, and it *will never be forgotten* (35:8–9; 35:5–6 in the Greek). God is, in Ben Sira's opinion, so moved by the fragrance of a well-cooked sacrifice that he never forgets the intentions that motivated the gift in the first place. Given the sort of power that resides within the sacrificial hearth, it cannot be surprising that Ben Sira recommends sacrifices during a time of need. For example, when one is ill, our sage urges that one "offer a sweet-smelling sacrifice and *a memorial portion* of choice flour, and pour oil on your offering, as much as you can afford" (38:11).

Ben Sira also employs the image of a memorial to explain the benefits of charity. As I have noted, Ben Sira believes that charitable deeds endure long after those who have done them have passed away. Regarding these anonymous "men of charity" (*hesed*), Ben Sira says, "with their offspring their goodness shall abide, and their inheritance [with their children's children]. Forever shall their *memory* abide, their charitable deeds [*tsedaqa*] [shall never be wiped out]" (44:11, 13).[9] Earlier in his book he told his students that the charity their fathers once showed "will never be wiped out," that is, its balance cannot be drawn down to zero. As a result, "in a day of trouble it will be *remembered* to you [by God] to cancel your sins as heat melts ice" (3:14–15).

Ben Sira provides us with a great example of how acts of charity are *stored* in heaven and later *remembered* by God to the advantage of the agent or his offspring. If we return to the sacrificial metaphor we have been following, these deeds of charity, like the memorial portions at the altar, remind God of the service that has been rendered him. They function as an ongoing appeal for mercy.

As we have seen, the biblical triad of sacrifice, prayer, and fasting was gradually replaced in the Second Temple period by alms, prayer, and fasting. In this grouping, alms had the greatest prestige because like sacrifice it involved direct commerce with God. Sacrifice provided food for God's table, whereas alms funded a treasury in heaven. Klaus Koch has argued, on the other hand, that Jewish texts of the Second Temple period understood the treasury as the place where the rewards for the keeping of *every* commandment were stored. I have suggested that Matthew 6 represents a mixture of these two positions.[10] The treasury image that was originally unique to almsgiving now governs the rewards that apply to the other two parts of a traditional triad: prayer and fasting.[11]

As David Lambert observes, this is a striking *novum* in biblical thinking. "The notion that almsgiving, prayer, and fasting are meritorious deeds," Lambert concludes, "is unique to postbiblical Judaism; it is not to be found in the Hebrew Bible." Fasting is an effective ritual in the Bible due to its ability to move the deity to mercy, not because it collects as a merit in a heavenly treasury. Things are far different in the Gospel of Matthew. There, Lambert argues, God "'sees' the meritorious deed but he is not moved to action by it; he allows its appropriate reward to accrue. Fasting has ceased to be a dialogical act and has become an act that is privately and personally beneficial and therefore, if performed in public, an ostentatious display of personal merit."[12] Though I have agreed with most of what Lambert asserts, I think he goes too far in declaring that the expressive value of fasting disappears once it becomes a meritorious act. As our discussion has shown, the character of the almsdeed (and by extension, the fast) includes both facets: it is both a monetary *deposit* in a heaven bank and a *memorial* of the originating act of mercy that continues to pull on the heartstrings of God.

We should not forget that the Greek Bible forever inscribes this double nature by translating the Hebrew term for merit (*tsedaqa*) as mercy (*eleēmosunē*). Koch's notion of the "thing-like" character of the good deed in biblical thought is certainly the point of origin for both these ideas. The question is what sort of "thing" is actually deposited in the heavenly bank. Here we cannot speak univocally; the texts we have examined can parse the matter both financially (a treasury) and emotively (a memorial).

CHAPTER ELEVEN

Sacrificial Giving

[The list of the corporal works of mercy in Matthew 25:31–46] reminds one of an anonymous Jewish interpretation of Psalm 118:19: "Open for me the gates of charity (*tsedeq*)." In the world to come, one will be asked: "What was your work?" If he answers, "I fed the hungry," then they will say, "This is the gate of the Lord" (v. 20)—Let the feeder of the hungry enter by it. If he answers, "I gave drink to the thirsty," then they will say: "This is the gate of the Lord"—Let the giver of drink to the thirsty enter by it. If he answers, "I clothed the naked," then they will say, "This is the gate of the Lord"—Let the one who clothes the naked enter by it.

—Ephraim Urbach

If giving alms is something like making a bank deposit to an account in heaven, then one might wonder how to maximize one's capital. One option is to follow the example of Tobit and make regular contributions so that a generous nest egg might accumulate. For if one's treasure is a hedge against an uncertain future, then there are very good reasons to keep your bottom line growing. And there is another advantage to regular donations to this account: the more regularly one contributes, the easier and more natural each donation will become. In this way one will be able to fulfill the commandment: "Do not let your eye *begrudge* the gift when you make it" (Tobit 4:7; cf. Deut 15:7b–8, 10a). It may be that St. Paul recalled this advice when he wrote, in his famous address on love, "If I give away all my possessions . . . but do not have love, I am nothing" (1 Cor 13:3).

But there are more variables on the table. As any wise investment officer will disclose, future holdings depend on prudent investments. And so for almsgiving. If our donations are to make a difference, they must be made responsibly. On the one hand, this requires careful scrutiny of the recipients. "To all those who practice righteousness," Tobit declares, "give alms from your possessions" (4:6–7). On the other hand, it is also important to give in proportion to one's means: "If you have many possessions, make your gift from them in proportion; if few, do not be afraid to give according to the little you have" (4:8). Should one give too much there would be the danger of cutting into the principal. If that is done too often, one will eventually become destitute and in need of alms oneself. It is this sort of prudential judgment that led the Rabbis to codify the principle that one should give no more than one-fifth of one's principal at first and afterward only one-fifth of the interest earned on that principal.[1] Such stewardship nearly guarantees that one can keep giving alms year in and year out without becoming destitute oneself.

Almsgiving and Sacrifice

Because almsgiving was a way of depositing money directly into a heavenly treasury, it also intersected, as we have seen, with another means of shipping goods to God—sacrifice. For one of the major purposes of the altar in ancient Israel was to convey the sacrifices made by an individual to God in heaven. For this reason the altar was thought to be the "most holy" (*qodesh-qodashim;* cf. Exod 40:10) of structures, a degree of holiness it shared with the inner sanctum of the temple, where God was thought to dwell. A particularly important biblical verse for the development of the idea that almsgiving intersects with sacrifice was Proverbs 19:17, "Whoever is *kind* to the poor *lends to the Lord,* and will be repaid in full."[2] This surprising text suggests that when one deposits coins in the hand of a poor person, they are simultaneously transferred to God in heaven. The almsgiver becomes the holder of a bond that has been "signed" by God himself. If ordinary investors are partial to U.S. treasury notes because the United States government stands behind them, then what about the security one ought to feel if the Holy One of Israel is the borrower?

The Christian theologian Irenaeus of Lyons (second century CE) saw in Proverbs 19:17 a dramatic act of loving condescension on the part of God. Although God does not need our sacrifices or our money, he uses the altar and the waiting hand of the poor person as the means by which he may be approached.

> Now we make offerings to Him [at the Eucharistic altar], not as though He stood in need of it. . . . And even [though] God does not need our possessions . . . we need to offer something to God; as Solomon says: *"He who is generous to the downtrodden, makes a loan to the Lord"* (Prov 19:17). For God, who stands in need of nothing, takes our good works to Himself for this purpose, that He may grant us a recompense of His own good things, as our Lord says: *"Come, ye blessed of My Father, receive the kingdom prepared for you. For I was hungry, and ye gave Me to eat; I was thirsty, and ye gave Me drink; I was a stranger, and ye took Me in; naked, and ye clothed Me; sick, and ye visited Me; in prison, and ye came to Me"* (Matt 25:34–36). As, therefore, He does not stand in need of these [services], yet does desire that we should render them for our own benefit, lest we be unfruitful; so did the Word give to the people that very precept as to the making of oblations, although He stood in no need of them, that they might learn to serve God: thus it is also His will that we, too, should offer a gift at the altar, frequently, and without intermission.[3]

In this text, Irenaeus links (1) sacrificial oblation (2) almsgiving as a loan to God (Prov 19:17) and (3) the depiction of the last judgment in Matt 25:31–46, a linkage that becomes standard and widespread among almost all patristic commentators.[4] According to Matthew, we will be judged on the basis of our generosity to Christ, who is present in the poor. Proverbs 19:17 serves as an Old Testament proof text for the picture Christ draws in Matthew 25. In giving alms to the poor, we are making a loan to the Son of Man. But it is important to note that Irenaeus thinks of this "loan" not as a financial matter but as a liturgical act. Placing an offering on the altar is like putting money in the hands of a poor person. Just as God did not need the sacrifice of animals in the temple but desired that we give them to Him for our own benefit, so God does not need the alms we give but demands them from us in order that we might have some concrete means of displaying reverence.

But if the giving of alms was akin to making a sacrificial donation, then one must wonder whether Tobit's advice about prudent stewardship is the only way to calculate the level of one's contribution. For some sacrificial laws, particularly those that concern obligatory contributions to deal with sin, there is a clearly constructed gradient as to what one must give and the crucial variable is the wealth of the donor (as in Lev 5). Some must offer an expensive animal, others a pair of birds, and still others can make do with just grain. But in nonobligatory sacrificial contexts, such as sacrifices that are vowed or freely given, the door is open for giving much more.[5] In this vein, one is reminded of the prophet Micah's sliding scale of values regarding sacrifice. He begins his oracle on this issue with a rhetorical question:

> With what shall I come before the LORD,
>   and bow myself before God on high?

In response, he provides three options:

> Shall I come before him with burnt offerings,
>   with calves a year old?
> Will the LORD be pleased with thousands of rams,
>   with ten thousands of rivers of oil?
> Shall I give my firstborn for my transgression,
>   the fruit of my body for the sin of my soul?" (6:6–7)

It is fine and good, Micah reasons, to offer a few animals as a burnt offering; even better would be thousands of rams, but the supreme sacrifice would be a firstborn son. As Abraham knew so well, that would be the most difficult thing to part with. No doubt for this very reason, some rabbinic texts could see the sacrifice of Isaac as the founding moment of the daily liturgy of the temple.[6]

A similar logic held true for the giving of alms. If almsgiving was analogous to an offering on the altar, then even a modest donation could have its effect. Yet among the truly devout there would certainly be some who would wish to go beyond the bare minimum.

The Rich Young Man and Jesus

There is no better example of this principle than the story of the rich young man found in the Synoptic Gospels.[7] I would like to discuss the version of the story found in the Gospel of Mark (10:17–31; cf. Matt 19:16–30, Luke 18:18–30). But before looking at the story, it is important to consider its literary placement. The discourse occurs at the very center of the Gospel (8:27–10:52), a section that deals with Jesus' journey toward Jerusalem, where he will spend his last week. In this position, it marks the crucial transition from Jesus' early ministry in the Galilee (1:1–8:26) to his last week in Jerusalem (11:1–16:8). This critical portion of the book is marked by three separate predictions of the passion, one near the beginning (8:31–33), one in the middle (9:30–32), and one at the end (10:32–34).

In all three of these predictions the disciples react in utter shock to what Jesus declares about the great suffering he must endure before his ignominious death at the hands of the religious elite. After the first prediction, Peter takes Jesus aside and tries to correct him. To this Jesus responds severely: "Get behind me, Satan! For you are setting your mind not on divine things but on human things" (8:33). After the next two predictions, the disciples are still puzzled but wisely keep silence ("But they did not understand what he was saying and were afraid to ask him" [9:32]). The disciples clearly presume that the Messiah of Israel would never have to suffer such a death. The cost of being the beloved Son of God will come as a complete surprise to them. But there is an additional irony here. Jesus adds that what is true for him will also hold true for those who wish to be his disciples: "If any want to become my followers, let them deny themselves and take up their cross and follow me. For those who want to save their life will lose it, and those who lose their life for my sake, and for the sake of the gospel, will save it" (Mark 8:34–35). Following Jesus means following him on the way of the cross.

Sandwiched between the second and third predictions is Jesus' encounter with the young man; indeed, it occurs immediately before the third and final prediction. As the great patristic commentator Origen (third century CE) already saw, this literary juxtaposition was hardly accidental.[8] The giving up of all one's wealth was construed to be one way of losing one's life on behalf of the Gospel. Just as the inner core of disciples found the crucifixion to be shocking, so the young man finds the giving up of all his wealth to be a sacrifice beyond calculation.

The story opens when a young man runs up to Jesus, kneels before him, and asks: "What must I do to inherit eternal life?" (10:17). Jesus redirects the man's attention to the Ten Commandments that Israel heard back at Mount Sinai:

> You know the commandments: "You shall not murder; You shall not commit adultery; You shall not steal; You shall not bear false witness; You shall not defraud; Honor your father and mother." He said to him, "Teacher, I have kept all these since my youth." Jesus, looking at him, loved him and said, "You lack one thing; go, sell what you own, and give the money to the poor, and you will have treasure in heaven; then come, follow me." When he heard this, he was shocked and went away grieving, for he had many possessions. (10:19–22)

Though the interaction with this man has now come to an end, the overall narrative does not. For the disciples are understandably shocked at the implications of what Jesus has said. If this is what is required, they reason, then what hope does anyone have? Jesus seems to be setting the bar very high. In response to their anxious query Jesus says,

> "For mortals it is impossible [to do this], but not for God; for God all things are possible." Peter began to say to him, "Look, we have left everything and followed you." Jesus said, "Truly I tell you, there is no one who has left house or brothers or sisters or mother or father or children or fields, for my sake and for the sake of the good news, who will not receive a hundredfold now in this age—houses, brothers and sisters, mothers and children and fields, with persecutions—and in the age to come eternal life. (10:27–30)

Three things in this story demand our attention:

First is the particular selection that Jesus makes from what is often known as the "second table" of the Ten Commandments. The list begins with the fifth commandment ("you shall not murder") and continues in serial order to the tenth ("you shall not defraud"), but then it doubles back at the end and appends the fourth commandment ("honor father and mother").[9] One obvious feature of these particular commandments is that they pertain to interpersonal matters rather than the relationship of man to God. By neglecting the "first table" of the Ten Commandments, which concerns human obligations to God, Jesus appears to emphasize the horizontal at the cost of the vertical. This is all the more surprising given that Jesus had begun his answer to the young man by using Deuteronomistic language that alludes to the Shema prayer ("The LORD is God, *there is no other besides him*" [Deut 4:35]): "Why do you call me good? *No one is good but God alone.*"[10]

Second is the fact that Jesus believes that keeping the specified commandments is not sufficient. Why, we must wonder, does Jesus add a new condition that he must give all that he has to the poor?[11]

The third and final point is the *motivation* that Jesus provides the man. He is not asked simply to give his goods to the poor as a purely altruistic act; rather he is encouraged to do so in order to acquire "a treasure in heaven." This treasury is not presented as an alternative to enjoying the goods of this world. Jesus does not say to suffer without these goods for now and revel in the wealth that will be waiting in the world to come. Instead he claims that one can enjoy the fruits of one's labors both now and in the hereafter.

We therefore have three themes to explore: the selection of commandments with their horizontal rather than vertical orientation, the reason for the additional command that Jesus gives, and the moral status of the treasury that Jesus promises. All three can be illuminated by rabbinic texts.

There Is No Limit to Almsgiving

The first rabbinic text that I would like to examine is from the Mishna, a compilation of Jewish law whose final redaction took place in the late second or early third century CE. According to tradition, it contains laws that had been passed on orally since Moses' time. Modern scholars doubt the historicity of that claim; a more reasonable supposition is that some of the laws (which ones in particular is a subject of great scholarly debate) go back to the turn of the Common Era, and some perhaps to a century or two before that.

In tractate *Peah* of the Mishna we find a discussion of the various biblical laws that have to do with donations to the poor.[12] It is titled *Peah* because one way of making a donation to the poor in biblical times was to leave a corner—that is, a peah—unharvested: "When you reap the harvest of your land, you shall not reap to the very edges [*peah*] of your field, or gather the gleanings of your harvest" (Lev 19:9). But the opening section of the tractate is very unusual, for it does not open with a consideration of *peah* per se, as we might expect. Rather its interest is in a formal feature that is shared by five commandments: "These are matters that have no specified amount: peah, first fruits, the festival offering, charitable deeds, and Torah-study."[13]

The order of the commandments that have "no specified measure" is not random. I would outline them as follows:

A. Peah—donation for the poor
  B. First fruits—temple
  B'. Festival offering—temple
A'. Charitable deeds—donation for the poor
C. Torah-study.

The first and fourth items (A and A'), which are provisions for the poor, constitute something of an outer frame for the inner two commandments (B and B') that concern the temple. The only item that does not fit is Torah-study, and that may be one of the reasons why the Mishna describes it as "equal in value to all the rest." It stands as a counterbalance to the first four.

There is yet an additional feature of this Mishnah to which we must attend. The opening line of the tractate states that these five commandments are distinguished by the fact that even the slightest level of observance will suffice to fulfill one's obligation for them. But why was this so noteworthy that the Mishna would make it the subject of its opening sentence? Saul Lieberman glossed this line, "The more one does, the more commandments one fulfills." In other words, for these commandments there is the possibility of making an *exceptional* display of one's piety, what Catholics would call works of supererogation. The more one does of any of them, the more merits (*zekut*) one accrues. Hanokh Albeck says nearly the same with his annotation, "The more one does, the more praiseworthy he becomes."[14] The feature that distinguishes these commandments is the fact that *they provide an individual the opportunity to put his deep devotion to God into action.* If we take the sacrificial paradigm seriously, then the truly devout Jew will not be interested in making a minimal donation to charity. He may wish to imitate the sacrificial donation of Abraham and give away all that he holds dear. If there is no limit to almsgiving, and every coin I give adds to my merit, why not go all the way and donate *everything* to the poor?[15]

Almsgiving Is *the* Commandment

The Mishna, as we noted, believes that the study of the Torah is equal in value to keeping all the rest of the commandments. It should be added that the Tosephta, a supplement to the Mishna, does not contain this assertion. This is because the Tosephta declares that "the giving of alms and works of charity are equal in value to all of the commandments in the Torah" (4.19). The Mishna and Tosephta, then, represent differing views as to what is the most important of all the commandments.

The Tosephta's position is hardly unique. The declaration that almsgiving is equal to all the other commandments is a motif found in every corner of rabbinic literature. Indeed, this claim is part and parcel of contemporary Hebrew and Aramaic idiom. Saul Lieberman, the leading Talmudist of the twentieth century, pointed out that the Hebrew and Aramaic term for commandment, *mitsva,* can often mean simply almsgiving.[16] What does it mean to keep the commandment?—give alms! Indeed, in Aramaic, the phrase *bar mitsveta* does not mean "a son of the commandment" or "a commandment keeper" but rather "a generous person," that is, one who is in the habit of giving alms. This is nicely exemplified in a fifth-century rabbinic commentary on the book of Leviticus known as *Leviticus Rabbah* (3:1):

> Better is he who goes and works and gives charity of that which is his own, than he who goes and robs and takes by violence and gives charity of that belonging to others. . . . It is his desire to be called a man of charity (*bar mitsveta*).

It is striking that the usage of "commandment" as a cipher for almsgiving is also attested outside the rabbinic corpus. There is a tradition found in the *Testament of Asher* (an apocryphal work of the early Christian era) that closely parallels our text from *Leviticus Rabbah,* showing us that the tradition could go back to the Second Temple period itself: "And by the power of his wealth he ruins many; and out of [the wealth he secured through] his excessive wickedness, he gives alms." The last phrase of this text reads literally in Greek, "he does the commandments." But this would make little sense. Lieberman is surely right when he observes that the term *commandment* in the *Testament of Asher* must be a cipher for the giving of alms.[17]

Even the book of Tobit is worth rereading with this concept in mind, for it can hardly be accidental that when Tobit provides his son with what he thinks will be his last instruction in Torah, he puts special emphasis on the value of almsgiving (4:5–11). And later in the tale, when Raphael gives his own instruction to Tobit, he summarizes the Torah in the command to give alms (12:8–10). At the end of the book, Tobit closes his deathbed address with the command to give alms (14:8–11). For the book of Tobit, almsgiving is *the* commandment.[18]

I would like to recall one other item that we have encountered several times already before closing this section on *Peah*. This tractate not only claims that alms can be given without measure but that to the category of charitable giving belongs both "principal and interest." The text in question reads: "Regarding the following matters, a man may enjoy their fruit in this world and his principal will remain for him in the next: honoring father and mother, charitable deeds, establishing peace between a man and his friend; Torah-study is equal to all of them." The striking feature for our purposes is the way in which almsgiving is treated as an item sui generis in the normal economy of sins (debits) and merits (credits). The credit that it creates behaves in a quite unexpected way. Though it has been securely deposited in a heavenly bank, it will nevertheless continue to provide benefits in this world without harming the principal.

The Gospel of Mark in Light of Mishna *Peah*

As noted, Mishna *Peah* makes several points about charitable giving. First, giving alms to the poor is comparable to making a sacrifice in the temple; both are conveyed directly to God. Secondly, almsgiving has a special position among the commandments in that there is no specified minimum amount. Because of this uncertainty, the religiously devout will be able to use this commandment as a means of demonstrating extraordinary piety, for as Lieberman remarked, the more alms that one gives, the more merits will be accumulated. Finally, almsgiving has a unique "ontological" status in the economy of heaven. It is not subject to the limitations that are part of a zero-sum economy. One can enjoy the fruits of one's merits in both this world and the next. With this in mind, let us return to the three questions raised by the story of the rich young man.

First, we noted that the majority of New Testament scholars have wondered why Jesus chose a set of commandments that function on a horizontal rather than a vertical plane. They concern what takes place between human beings rather than between human beings and God. But such a characterization does not fit the way almsgiving was viewed in contemporary Jewish material. To give alms to a poor person was just like bringing a gift to the temple. Just as the altar was a direct conduit of sacrificial donations to heaven, so, too, was the role of the poor person who receives another's coins. I would suggest that Jesus' injunction to give alms was meant to turn the young man's earthly focus heavenward through the agency of the poor. This would be in keeping with the contextual placement of this story amid three predictions of the passion. Just as the crucifixion constitutes the highest form of sacrifice Jesus could make, so for the distribution of *all* one's goods to the poor.[19] What Christ offers to his divine Father, this young man is called to donate to the poor.

Our second question concerned why Jesus felt the need to add another commandment to the six he drew from the Ten Commandments in order to see whether the young man was worthy of the Kingdom of God. To answer this, recall the opening line of Mishna *Peah*, which I paraphrase: "These are the commandments that have no fixed level of observance." If one of the distinctive features of almsgiving is the opportunity to distinguish oneself through generosity, then it is not surprising that Jesus would advise a prospective disciple to do just that. As the text recounts, the young man was able to keep the "second table" of the Ten Commandments with seemingly little effort.[20] After all, it is not that difficult to abstain from murder, adultery, theft, and fraud. But Jesus was looking for an additional command that would allow the man's true love for God to surface. And almsgiving was just such a commandment.

Finally, the third query we raised about Jesus' teaching on alms was his promise that what was given to the poor would fund a heavenly treasury that would yield a hundredfold in this world and still more in the next. This fits hand in glove with the tradition we have followed in *Peah*. Although every act of Torah obedience will yield a merit (*zekut*), the uniqueness of almsgiving is that the merit it earns spins off interest in this world while maintaining its principal for the world to come.

Many interpreters have stumbled over this teaching of Jesus because it appears to violate a central tenet of altruism: one should be generous to the poor simply for its own sake, not because of an expected reward. But as I have been at pains to show over the course of this book, the concept of the treasury in heaven focuses not on the moral status of the charitable act but on the ontological character of the world God has fashioned. The economy of the Kingdom of Heaven, Jesus teaches, reflects the type of world God has created. Showing mercy to the poor taps into the larger font of mercy that governs God's providential hand. It is for this reason and this reason alone that funding such a treasury leads to unimagined compensation.

Jesus closes this literary unit by providing the disciples with an "insider tip" on how the heavenly economy works. The way to prosper in this market is to sacrifice all that one has. Although the initial risk is considerable, the reward is beyond imagining ("you will receive a hundredfold *now* in this age . . . and *in the age to come*, eternal life"). The Kingdom of Heaven runs by its own unique set of rules. That which is given benefits both donor and recipient—again we see a confluence between almsgiving and sacrifice. As I have argued elsewhere, the logic that governs donations to the temple is: "I have given so little (a mere animal) and you have requited me so bountifully (fullness of life)."[21]

The Great Judgment (Matt 25:31–46) and Almsgiving as Sacrifice

There is one more detail that needs attending to. As I have noted throughout this book, almsgiving is thought of as a form of sacrificial exchange. Basic to the concept of the almsdeed as loan is the notion that the charitable deed has a vertical focus. When one assists the poor, one meets God Almighty himself. Ancient interpreters were often more aware of this element than their modern counterparts.

We saw at the beginning of this chapter that Irenaeus understood the famous text of Matthew 25:31–46 through the lens of Proverbs 19:17, an interpretive move that was followed by nearly all the fathers of the church. Whether Matthew himself was thinking specifically of Proverbs 19:17 need not detain us. What is crucial, however, is the theological logic that led early Christian interpreters to this intertextual comparison. Beginning with the books of Tobit and Sirach and continuing into rabbinic Judaism and early Christianity there was a very close association between charity and service of the altar. As we saw earlier, Irenaeus specifically compares the almsdeed to a sacrifice when he writes: "Now we make offerings to Him [at the Eucharistic altar], not as though He stood in need of it. . . . And even [though] God does not need our possessions . . . we need to offer something to God; as Solomon says: 'He who is generous to the downtrodden, makes a loan to the Lord'" (Prov 19:17). Justin Martyr (also mid–second century CE) observes that at the celebration of the Eucharist, money is collected for distribution to the poor, indicating the close nexus between sacrifice and charity.[22]

Because we possess such a broad swath of sources that construe alms-giving as a gift to God (and for this reason it brought about extraordinary rewards), it is difficult to presume that Matthew was an exception, espe-cially given the fact that he shares a similar construal of the treasury in heaven. On this basis, I would claim that Matthew's depiction of the last judgment presumes a high understanding of the person of Christ. The text teaches that the one who provides food, drink, and clothing to the poor is really giving them to Jesus. As the great New Testament scholar Rudoph Bultmann observed, the basic plot of the story is through and through Jewish, the key transformation being Matthew's insertion of the title "Son of Man" where his original source would have had "God."[23] If Bultmann is correct, then we have another piece of evidence for Matthew's high view of the person of Christ. Because New Testament scholars have missed the sacrificial character of almsgiving, they fail to see its implications for Matthew's Christology. W. D. Davies and Dale Allison summarize this position when they write:

> The application of the word "God" to Jesus is extremely rare in the NT, and it is not found in the First Gospel. Is it, however, there implied? Should one hazard

that "deity" was a significant implication of Matthew's Christology, as it was of John's? We only ask the question. We do not answer it.[24]

If my book has been fair in its characterization of charity in the Second Temple period, we can do more than simply ask the question. The evidence of Tobit and Ben Sira suggests a vigorous "yes."

CHAPTER TWELVE

Deliverance from Purgatory

An Indulgence is a remission before God of the temporal punishments due to sins whose guilt has already been forgiven which the faithful Christian who is duly disposed gains under certain prescribed conditions through the action of the Church which, as the minister of redemption, dispenses and applies with authority the treasury of the satisfactions of Christ and his saints."

—*Catechism of the Catholic Church* (§1471)

(Leah) commanded from her sickbed close to death that all the revenue (of her trust) would go to assist marrying orphans or for clothing the poor and similar causes—these are commandments which elicit reward from God.

—(A Jewish will from medieval Spain)

A few years ago the Methodist philosopher Jerry Walls wrote an article ("Purgatory for Everyone") in which he encouraged his fellow Protestants to reconsider their aversion to the doctrine of purgatory.[1] He began by addressing a context with which everyone is familiar: listening to a homily at a funeral in which the pastor confidently asserts that a particular uncle is enjoying all the delights of heaven regardless of the type of life he might have lived on earth. On the one hand, it is easy to see the pastoral reasons that would generate such buoyant optimism about a family member who has died, but on the other hand one is saddened at how sentimental efforts like this trivialize what the Christian tradition has taught about the seriousness of the choices we make in this world.

162

On purely pastoral grounds, one can make a case for the doctrine of purgatory, for this teaching allows us to give voice to the deep and legitimate hopes that are shared by the family and friends of the deceased while at the same time acknowledging that the work of spiritual transformation does not come to closure at death. The task of being transformed into the image of Christ continues even after our departure from this life.

But a pastoral case should not be confused with a theological justification. For that, we need to look a little deeper. Most Protestants will concede, and many will vigorously insist, that there is inextricable connection between "justification by faith" (God's declaration of our righteousness based on the merits of Christ) and "sanctification" (our growth in holiness of life).[2] Saving faith cannot be simply an intellectual assent, nor can it be limited to a one-time decision. Somehow it must press forward to remake the entire person in the image of Christ.

This leads Walls to pose what he calls an indiscreet theological question: "If salvation essentially involves transformation—and, at the same time, we cannot be united with God unless we are holy—what becomes of those who plead the atonement of Christ for salvation but die before they have been thoroughly transformed?" Appealing to the forgiveness of sins alone "does nothing to address the fact that many Christians are imperfect lovers of God (and others) at the time of their death." What began as a *pastoral* problem has now become a *theological* challenge. Being forgiven—which occurs most prominently at baptism—is a profound moment of grace, but it does not transform *completely*. For this reason, the words of C. S. Lewis (a Protestant in good standing!) ring particularly true:

> Our souls *demand* purgatory, don't they? Would it not break the heart if God said to us, "It is true, my son, that your breath smells and your rags drip with mud and slime, but we are charitable here and no one will upbraid you with these things, nor draw away from you. Enter into the joy"? Should we not reply, "With submission, sir, and if there is no objection, I'd *rather* be cleansed first"? "It may hurt, you know."—"Even so, sir."[3]

At the heart of Walls's argument lies the deep Wesleyan conviction that those who are called in Christ are called to a journey toward sanctification. As he puts the matter: "Wesleyans insist that God not only forgives us but also changes us and actually makes us righteous. Only when we are entirely sanctified or fully perfected in this sense are we truly fit to enjoy the beatific vision of heaven." Though it is perhaps theoretically true that God could complete our sanctification at point of death with a snap of his fingers, Walls asserts that this would entail a complete trumping of our free will. And sanctification is achieved by the cooperation of the human agent with the power of the Holy Spirit; the person is not transformed against his will. If this is the manner in which God has chosen to heal us in this life, why would that process suddenly stop with our death? Indeed, if God is willing to dispense with our free will in the next life, "it is hard to see why He would not do so now, particularly in view of the high price of freedom in terms of evil and suffering." This logic constitutes a compelling argument for a period of purgation after death that allows the person to complete the transformation begun at baptism.

And what then of the classic Reformation rebuttal that scripture provides us with no clear-cut support for such an idea? In Walls's mind this is not sufficient to settle the matter. "The deeper issue," he argues, "is whether it is a reasonable inference from important truths that are clearly found [in scripture]. If theology involves a degree of disciplined speculation and logical inference, then the doctrine of purgatory cannot simply be dismissed on the grounds that Scripture does not explicitly articulate it."

Walls has provided some very good arguments for why the contemporary Christian might wish to rethink his wariness about purgatory. (And I use the term *Christian* rather than *Protestant* intentionally. For though the doctrine of purgatory remains an official teaching of the Catholic Church [*Catechism* §§1030–32], it has almost fallen into desuetude among practicing Catholics.) What I would like to suggest is that the argument for this doctrine goes deeper than just "disciplined speculation" and "logical inference." It is my thesis that purgatory depends upon a robust understanding of sanctification and merit, an understanding that is deeply grounded in the biblical narrative.[4]

The Forgiveness of King David

The first point to be made concerns the issue of forgiveness. There is a widespread assumption that forgiveness in the Bible is a yes or no proposition. One is either forgiven or not, end of question. In certain Protestant circles this is often associated with what is known as the "forensic" theory of the atonement. On this view, forgiveness is likened to a judge declaring an accused party innocent. The legal declaration depends not on the spiritual constitution of the forgiven, but on the authority of the judge. This is, of course, at considerable variance from the process of sanctification that Walls has taken such care to outline. Forgiveness is not so much a forensic declaration as a process. It begins at baptism with the infusion of justifying grace but presses on toward the complete transformation ("sanctification") of the individual. It is not, in any sense of the word, a simple yes or no proposition; it is not the "cheap grace" that Dietrich Bonhoeffer worried about. Salvation entails shedding the old Adam in favor of the new.

But it is important to emphasize that this does not mean that God's grace is active solely at conversion and afterward the person presses forward on her own. The Catholic-cum-Wesleyan tradition has often been accused of this Pelagian tendency. Rather, God's grace is understood to have spurred the will of the individual at conversion and continued to enable her to make those choices that lead to sanctification. To paraphrase St. Augustine: Command of me, O God, whatever you will, but give me the grace to pull it off.[5]

Perhaps the best place to see the way in which this process works in the Bible is in the story of David. As careful readers of the books of Samuel have long noted, God's choice of David as his anointed comes at the cost of the rejection of Saul. On the face of it, one might think that this choice was decidedly unfair because David does not seem to be a character worthy of the office God has bestowed upon him. Saul, to be sure, has his faults— he twice violates the ritual commands that the prophet Samuel gives him (1 Sam 13 and 15)—but these sins seem minor compared with those of David. In the event that will define his tenure as king, David spies Bathsheba bathing outdoors, has her summoned to his quarters, and sleeps with her; then, when he learns she has become pregnant, he has her husband murdered to cover his tracks. An unhappy chain of events to say the least. How could God prefer David over Saul?

The only way to make sense of what the Bible is doing here is to attend not to the sins themselves but to how these two kings respond to the reprimands made by their respective prophets. In Saul's case, the chief concern is personal vanity. Though he has the good sense to admit straightaway that he has failed ("I have sinned; for I have transgressed the commandment of the LORD and your words"), he qualifies the nature of his fault by foisting blame on his soldiers ("I feared the people and obeyed their voice" [1 Sam 15:24]). He then begs Samuel to accompany him to the altar to worship their Lord. When Samuel refuses, Saul reaches out to pull him back but instead catches his robe and tears a piece from it. The reader is taken aback by this sort of desperation. The story ends as abruptly as it began: "Samuel did not see Saul again until the day of his death," our narrator reports. "And the LORD was sorry that he had made Saul king over Israel" (v. 35).

When David is confronted by Nathan, he, too, is condemned for his deeds, and in far harsher terms. Speaking in God's voice, the prophet tells David that a host of evils shall now bedevil him the remainder of his days in the royal office: "I will raise up trouble against you from within your own house; and I will take your wives before your eyes, and give them to your neighbor, and he shall lie with your wives in the sight of this very sun. For you did it secretly; but I will do this thing before all Israel, and before the sun" (2 Sam 12:11–12). David immediately confesses, as Saul had done, and Nathan rescinds the penalty of death that was David's due, but the other consequences of David's misdeeds cannot be so easily dismissed. As the story continues to unfold, we learn that his tempestuous relationship with his son Absalom leads to a successful coup d'état. In order to solidify his reign, Absalom gathers all of David's women onto the roof of the royal palace in order to sleep with them in full view of those in the city. David, meanwhile, flees the city in fear for his life.

What is striking, however, is the attitude of David as he makes his way down from Mount Zion into the Kidron Valley and then ascends the Mount of Olives, from which he turns eastward toward the Jordan Valley. He does not begrudge his lot in any way, shape, or form. All that is unfolding, he realizes, is the consequence of his own shameful actions.

Two moments in particular are quite revealing as to the state of his soul. First, the priests who have been in the employ of David are naturally anxious about the loss of their sacerdotal responsibilities. Chief among them would be service of the Ark of the Covenant, the most sacred object within the Tent of Meeting. Zadok, the chief priest of that time, takes care to fetch the Ark before the exodus from the city and brings it to David as he heads east out of the city. But David is not pleased by his efforts. "Carry the ark of God back into the city," he commands. "If I find favor in the eyes of the LORD, he will bring me back and let me see both it and the place where it stays. But if he says, 'I take no pleasure in you,' here I am, let him do to me what seems good to him" (2 Sam 15:25–26). Scholars have long noted the parallels of these lines to those of Jesus in the Garden of Gethsemane. Each speaker is eager to do his Lord's bidding, even at the highest possible cost to his own person. And both submit themselves to

God's providence while following identical paths out of the holy city. David is to be especially commended for the way in which he puts his entire future as Israel's king in the hands of his God; this was the sort of piety God had hoped for when he took the risk of appointing a king back in the opening chapters of 1 Samuel. It was not the sort of piety that Saul was capable of displaying.

The second moment comes when David makes his way over the summit of the Mount of Olives. There he is met by Shimei, an opponent of David's from the beginning of his royal rule. As David marches along with his able warriors on both his left and his right, Shimei lunges forward and curses David: "Out! Out! Murderer! Scoundrel! The LORD has avenged on all of you the blood of the house of Saul, in whose place you have reigned. . . . See, disaster has overtaken you; for you are a man of blood" (2 Sam 16:7–8). Not satisfied with expressing his contempt in words alone, he throws stones and flings dirt at David and those gathered beside him. David's military advisers are understandably shocked at this rude behavior and, noticing the vulnerability of this fellow, seek David's permission to do him in. But David will hear none of it. "My own son seeks my life," David reasons; "how much more now may this Benjaminite! Let him alone, and let him curse; for the LORD has bidden him" (v. 11).

One stands in amazement at the response of David. He is the bearer of an eternal promise of God (2 Sam 7). He knows, in a way Saul never did, that his throne is invulnerable. Yet in spite of this (or precisely because of it?), David will not use his favor with God as a pretext for exempting himself from the humiliating consequences of his sins. David proves himself worthy of the high calling God has granted him by virtue of his indifference to the perquisites of that office.

But we can say more. Though Nathan had rescinded the penalty of death that threatened David, not all the consequences of his actions could be undone. The effects of sin endure long after their perpetration.[6] One can take consolation in being forgiven, but one should not confuse forgiveness with the *process* of spiritual repair. Though one could say that David had to pay the full price for his sin, it would be misleading to leave it at that, as though the punishment David had to endure was similar to a wayward adolescent taking his licks at the woodshed. For God's punishment is never solely punitive in effect. The pain that David must endure is nothing other than the logical consequence of what he has done, and by submitting to this terrible moment of humiliation, David allows himself to be refashioned in the image of the God he longs to serve. Fleeing the city and humiliated by his adversaries, David puts his future solely in the hands of God. "If I find favor in the eyes of the LORD," David confesses, "he will bring me back" (2 Sam 15:25). Put simply: not my will, Lord, but thine.

For someone committed to a forensic understanding of the atonement, the story of David's penance will remain an enigma. For according to this theory, once Nathan pronounced the words of absolution, the matter should have been closed. God had acted; human deeds can make no material contribution to the process. But for those beholden to a robust doctrine of sanctification, every detail in this story about David can be pondered and savored. Salvation is not limited to the punctiliar experience of forgiveness or justification (being declared "innocent"); it involves gradual moral and spiritual transformation—something like purgatory for David, at least in this world.

Almsgiving and Sanctification

So far I have made two points. The doctrine of purgatory depends on a robust understanding of sanctification, and this doctrine of sanctification is deeply grounded in biblical narrative. Forgiveness is not merely forensic; it entails transformation of the self. Yet one of the shortcomings of the example I provided about David is that one might get the idea that sanctification is simply a process of coming to terms with the effects one's sins have had on oneself and others. David's role, in the narrative we examined, is in many respects passive—he must *patiently await* what Nathan has prophesied to come about in order to demonstrate his spiritual growth. But the Bible knows of another, more activist strategy—the giving of alms. In order to understand how this comes about, we need to consider how sins are understood in the later sections of the Old Testament.

As I have recently argued, the Bible does not understand sin as a purely philosophical concept but always explains both its gravity and means of repair by way of metaphor.[7] At the close of the Old Testament period and on into the New, the predominant metaphor is that of a debt. So the famous words of the Our Father, "Forgive us our debts as we forgive our debtors," or the many stories that Jesus tells about forgiveness that involve debtors and creditors. On this understanding, when one sins, one incurs a debt to God, and forgiveness will involve the repayment of what is owed. The means of repayment will vary depending on the story that we consult, but one particularly esteemed means of paying down the debt can be through charity to the poor.

There are a number of reasons one could give for the high esteem that almsgiving has enjoyed in the Christian tradition. But pride of place should go to scriptural precedent: when King Nebuchadnezzar approaches the prophet Daniel in deep contrition over his errors, he pleads for a way to make amends. Daniel famously advises: "Pay off the debt you owe for your sins through charity toward the poor" (4:27; Aramaic original v. 24). (Nebuchadnezzar, we might add, was the model penitent sinner in early Christian homiletic literature for obvious reasons: if this heinous sinner could be forgiven, then anyone could.)[8]

The novelty of Daniel's advice should not escape us. In this text, we have stumbled upon a major revolution in the way in which the Bible understands sin. Whereas David had to make amends for what he had done by graciously *enduring the consequences*, Nebuchadnezzar was given the option of *taking active steps* in the repair of his own soul. Forgiveness was no longer dependent on awaiting what the future might bring, but could be achieved by putting into effect a set of spiritual disciplines revealed by God.

Traditionally, Protestant interpreters have been uncomfortable with the advice Daniel provides because it seems to convey a form of "works-righteousness." Nebuchadnezzar is able to buy his way out through his acts of charity. But in order to blunt these worries, we need to recall how the Bible understands almsgiving. For the Bible, charity to the poor is an act of mercy that generates a merit. The paradox is captured well by the translation of the Semitic original into Greek. The Hebrew term for almsgiving, *tsedaqa* (*tsidqa* in the Aramaic of Daniel), originally referred to a merit or credit that registered to the individual and was translated into the Greek as *eleēmosunē*, which meant an act of mercy. Frequently in the Greek Bible we see the term *eleēmosunē* used in contexts in which we would have expected a word for merit or credit.[9] The conclusion is as obvious as it is paradoxical: acts of generosity to another that are entirely undeserved (sola gratia!) generate a "merit" for the doer of the deed.

St. Augustine would have had no trouble with this improbable juxtaposition of grace and merit. He believed that grace enabled human beings to participate in the work of God. Though they win merits for themselves, the merits are nothing other than gifts in the first place. A close analogy might be the young girl who buys a Christmas gift for her mother with all her allowance money. From one perspective it is no gift at all; the mother simply gets back what she provided in the first place. But from another perspective the gift allows the child to participate in the exchange of love that is basic to the family itself. Augustine expresses the same notion from a more theological vantage point when he writes: "You [O, God] are glorified in the assembly of your Holy Ones, for in crowning their merits you are crowning your own gifts."[10]

And so the revolution that the book of Daniel sets in motion. Whereas David has to *await* what the future will bring in order to complete the repair of his soul, Nebuchadnezzar can *initiate* that process on his own. This is the reason that almsgiving became such a prestigious act in the spirituality of Judaism and Christianity. It allowed the individual to enact the miracle of God's grace in his own life and assume the role of an active participant in the repair of the world.

The Raising of Tabitha

The book of Daniel shows how almsgiving pays down the debt of sin. But the Bible teaches us another important lesson about the power of almsgiving—its ability to deliver one from death (Proverbs 10:2). In the book of Tobit, as we saw in an earlier chapter, this was primarily understood as restoring vision to Tobit and allowing him to see his son return home safely and then sire numerous grandchildren. In the wake of the bodily resurrection of Jesus, this proverb assumed a different meaning. In order to see this in bold relief, let's take a look at the story of the raising of Tabitha in the book of Acts.

> Now in Joppa there was a disciple whose name was Tabitha, which in Greek is Dorcas. *She was devoted to good works and acts of charity.* At that time she became ill and died. When they had washed her, they laid her in a room upstairs. Since Lydda was near Joppa, the disciples, who heard that Peter was there, sent two men to him with the request, "Please come to us without delay." So Peter got up and went with them; and when he arrived, they took him to the room upstairs. *All the widows stood beside him, weeping and showing tunics and other clothing that Dorcas had made while she was with them.* Peter put all of them outside, and then he knelt down and prayed. He turned to the body and said, "Tabitha, get up." Then she opened her eyes, and seeing Peter, she sat up. (Acts 9:36–40)

Most New Testament scholars ignore the references to Tabitha's generosity that I have put in italics and focus their attention solely on the power of Peter, acting in *imitatio Christi*, to raise someone from the dead.[11] But this ignores an important dimension of the way in which the story has been told. She was not just a woman of faith, but as the author of Acts emphasizes, "She was devoted to good works and acts of charity." Furthermore, when Peter comes to her dead body, the biblical author takes care to place the recipients of her charity alongside the apostle: "All the widows stood beside him, weeping and showing tunics and other clothing that [Tabitha] had made while she was with them." To whom were they showing their tunics? Certainly Peter, but it is not hard to imagine that God was also being urged to take notice. That almsgifts could intercede on one's behalf was well known in contemporary Judaism and confirmed just a few verses later when in a different episode an angel tells the centurion Cornelius that both "your prayers and your alms have ascended as a *memorial* before God" (10:4).

Artists were also careful to draw our attention to the role of almsgiving in facilitating Peter's command that she rise from her bed, as the mosaic from the Palatine Chapel in Palermo so graphically shows (figure 4). In this image Peter stands at the left, his right foot striding toward the viewer while his left points in the direction of Tabitha. He raises his right hand in blessing while his left grabs Tabitha's wrist and pulls her forward. Behind the figure of Tabitha is a garment that is draped over the back of what appears to be a piece of furniture with spindles. (Perhaps a stand to display a piece of clothing?) That the garment belongs to Tabitha is clear from the fact that it wraps around her waist. But that it also belongs to the widows is obvious from the way in which it has been placed directly in front of them. That the intercession of the garment is at least as important as the prayers of the widows themselves is evident from the fact that it dwarfs the widows. One gets the impression that the garment has been cast as an independent actor in the scene; besides praying with the widows, it appears to lift Tabitha up from her temporary repose.

Cyprian, the bishop of Carthage (third century), was also very sensitive to the important role charity plays in our story. He begins his discussion by citing the words of Raphael in the book of Tobit about the power of almsgiving. It is superior to prayer and fasting because it not only can garner the attention of God but also can redeem from the power of death. He then turns to the story of Tabitha as a concrete example of Raphael's teaching. His retelling of the story takes care to put special emphasis on the intercessory character of the garments that Tabitha had woven: "When,

Figure 4 *The Raising of Tabitha by the Apostle Peter;* wall mosaic from
the Palatine Chapel (1166–89), Palermo, Italy (Photograph courtesy of
Paul Williams of Funkystock Picture Library)

in keeping with his apostolic kindness, [Peter] had come quickly, the widows stood about him weeping and beseeching, showing the cloaks and tunics and all those garments which they had earlier received, and *interceding for the dead woman not with their voices but with her corporal works of mercy."*[12] Peter, for his part, Cyprian concludes, is aware of the power that these almsdeeds possess. Cyprian continues: "Peter judged that what was asked for in this fashion could be obtained, and that Christ would not fail to grant the widows' intercession, since He Himself had been clothed in the person of the widows" (see Matt 25:40). Cyprian concludes his retelling of Tabitha's resurrection by bringing his readers back to the principal point—the miraculous powers of charity: "Such was the miracle wrought by the merits of mercy, such was the power of just works. She, who had bestowed on suffering widows the means of life, merited to be recalled to life by the entreaty of the widows." In Cyprian's mind one must not divorce the generosity of Tabitha from the reward it generated—her being raised from the dead. To be sure, Peter had acted in imitation of Christ and it was through his grace that she rose to new life. But Tabitha was no passive agent; her deeds literally spoke for themselves. Almsgiving rendered her ripe for resurrection.

The picture that I have been painting is just about complete. As the example of King David has shown, forgiveness in the Bible is far more than just being declared innocent; it requires a *process* of spiritual transformation. For David this meant dealing with the consequences of what he had done wrong as they slowly surfaced over his lifetime. Punishment was nothing more than a means to the larger goal of being fashioned anew. At the end of the biblical period the prophet Daniel shows us that this process can be accelerated through the act of almsgiving. Finally, Tabitha's example teaches us that charity allows one to amass a treasury of merit that can provide deliverance even from the bonds of death. But one essential element has not been explicitly addressed in the Bible—what happens to the person who dies before being able to amend fully his or her life as David was privileged to do? Here the church had to use the hints provided in scripture to extend the scope of its witness. We can see the results of such a reasoning process in the *Apostolic Constitutions*, a text from the fourth century that provides a number of theological answers to issues about which the Bible had not spoken clearly. In regard to the rites to be observed for the dead we read: "Let the third day of the departed be celebrated with psalms, lessons, and prayers on account of [Jesus] who arose within the space of three days. . . . And let alms be given to the poor out of his goods *as a memorial* before God on his behalf."[13] Like Tabitha's gifts to the poor widows in the book of Acts, alms given on behalf of the deceased function as prayers that continue to have their effect after death. No wonder that Henry VIII, even though he rejected the power of the Mass to deliver one from purgatory, made sure his will included instructions for substantial postmortem almsgiving.[14]

Almsgiving as Suffrage

We now have enough of the puzzle pieces in hand to tackle a larger theological problem that dogs anyone who wishes to understand purgatory. The Reformers rejected this doctrine on two essential grounds: first, it gave one the idea that one could purchase one's salvation, and, second, it allowed one to transfer good deeds from one party to another. We have already addressed the first issue, so let's turn to the second.

As we saw, one of the major concerns of E. P. Sanders's treatment of merit making in rabbinic Judaism was to deny the idea that merits could be transferred from one party to another at the time of the final judgment. He rightly indicated that this soteriological concern was not central to rabbinic sources. But in making that point he went too far in saying that early rabbinic sources did not understand the transfer of merits in financial terms at all. As we say, this was clearly contradicted by the evidence of both rabbinic sources and Ben Sira as well. The notion of accumulating a treasury in heaven was not simply to secure merit for one's own person but to be able to pass on that merit to one's offspring. I have argued that this is the key to understanding Tobit's sending of Tobias to Media. I have claimed that the biblical presumption that deed and consequence are inextricably linked prepared the way for this development. For the Bible clearly teaches that the deeds of one's forefathers play a significant role in shaping the fate of succeeding generations. Transferability is unquestionably a biblical idea. As for almsgiving, we have seen that Ben Sira, Jesus, and the Mishna claim that it is unique among the commandments in that it funds a treasury whose endowment can never be zeroed out. Charity is a gift that keeps on giving.

So if we can accept that transferability is not problematic in terms of biblical precedent, what about the matter of almsgiving delivering one from final damnation? As I noted, Sanders was quite right to emphasize that the Jewish notion of "the merits of the fathers" never understood the heavenly treasury in this fashion. Protestant polemicists, however, frequently accused Catholics (and, by extension, Jews) of making precisely this claim.

Traditionally, the church taught that there were three possible destinations for the deceased: (1) heaven, for the few who had achieved what John Wesley would call Christian perfection; (2) purgatory, where most would go and await the moment of their completed sanctification; and (3) hell, where there was no chance of redemption. One could assist those in purgatory because, like King David, through repentance they had benefited from the grace of Christ and had received the promised salvation. What they awaited in the interim was their full sanctification.

But we must say even more than this. Purgatory has also been criticized as having provided a mechanical model for understanding the process of sanctification. Gunther Bornkamm, the highly esteemed New Testament scholar of a generation back, condemned Judaism and Catholicism on this ground, claiming that in this system the reward ceases to follow from the grace of God but rather "becomes a form of financial capital which individual observers of the law acquire for themselves in heaven and whose payout they can await with certainty."[15] In Bornkamm's mind, the problem with a concept like purgatory is that it allows the religiously minded person to think his good deeds have forced God to reward human works.

In order to respond to the worries of Bornkamm, one must note two things. On the one hand, it is true that for Catholics and Jews obedience to the divine law yields a "merit" that God has promised to reward. But this hardly compromises the freedom of God, for the rewards are based on a choice God already made regarding the order of salvation. Even Calvin is willing to say that Tabitha was raised by virtue of her good works as long as one bears in mind that those works were the result of a faith in God and the promises he has made. God has ordered the way of salvation in such a manner that human beings participate in the grace he has to offer. Acts of charity to the poor are a privileged way of participating in the love of God and thus constitute a claim to a future reward. On the other hand, things are quite different when we begin to speak about the transfer of merits from the agent who earned them to a second party, a matter of grave concern for Sanders. Here Bornkamm's worries are weighty and in need of clarification. The Dominican preacher Johann Tetzel (1465–1519) set the framework for Martin Luther's posting of his famous ninety-five theses by proclaiming that "as soon as the coin [you offer] in the coffer rings, the soul from Purgatory springs." By this witty saying, Tetzel implied that one could assure the release of a loved one from purgatory by a simple financial transfer. Yet as scholars have long noted, the rhetorical excesses of preachers like Tetzel did not fully represent the teaching of the Catholic Church in the sixteenth century. Performing an indulged action on behalf of another does not mechanically generate an intended reward.

When undertaken to benefit souls in purgatory, the giving of alms on behalf of the dead was identified as a suffrage, that is, an *appeal* for mercy. The indulged charitable deed was simply a prayer manifested in human action. Consider the words of Bonaventure on the relationship of indulgences to treasury of merits. Though he concedes the power of the pope (as holder of the "keys" of the kingdom [cf. Matt 16]) over the distribution of goods from the divine treasuries, his power does have limits. "Because the dead are outside the forum of the Church and of ecclesiastical judges," he writes, "it seems that absolution [of the temporal punishment due to one's sins] is not possible for them, except as a prayer for pardon; and so, to speak properly, indulgence is not granted to them." He goes on to say that if an indulgence can be called a "dispensation of the goods of the Church," one must concede that some concrete good has been extended to the intended party, but the church acts not as a "judge" (over the state of the deceased—that being solely the domain of God) but as a "supplicant."[16]

What we see here is a standard worry in the Bible about protecting the freedom of God. There is a reason why the captain of the ship on which Jonah had taken refuge exhorts Jonah to prayer, saying, "Get up, call on your god! *Perhaps* [your] god will spare us a thought so that we do not perish" (1:6). And the king of Nineveh similarly orders his citizens to fast, saying: "*Who knows*, God *may* relent and change his mind . . . " (3:9). Prayer and fasting certainly raise the odds of deliverance—they are merit-worthy actions—but they provide no hard and fast guarantee. And so for the giving of alms. In biblical terms they are meant to establish a memorial in heaven that God *may* be pleased to consult.[17] Like the widows who gathered around the bier of Tabitha, those deeds can become living prayers to God but never rigid financial instruments that compel his action. Though the notion of giving alms to fund a treasury in heaven is built on a metaphor of accounting, it can't be reduced to purely monetary terms. When it works, it is because of God's gracious decision to honor the merits of his saints;

when it doesn't, it remains a testimony to God's unfathomable freedom: "I will show mercy upon whom I will show mercy." A divine treasury does not compromise God's freedom; rather, it grounds that freedom in a manner that makes human supplication on behalf of the dead intelligible. A Protestant who ponders carefully what Bonaventure says should have no principled reason to reject prayers and alms for the dead tout court.

Purgatory in Judaism

So where does all of this leave us? Is purgatory a retrievable notion for Christians in the twenty-first century? The answer to that question will surely be a matter of personal taste and ecclesial affiliation. But perhaps the recent joint declaration on the subject of justification by Catholics and Lutherans will lead more Protestants to reopen this door.[18] As a goad to that end, let me return to the evidence of Judaism. Over the course of the past decade or so, there have been a number of studies that have high-lighted the surprising interdependence of Jews and Catholics on this doctrine. Judah Galinsky, for example, an Israeli scholar of rabbinic culture, has shown that in the mid-thirteenth to fourteenth centuries Jewish communities in Spain began to imitate the Christian practice of leaving sizable charitable bequests in their estate "for the benefit of their souls" after death.[19] The language used in these wills is so patently close to the words found in their Christian counterparts that it cannot be doubted from which direction the influence has come. Similarly, Stephen Greenblatt and Leon Wieseltier have noted that the traditional Jewish practice of having the son pray on behalf of a dead parent for eleven months after the parent's death ("kaddish") appears at roughly the same time that the doctrine of purgatory was gaining tremendous momentum.[20]

In the Jewish folklore that arises in the wake of this practice, it becomes clear that the father's safe arrival in the World-to-Come is dependent on his son saying these words in synagogue. In Wieseltier's moving account of the year in which he said kaddish for his own father, he spends a good proportion of his narrative exploring a tale that probably emerged in the early Middle Ages and was disseminated in an extraordinary number of copies and elaborated in many variants. In the version from an eleventh-century prayer book known as the *Mahzor Vitry,* Rabbi Akiva is walking in a cemetery when he meets a naked man, black as coal, carrying a large amount of wood on his head. The rabbi stops him and asks why he is working so hard, offering to buy him from his master if he is a slave. The man answers, "The man whom you are addressing is a dead man. Every day they send me out to collect wood and use it to burn me." Why such a terrible fate? The man explains, "I was a tax collector and I would favor the rich and kill the poor."

"Have your superiors told you nothing about how you might relieve your condition?" Rabbi Akiva asks, and the man begs the rabbi not to detain him, because that will anger his tormentors.

> For such a man [as I], there can be no relief. Though I did hear them say something—but no, it is impossible. They said: If this poor man had a son, and his son were to stand before the congregation and recite [the prayer] "Bless the Lord who is blessed!" and the congregation were to answer amen, and the son were also to say "May the Great Name be blessed!" [a sentence from the kaddish], they would release him from his punishment. But this man never had a son. He left his wife pregnant and he did not know whether the child was a boy. And if she gave birth to a boy, who would teach the boy Torah? For this man does not have a friend in the world.

Deeply troubled by this, the rabbi traveled to the man's hometown and found that he had a son, but that the people of the town had not circumcised him. Rabbi Akiva promptly circumcised him and tried to teach him Torah, but he refused to learn. Rabbi Akiva fasted for forty days. A heavenly voice asked him, "For this you mortify yourself?" and the rabbi replied, "But Lord of the Universe, it is for You that I am preparing him." The Lord opened the boy's heart. Rabbi Akiva taught him Torah and the prayers and presented the boy to the congregation. When the boy recited the prayer "Bless the Lord who is blessed!" his father was released from his punishment.

The man then appeared to Rabbi Akiva in a dream and said: "May it be the will of the Lord that your soul find delight in the Garden of Eden, for you have saved me from the sentence of Gehenna." Rabbi Akiva responded: "Your Name, O Lord, endures forever, and the memory of You through all the generations!"[21]

The major theme of the story is evident to even the casual reader: "That the dead are in need of spiritual rescue; and that the agent of spiritual rescue is the son; and that the instrument of spiritual rescue is prayer, notably the kaddish."[22] So important was the practice that if a father lacked sons, or worried that his son might not fulfill the obligation of saying the appropriate prayers, he would leave money in his will to have someone else say the prayers. In some circles, the firstborn son of a Jewish family was referred to as his "kaddish." Should a man die childless, one could say he left this world without a kaddish.[23] This practice sounds a lot like the Catholic custom of having Masses said in one's name, an ancient Christian practice that St. Augustine already alludes to when he speaks of his mother's death in book 9 of his *Confessions.*

Yet the key point, as both Galinsky and Wieseltier observe, is not the observation of the interreligious borrowing, but the nature of Jewish mourning practices that made this possible. After all, there are many Christian practices that Judaism showed no interest in whatsoever. Why practices that one associates with the doctrine of purgatory? As it turns out, there is evidence stretching back to Talmudic times that almsgiving was thought to benefit the journey of the deceased after his death. Mar Uqba, for example, was queried as to why he had designated such a high percentage of his money for the poor in his will. "My provisions are scanty," he replied, "but the road is long."[24]

Even more illuminating is the *responsum* of Rabbi Sherira Ha-Gaon, a leading authority of the Jewish community in Babylon during the tenth century CE. (A responsum is an authoritative rabbinic figure's response to a question formally submitted to him.) He said that alms given in the name of a particular deceased man could provide benefit. "If a Holy Man seeks mercy for the deceased whether with alms for the poor or without [that is, by prayer]," Rabbi Sherira writes,

> it is *possible* that the Holy One (Blessed be He!) will lighten his punishment in recognition of that meritorious person's merit. But if no [such person is available], we take the poor [who received alms on his behalf] to [his grave] to petition that he be granted mercy. If one of them has [sufficient] merits . . . they may *possibly* help him; but there is *no presumption* that it will help: May it be God's will that He accede to their petition.[25]

What comes out clearly in this responsum is that rabbinic Judaism clearly imagines that the state of the person is not always settled at time of death and that there is a period of time during which further purgation from sin is possible. Judaism, like early Christianity, imagines that specific human actions like prayer and the offering of alms *could* have an effect.

Once again we see some of the crucial elements of the doctrine of purgatory: sins require not just forgiveness but transformation, a process that can extend beyond the confines of a finite human life. That transformation, in turn, can be abetted by acts of mercy toward the unde-serving (alms), deeds which generate merits that can deliver one from death. The final move is one in which these merits are potentially transfer-rable to another person. That final move goes beyond the explicit teaching of the Bible. Christians have the example of Christ to draw upon. The merits won by his passion and death apply to us. But it is striking that Jews come to a similar conclusion about the way in which merit can be commu-nicated from one person to another. The fact that both faiths drew out such a similar implication argues strongly in favor of its roots in the common scriptural inheritance that Jews and Christians share.

The Enduring Appeal of Purgatory

I have tried to suggest that the practice of giving alms on behalf of the deceased is an ancient practice that built on biblical texts such as Daniel 4:27 (v. 24 in the original Aramaic) and Proverbs 10:2. The terrible detritus left in the wake of one's sins can be redeemed by showing mercy to the poor, and charity provides the basis for the promise of resurrection. Such practices need not ruffle the feathers of anyone committed to a high doctrine of salvation *sola gratia*. Almsgiving was meant to participate at the human level in what has been done for us through Christ at the divine level. Certainly this is one of the main reasons why artistic depictions of purgatory in the Middle Ages paired the sacrifice of the Mass with the charity shown toward the poor: both actions are about showing mercy to the undeserving.

And finally, there do remain the pastoral considerations. It is striking that Stephen Greenblatt, a nonobservant, secular Jew, was drawn back to the ancient Jewish ritual of saying kaddish for his deceased father in light of what he learned from his study of purgatory. At the close of his prologue he writes: "This practice, then, which with a lightly ironic piety I, who scarcely know how to pray, undertook for my own father, is the starting point for what follows."[26] Later on in his narrative, when addressing the deeper human reasons for the development of such practices with the Church, he writes,

> Anyone who has experienced the death of a close friend or relative knows the feeling; not only the pain of sudden, irrevocable loss but also the strange, irra-tional expectation of recovery. . . . These are not merely modern feelings; in fact

it is startling that we continue to have them so vividly, since everything in the contemporary world works to suppress them. They were not suppressed in the past. The brilliance of Purgatory . . . lay in its institutional control over ineradicable folk beliefs and in its engagement with intimate, private feelings. . . . The notion of suffrages—masses, almsgiving, fasts, and prayers—gave mourners something constructive to do with their feelings of grief and confirmed those feelings of reciprocity that survived, at least for a limited time, the shock of death."[27]

Greenblatt's reflections bring us back to the profoundly pastoral dimension in the doctrine of purgatory. Who among us does not desire to show some sign of love for our friends and family whom we mourn at graveside? Both Judaism and Christianity have long held that the prayers and alms of the faithful can be a benefit for our beloved dead. Salvation, after all, is both individual *and* communal in nature, and the doctrine of purgatory reminds us that our lives are not ours alone. We are linked in a great chain of being (one body, many members, to invoke the Pauline metaphor) to all of our beloved ancestors. We don't have to pretend that all are saved and by so doing make a mockery of our moral choices, but neither must we consign our beloved to eternal suffering.

Purgatory makes Christ's atoning sacrifice come alive in our religious practices. C. S. Lewis put the matter just about perfectly when he wrote:

Of course I pray for the dead. The action is so spontaneous, so all but inevitable, that only the most compulsive theological case against it would deter me. And I hardly know how the rest of my prayers would survive if those for the dead were forbidden. At our age, the majority of those we love best are dead. What sort of intercourse with God could I have if what I love best were unmentionable to Him?[28]

Yes, spontaneous, perhaps inevitable—but also biblical.

CHAPTER THIRTEEN

Conclusion

Your Alms Are a Memorial

For man with-owt marcy, of marcy shalle misse;
And shall have marcy, that marcyfyll is.

—Traditional English carol

For the highest saints of God are least in their own sight, and the more glorious they are, so much the lowlier are they in themselves. . . . And they who ascribe unto God all the good which they have received, "seek not glory one of another, but the glory which cometh from God only."

—Thomas à Kempis, *The Imitation of Christ*

I have contended that charity was construed as a loan to God, which was then converted into a form of spiritual currency and stored in an impregnable divine bank. This idea is first attested in books of the Second Temple period and continues through the rabbinic and patristic periods. Only by the time that we reach the early Middle Ages do we see the conception begin to wane.[1] From this commercial metaphor we are able to understand why Daniel could advise King Nebuchadnezzar to give alms as a means of repaying his spiritual debts—it restocks a nearly depleted divine treasury.

The Heavenly Treasure as an Equivocal Term

But as helpful as this financial construal might be, its application is by no means uniform across our sources. Or to put the matter in Aristotelian terms, the treasury in heaven functions not univocally (meaning one thing and one thing only) but equivocally (vacillating between two or more meanings depending on context). This can be seen in the book of Tobit, a work that is more or less contemporary with the invention of the category itself. The first time the term is used is when Tobit is teaching his son Torah. Having just mentioned the commandment to give alms, he says: "[in so doing] you will be laying up a good treasure for yourself against the day of necessity. *For almsgiving delivers from death and keeps you from going into the Darkness*" (4:9–10). The second occurrence is the instruction that the angel Raphael gives before departing for heaven: "Prayer with fasting is good, but better than both is almsgiving with righteousness. A little with righteousness is better than wealth with wrongdoing. It is better to give alms than to lay up gold. *For almsgiving delivers from death and cleanses one's account from every sin*" (12:8–9).[2]

In the former case, Tobit glosses the line from Proverbs, "almsgiving delivers from death" with the phrase, "and keeps you from going into Darkness." This, of course, accords perfectly with Tobit's own situation. He has been rendered blind and as a result despairs of his life and believes that he is on the threshold of death. The narrative at this point is decidedly Joban; Tobit suffers innocently. His almsgiving, to be sure, has been stored in a heavenly treasury, but not in order to make good on the debts his sins have wrought. Tobit's problem is not his sins. In this particular situation, Koch's notion of the deed-consequence connection is put to the test. The question is whether those who act charitably have reason to expect that a positive outcome will naturally follow. Tobit's acts of mercy toward the poor, on this understanding, should have preserved him from such indignities. Sadly, they did not. The question on the table is whether Tobit will persevere in this teaching in spite of its not having proven true within the span of his own life.

In the case of Raphael's instruction, the focus is quite different. Raphael began his instruction to Tobit and Tobias with the urgent plea that Tobit not keep the miracle that God had wrought for him to himself. It is imperative, Raphael declares, that Tobit broadcast the news of his redemption to the entire nation. Tobit, in fact, fulfills this command as soon as Raphael has departed in the form of a long, extended hymn of praise (chapter 13). The function of this hymn is to encourage the people of Israel to repent of apostasy and turn to the Lord. Just as God had redeemed Tobit from his brush with death, so would God restore his chosen people from exile. Tobit, in short, can be viewed as personifying the people Israel. What God did through this just man becomes a pledge of what he intends to do for his sinful people. One means of hastening this moment of restoration, Raphael declares, is giving alms because almsgiving "cleanses one's account from every sin." In this instance, almsgiving functions exactly as it did in the book of Daniel: it repays the debts one has accumulated due to sin.

What we see in this instance are two ways in which the treasury in heaven can function. In the first instance, it is simply a guarantee that one's charitable deeds will be rewarded in the end. The monetary dimension of the treasury is not a matter of distinct emphasis. In the second instance, the charitable deeds can do their job only by erasing the debt that Israel owes. The commercial dimension is front and center.

But even when the commercial dimension attains such prominence, it is not necessarily the case that the monetary element functions exactly like coinage (that is, univocally). The tradition has taken considerable care to distinguish those instances when "money" earned by charity can be counted on to purchase goods and those instances when the money functions more like a suffrage, that is, a *plea* before the throne of God for mercy. The favored term in the Bible for this suffrage aspect is *memorial* (*mnēmosunon* in Greek; it translates words from the root *zakar* in Hebrew).

In one of the more momentous events in the book of Acts, an Italian centurion named Cornelius is baptized by Peter and so becomes the first non-Jew to join the evolving Christian movement. But God's choice of Cornelius is not without reason, as we learn at the beginning of the story:

> In Caesarea there was a man named Cornelius, a centurion of the Italian Cohort, as it was called. He was a devout man who feared God with all his household; he gave alms generously to the people and prayed constantly to God. One afternoon at about three o'clock he had a vision in which he clearly saw an angel of God coming in and saying to him, "Cornelius." He stared at him in terror and said, "What is it, Lord?" He answered, "*Your prayers and your alms have ascended as a memorial* [*mnēmosunon*] *before God*. Now send men to Joppa for a certain Simon who is called Peter; he is lodging with Simon, a tanner, whose house is by the seaside." (Acts 10:1–6)

We should recall that Tobit's and Sarah's prayers and deeds of charity are answered when their memorial is placed before God in heaven: "When you and Sarah prayed, it was I who brought the *memorial* [*mnēmosunon*] of your prayer before the glory of the Lord, and likewise whenever you would bury the dead" (Tobit 12:12; my translation). Similarly, when Cornelius's prayers and alms have been favorably received in Heaven, Peter is sent to his household in order to baptize the family. In both Tobit and Acts the almsdeed functions as a memorial that prompts God to intervene. It is worth noting that this story of the conversion of Cornelius (Acts 10:1 ff.) takes place immediately after the raising of Tabitha (9:36–43). In both cases, the almsdeed functions as a suffrage or prayer that God can either heed or ignore. God retains his freedom "to show mercy upon whom he will show mercy" (Exod 33:19; cf. Rom 9:15).

The function of alms as a memorial is also present in the discussion about the state of the deceased in the *Apostolic Constitutions*. As is well known, the Bible declares that the dead will be tested by fire (1 Cor 3:11–15), an image that many Christian interpreters took as proof of a postmortem purgatorial process. This interpretation, however, has been questioned. Second Maccabees 12:42–45 gives us a bit more information. It teaches that prayer can assist the dead but says nothing about alms.[3] Given scripture's assurance that almsgiving delivers one from death, it is altogether natural that the early church wondered whether alms could be effective after one had died. This question was answered in the *Apostolic Constitutions*: "Let alms be given to the poor out of the goods [of the deceased] for a *memorial* of him." Significantly, this text goes on to declare that almsdeeds can benefit only those destined for eternal salvation. In regard to the wicked, even if one were to give "all the world to the poor," it would "not benefit [them] at all." This confirms what we saw with respect to King David—forgiveness of sins is granted to the just for the purpose of their moral and spiritual sanctification.

The idea that alms functioned as a memorial or suffrage for the deceased was a commonplace in classical medieval theology. Even Martin Luther conceded this when he posted his ninety-five theses to the Wittenberg door (1517). At that time he was still within the ambit of Catholic teaching on the subject. Only later would his thinking take a more radical direction.[4]

For the medieval church, almsgiving was linked to the foundational sacrifice of Christ. It was that act that ultimately funded the heavenly treasuries. Only through the power of God's grace could individual Christians participate by their own deeds of mercy. Because Christ's merciful self-donation was continually re-presented in the sacrifice of the Mass, it was standard for Christian writers and artists to correlate the Eucharist with the seven corporal acts of mercy (Matt 25:31 ff.). At the center of each was a display of compassion for those in need.

The Middle English drawing we considered in Chapter 8 provides a striking illustration of this correlation. Let us recall that the acts of alms-giving and the Eucharist were paired on one side of that drawing by means of a rope that led up to an enclosure in heaven where Christ and the saints reside, and then descended on the other side to a large tub that held souls being lifted out of purgatory. But the clarity of the image is also a weak point: for some, it illustrates the very heterodoxy of purgatory. Tetzel's words return with all their troublesome ramifications: "as soon as the coin in the coffer rings, the soul from Purgatory springs."

One of the limitations of religious art is that it can only make connections between ideas; it cannot offer a definitive commentary as to how they function. Tetzel's words provide one way to read this image, but let me suggest another, this time drawn from Augustine.

The Death of Monica in Augustine's *Confessions*

At the close of book 9 of his *Confessions,* Augustine spends three paragraphs on the death of his mother, Monica.[5] In the first paragraph (35) he attends to her sins and gives pride of place to the words of the Our Father. He writes: "I know that she dealt mercifully with others and from her heart *forgave her debtors their debts; do you then forgive her any debts* she contracted during all those years after she had passed through the saving waters." I had read this text many times without catching the significance of why Augustine joins the observation of her merciful deeds (*misericord-iter operatam*) and the fact that she had forgiven her debtors. For Augustine this is no casual juxtaposition. In his mind, showing forgiveness to another is one of the acts of corporal mercy. This can be gleaned from his discussion of charity in *The Enchiridion*:

> [Saying the Our Father] entirely cancels tiny daily sins. It also cancels those from which the faithful turn away by penance and reform, even though they have lived wickedly, provided that, as they truthfully pray, Forgive us our sins— for they have no lack of sins to be forgiven—they are also speaking the truth

when they say, as we forgive those who sin against us, that is, provided what they say is what they do, *for to forgive a person who asks for pardon is itself a work of charity*. And so the Lord's words, Give alms, and everything is clean [that is, forgiven] for you (Luke 11:41), apply to any work of mercy that benefits somebody. Not only somebody who offers food to the hungry, drink to the thirsty . . . *but also one who offers pardon to the sinner, is giving alms.*[6]

Pardoning the sins of another, then, like the other corporal acts that Matthew 25 outlined, was a merit-worthy deed. But whatever merits Monica may have secured through this action and others like it, Augustine never loses sight of the fact that they remain tokens of mercy shown toward the undeserving. And so he closes this opening paragraph not with a spreadsheet of what Monica has earned but with a plea for the mercy he hopes the Lord will show in return. I have put the terms for mercy in italics in order to bring out the surprising density of their occurrence. But it is important to note that the opening double imperative ("forgive her . . . forgive") picks up on the citation of the Our Father earlier and follows from the confession that Monica herself has shown such forgiveness to others:

> Forgive her, Lord, forgive, I beg you, and do not arraign her before you. Let *mercy* triumph over judgment, for you, whose utterances are true, have to the *merciful* promised *mercy*. Since their very power to be *merciful* was your gift to them in the first place, you will be showing *mercy* to those with whom you have yourself dealt *mercifully*, and granting pity to those toward whom you have shown *pity* first.

In the second paragraph (36), Augustine turns his attention to the sacrifice of Christ on the cross and its continual re-presentation on the altar of the church,

> On the day when her release was at hand she gave no thought to costly burial or the embalming of her body with spices, nor did she pine for a special monument or concern herself about a grave in her native land; no, that was not her command to us. She desired only to be remembered at your altar, where she had served you with never a day's absence. From that altar, as she knew, the holy Victim is made available to us, *he through whom the record of debt that stood against us was annulled*. (Colossians 2:14)

Given the significance of the debt metaphor in early Christianity, it is quite natural that Augustine (along with many others in his day) should see the text of Colossians 2:14 as definitive of what Christ had accomplished on the cross. I do not want, however, to dwell on the debt metaphor. What is crucial is the fact that Monica put no trust in human means of remembrance—the embalming of the body, burial in one's own homeland, or a costly gravestone. Rather, Monica's sole desire was that when her loved ones gathered at the Eucharistic altar, they would remember her name. To that very sacrament, Augustine emphasizes, Monica had "made fast her soul with the bonds of faith. Let no one wrench her away from your protection."

In the third and final paragraph (37) of this section and of Book 9 itself, Augustine turns to his readers and urges them all to heed the desires of his mother and remember her in their prayers around the altar:

> Inspire your servants who are my brethren, your children who are my masters, whom I now serve with heart and voice and pen, that as many of them as read this may remember [Monica], your servant, at your altar, along with Patricius, sometime her husband. From their flesh you brought me into this life, though how I do not know. Let them remember with loving devotion these two who were my parents in this transitory light, but also were my brethren under you, our Father, within our mother the Catholic Church, and my fellow-citizens in the eternal Jerusalem, for which your people sighs with longing throughout its pilgrimage, from its setting out to its return. So may the last request she made of me be granted to her more abundantly by the prayers of many, evoked by my confessions, than by my prayers alone.

If we compare these words of Augustine about his mother to the illustration of purgatory with which we had begun, we will see an amazing set of parallels. In the first two paragraphs (35–36) Augustine attends to two things: Monica's charitable deeds and her continual presence at the Lord's altar. This recalls the left-hand side of our illustration, where deeds of charity and the sacrifice of the Mass are conceived of as agents tugging on a rope. Augustine's last paragraph (37) is an impassioned plea that his readers not remain indifferent to the account they have just heard but also "tug on that rope" by recalling Monica's name while gathered before the altar. Augustine presumes that those prayers, joined to Christ's sacrifice and Monica's deeds of charity, will help convey her speedily to heaven.

At no point in this account does Augustine put on the eyeshades of an accountant, total up Monica's merits, and demand her reward. The words of Thomas à Kempis from this chapter's epigraph capture the spiritual disposition of Augustine just about perfectly. The greatest of the saints certainly abound in merit-worthy deeds; their treasuries are overflowing.

But this is precisely because of their humility ("the more glorious they are [in God's eyes], so much the lowlier are they in themselves") about their accomplishments. They realize that whatever merits they have acquired, they have been purchased solely through the aid of divine grace. In another portion of his justly famous book Thomas writes: "[The saints] do not glory in their own merits, for they attribute no good to themselves but all to Me, because out of My infinite charity I gave all to them. . . . Therefore, you find it written that they cast their crowns before God, and fell down upon their faces before the Lamb, and adored Him Who lives forever."[7]

For this reason Augustine brackets the merit-worthy deeds of his mother and focuses solely on God's mercy. Divine freedom is never compromised. But neither are Monica's charitable deeds. There is something substantial (in the etymological sense of having substance) and thus durable about them. Because she showed mercy toward her debtors, she has shown herself worthy of being treated mercifully in return. Or, rephrased in an Augustinian idiom, because God inspired and empowered her to be gracious toward the poor, God has every good reason to bestow the reward she has earned with his help.

It is this subtle dialectic that Augustine weaves between reward and mercy that constitutes the very fabric of what the treasury in heaven means. Only the reader who possesses a robust theology of the relationship between human merit and divine grace can make sense of this biblical concept.

Notes

Nearly all of the quotations from the Bible are taken from the New Revised Standard Version. Some, however, are my own translations; I have identified these in the notes.

1. The Challenge of Charity

1. For Judaism, see the classic essay of E. Urbach, "Religious and Social Tendencies in Talmudic Concepts of Charity" [Hebrew], *Zion* 16 (1951): 1–27, rpt. in *The World of the Sages: Collected Studies* [Hebrew] (Jerusalem: Magnes, 2002). More recent surveys include Michael Satlow, "'Fruit and Fruit of Fruit': Charity and Piety Among Jews in Late Antique Palestine," *Jewish Quarterly Review* 100 (2010): 244–77, and A. Gray, "Redemptive Almsgiving and the Rabbis of Late Antiquity," *Jewish Studies Quarterly* 18 (2011): 144–84. For Christianity, the classic treatment is that of H. Bolkestein, *Wohltätigkeit und Armenpflege im vorchristlichen Altertum* (Utrecht: A. Oosthoek, 1939). For more recent treatments, see R. Garrison, *Redemptive Almsgiving in Early Christianity* (Sheffield, U.K.: Sheffield University Press, 1993); S. Holman, *The Hungry Are Dying: Beggars and Bishops in Roman Cappadocia* (Oxford: Oxford University Press, 2001); P. Brown, *Poverty and Leadership in the Later Roman Empire* (Hanover, N.H.: University Press of New England, 2002); R. Finn, *Almsgiving in the Later Roman Empire: Christian Promotion and Practice, 313–450* (Oxford: Oxford University Press, 2006); Christopher Hays, "By Almsgiving and Faith Sins Are Purged? The Theological Underpinnings of Early Christian Care for the Poor," in *Engaging Economics: New Testament Scenarios and Early Christian Reception,* ed. B. Longnecker and K. Liebengood (Grand Rapids, Mich.: Eerdmans, 2009), 260–81; Helen Rhee, *Loving the Poor, Saving the Rich: Wealth, Poverty, and Early Christian Formation* (Grand Rapids, Mich.: Baker Academic, 2012); and finally, Peter Brown's magnum opus, *Through the Eye of a Needle: Wealth, the Fall of Rome, and the Making of Christianity in the West, 350–550 AD* (Princeton: Princeton University Press, 2012).

2. For the question of the "prosperity Gospel" see Simon Coleman, *The Globalisation of Charismatic Christianity: Spreading the Gospel of Prosperity* (Cambridge: Cambridge University Press, 2000); Milmon F. Harrison, *Righteous Riches: The Word of Faith Movement in Contemporary African American Religion* (New York: Oxford University Press, 2005); and Shayne Lee and Phillip Sinitiere, *Holy Mavericks: Evangelical Innovators and the Spiritual Marketplace* (New York: New York University Press, 2009).

3. For the saying of Antigonus see Mishnah *Avot,* 1.3. The translation of the last word, *gift,* is difficult. I have adopted the standard way this saying has been received in the tradition. For a fuller account of the problem, see Elias Bickerman, "The Maxim of Antigonus of Socho," *Harvard Theological Review* 44 (1951): 153–65. Also, compare Maimonides' famous statement about the different motivations for making a charitable gift. See his *Mishneh*

Torah. Book Seven: The Laws of Agriculture (New Haven: Yale University Press, 1979) 10:1–14.

4. The translation is my own and reflects the way this proverb was heard in Second Temple Judaism. For a justification, see page 54 and page 197, note 1.

5. Citations are taken from Pinker's "The Moral Instinct," which appeared as the lead article in the *New York Times Magazine,* January 13, 2008, http://www.nytimes.com/2008/01/13/magazine/13Psychology-t.html.

6. This quotation is taken from K. Spink's excellent (and authorized) biography, *Mother Teresa* (San Francisco: HarperCollins, 1997).

7. Maureen Flynn, *Sacred Charity: Confraternities and Social Welfare in Spain, 1400–1700* (Ithaca, N.Y.: Cornell University Press, 1989). See also the excellent studies of John O'Malley, *The First Jesuits* (Cambridge: Harvard University Press, 1993), 165–99, and David D'Andrea, *Civic Christianity in Renaissance Italy: The Hospital of Treviso, 1400–1530* (Rochester, N.Y.: University of Rochester Press, 2007).

8. For a discussion of Jewish confraternities see M. Cohen, *Poverty and Charity in the Jewish Community of Medieval Egypt* (Princeton: Princeton University Press, 2005), 197–98, and Y. Ben-Naeh, "Jewish Confraternities in the Ottoman Empire" [Hebrew], *Zion* 63 (1998) 277–318, extensive bibliography at n. 113.

9. In this respect, the Marxist broadside against charity as a practice that accepts poverty rather than trying to eliminate it merits hearing and can be sustained. But, perhaps somewhat paradoxically, it was precisely the singular focus that the church put on the plight of the poor that generated the sensitivity for social justice that has come to animate so many in the modern era. Some have wondered, however, with the waning of Christianity in the West, whether this sensitivity to the poor will remain a central focus of the modern nation-state. Has the modern West been cruising along unawares on the moral capital of a Judeo-Christian past? Can that accumulated capital be exhausted? The growing sympathy for various forms of economic libertarianism among the young might suggest that this may be the case. For a penetrating analysis of this problem, see Christian Smith, "Does Naturalism Warrant Moral Belief in Universal Benevolence and Human Rights?" in *Scientific, Philosophical, and Theological Reflections on the Origin of Religion,* ed. J. Schloss and M. Murray (Oxford: Oxford University Press, 2009), 292–317.

10. John Calvin, *Commentary on a Harmony of the Evangelists,* cited in Flynn, *Sacred Charity,* 143–44.

11. Steven Ozment, "German Austerity's Lutheran Core," *New York Times,* August 12, 2012. Ozment's sentiments are widely shared. One of the major features of the early Protestantism was its claim to handle the problem of the poor in a better way. For a good example of this see the aptly titled book of the Lutheran scholar Carter Lindberg: *Beyond Charity* (Minneapolis: Fortress, 1993). Also worth consulting is Lee Wandel, *Always Among Us: Images of the Poor in Zwingli's Zurich* (Cambridge: Cambridge University Press, 1990); and Stephen Greenblatt's narrative, in *Hamlet in Purgatory* (Princeton: Princeton University Press, 2001), 10–35, about the polemical tract that Simon Fish published anonymously in 1529, *Supplication for the Beggars.*

12. From Sermon 10, the translation is taken from J. Mark Armitage, *A Twofold Solidarity: Leo the Great's Theology of Redemption* (Strathfield, Australia: St. Paul's Publications, 2005), 175. It is worth noting that this emphasis on mercy made Catholic thinkers less worried about whether the recipients of charity deserved the goods they got. St. Ambrose (fourth century CE), for example, had written: "Mercy is accustomed not to judge on merits but to assist in situations of need, not to be on the lookout for righteousness but to help the one who is poor." It is ironic that it was the Catholics who were concerned that reforms of charitable practice would mean that only the *deserving* poor could receive alms, for presumably they were the ones committed to the idea that grace had to be earned! The theology of late medieval almsgiving makes this prejudicial notion hard to sustain. For

a penetrating account of how Catholic theologians in Spain reacted to "welfare reform" in the Early Modern period, see M. Flynn, *Sacred Charity*, 75–114.

13. For Hoppay's will, see Eamon Duffy, *The Stripping of the Altars: Traditional Religion in England, 1400–1580* (New Haven: Yale University Press, 1992), 506–7; for that of Henry VIII, see Greenblatt, *Hamlet in Purgatory*, 23.

14. Jonathan Z. Smith, *Drudgery Divine: On the Comparison of Early Christianities and the Religions of Late Antiquity* (Chicago: University of Chicago Press, 1990), 34; italics Smith's.

2. Charity as Service to God

Epigraph: The quotation from John Chrysostom can be found in *A Select Library of the Nicene and Post-Nicene Fathers of the Christian Church*, 14 vols., ed. Philip Schaff (Grand Rapids, Mich.: Eerdmans, 1978), 12: 374.

1. Paul Veyne, *Bread and Circuses* (London: Penguin, 1976), 19.

2. Ibid., 33.

3. Cited in Ephraim Urbach, "Religious and Social Tendencies in Talmudic Concepts of Charity," in *The World of the Sages: Collected Studies* [Hebrew] (Jerusalem: Magnes, 2002), 97. This article originally appeared in *Zion* 16 (1951): 1–27.

4. On almsgiving as *the* commandment, see Saul Lieberman, "Two Lexical Notes," *Journal of Biblical Literature* 65 (1946): 67–72, esp. 69–72. For the rabbinic statement about the importance of alms, see Tosephta *Peah* 4:19.

5. The citation is from *The Works of the Emperor Julian*, trans. Wilmer C. Wright, 3 vols. (Loeb Classical Library; New York: Macmillan, 1913), 3: 71. For an introduction to the historical figure of Julian, see Glen Bowersock, *Julian the Apostate* (Cambridge: Harvard University Press, 1978).

6. Rodney Stark writes (*The Rise of Christianity* [Princeton: Princeton University Press, 1996], 88), "It was not that the Romans knew nothing of charity, but it was not based on service to the gods. Pagan gods did not punish ethical violations because they imposed no ethical demands—humans offended the gods only through neglect or by violation of ritual standards." On this point Stark references Ramsey MacMullen (*Paganism in the Roman Empire* [New Haven: Yale University Press, 1981], 58), who writes that sin is restricted to issues concerning "ritual purity or the sacredness of the god's own dwelling. Perjurers will be caught only if they sin in the very face of the god, the virgin-not-a-virgin, only if she immerses herself in sacred waters. When people expect divine vengeance, it is usually in circumstances of this sort, not through supposing that the human and divine sense of right and wrong will be identically offended and that retribution will thereupon reach out to catch the criminal wherever he may be. Of such a grander faith there are very few signs indeed, at least in cults untouched by Judaism."

7. For a convenient introduction to Tobit and Ben Sira, see Daniel Harrington, *Invitation to the Apocrypha* (Grand Rapids, Mich.: Eerdmans, 1999), 10–27, 78–91. For the subject of charity in Ben Sira, see Bradley Gregory, *Like an Everlasting Signet Ring: Generosity in the Book of Sirach* (Berlin: de Gruyter, 2010). For an in-depth discussion of the text of Tobit and a full bibliography on the history of its interpretation, see Joseph Fitzmyer, *Tobit* (Berlin: de Gruyter, 2003).

8. Paul Deselaers offers a detailed (and improbable) redactional history of the composition of the book (*Das Buch Tobit. Studien zu seiner Entstehung, Komposition und Theologie* [Göttingen: Vandenhoeck and Ruprecht, 1982]). In his mind, vv. 4–8 belong to a third stage of expansion of the basic narrative (452–58). Compare also Merten Rabenau, *Studien zum Buch Tobit* (BZAW 220; Berlin: de Gruyter, 1994). I should also note that verses 10–15 complicate the picture I have drawn a bit, but not unduly so. The author clearly wishes to alert

the reader of Tobit's devotion to Torah in the Diaspora. He does this by flagging his acts of charity at the beginning (v. 3), turning to his devotion to the foods laws in vv. 10–15, and then returning to charity in vv. 16–17. In between this account of his prodigious obedience outside the land of Israel is inserted a brief account of his comportment prior to his exile (vv. 4–9).

9. *Avot deRabbi Natan,* 4:5; italics mine.

10. On Ben Sira's relationship to the priesthood, see Helga Stadelmann, *Ben Sira als Schriftgelehrter* (Tübingen: Mohr Siebeck, 1981); Saul Olyan, "Ben Sira's Relationship to the Priesthood," *Harvard Theological Review* 80 (1987): 261–86; and Benjamin Wright, "'Fear the Lord and Honor the Priest': Ben Sira as Defender of the Jerusalem Priesthood," in *Praise Israel for Wisdom and Instruction: Essays on Ben Sira and Wisdom, the Letter of Aristeas and the Septuagint* (Leiden: Brill, 2008), 97–104. On almsgiving as a form of sacrifice in Ben Sira, see Otto Kaiser, "Kultische und Sittliche Sühne bei Jesus Sirach," in *"Einen Altar von Erde mache mir . . ." Festschrift für D. Conrad zu seinem 70. Geburtstag,* ed. J. Diehl, R. Heitzenröder, and M. Witte (Waltrop: Harmut Spenner, 2003), 151–67, esp. 161–63; and Robert Hayward, "Sacrifice and World Order: Some Observations on Ben Sira's Attitude to the Temple Service," in *Sacrifice and Redemption: Durham Essays in Theology,* ed. S. Sykes (Cambridge: Cambridge University Press, 1991), 22–34.

11. Stephen Greenblatt, *Hamlet in Purgatory* (Princeton: Princeton University Press, 2001).

12. The oft-cited text can be found in John's homilies on I Corinthians. The excerpt is from Homily 20, which can be found in Schaff, *Nicene and Post-Nicene Fathers,* 12:374. The translation has been updated with the help of my graduate assistant, John Sehorn.

13. On the altar as a conduit to God, see Gary A. Anderson, "Sacrifices and Offerings," in *Anchor Bible Dictionary* (New York: Doubleday, 1992), 5: 870–86. As for the theological logic that governs this anthropomorphic language, we can do no better than Thomas Aquinas. When considering the question whether the practice of religion requires external acts, he writes: "We pay God honor and reverence not for His sake (because He is of Himself full of glory to which no creature can add anything), but for our own sake, because by the very fact that we revere and honor God, our mind is subjected to Him. . . . Now the human mind, in order to be united to God, needs to be guided by the sensible world, since *invisible things . . . are clearly seen, being understood by the things that are made,* as the Apostle says (Rom 1:20). Wherefore in the Divine worship it is necessary to make use of corporeal things, that man's mind may be aroused thereby, as by signs, to the spiritual acts by means of which he is united to God" (*Summa Theologica* II-II, Question 81. Article 7; for the translation, see *St. Thomas Aquinas: Summa Theologica* [Notre Dame, Ind.: Ave Maria, 1981], 3: 1527; italics in original). I would like to thank John Sehorn for pointing me to this text.

14. On this phrase, see Alyssa Gray, "Redemptive Almsgiving and the Rabbis of Late Antiquity," *Jewish Studies Quarterly* 18 (2011): 155–57.

15. Gerhard von Rad, *Deuteronomy: A Commentary* (Old Testament Library; Philadelphia: Westminster, 1966), 160–61; italics mine.

16. On the role of interest-free loans as a means of assisting the poor, see the classic essay of Isac Seeligmann, "Darlehen, Bürgschaft und Zins in Recht und Gedankenwelt der Hebräischen Bibel," in *Gesammelte Studien zur Hebräischen Bibel* (Tübingen: Mohr Siebeck, 2004), 319–48.

17. *Midrash Tannaim zum Deuteronomium,* ed. D. Hoffmann (Berlin: Ittzkowksi, 1908), 84, citing Deut 15:10. My translation is not completely literal but somewhat periphrastic.

18. The very word for alms in Arabic, *zakat,* is a loan word from Jewish Aramaic (*zakuta*). Mohammad likewise characterizes the act of charity as a loan made to God. Let me illustrate this with two Quranic texts: "God took compact with the Children of Israel; and We raised up from among them twelve chieftains. And God said, 'I am with you. Surely, if you perform the prayer, and pay the alms (*zakat*), and believe in My Messengers and succor them, and lend to God a good loan, I will acquit you of your evil deeds, and I will admit you to gardens

underneath which rivers flow. So whosoever of you thereafter disbelieves, surely he has gone astray from the right way'" (5:12). And also: "Who is he that will lend to God a good loan, and He will multiply it for him, and his shall be a generous wage" (57:11). The translation is that of A. J. Arberry, *The Koran Interpreted: A Translation* (New York: Simon and Schuster, 1996).

19. The following text from St. Basil is taken from his second sermon on Psalm 14 (15 in the Hebrew and most English versions), section 5. I have made some minor modifications to the translation found in *Saint Basil: Exegetic Homilies*, trans. Agnes Clare Way (*Fathers of the Church*, 46; Washington, D.C.: Catholic University of America Press, 1963).

20. The text in from Dom Edmund Beck, *Des Heiligen Ephraem des Syrers. Hymnen auf Abraham Kidunaya und Julianos Saba*, (CSCO 322–23; Louvain: Imprimerie Orientalische, 1955), hymn 1, lines 5–8. For a good introduction to the figure of Ephrem within the context of Syriac Christianity, see Sebastian Brock, *The Luminous Eye: The Spiritual World Vision of Saint Ephrem* (Kalamazoo, Mich.: Cistercian Publications, 1992). For the figure of Abraham Kidunaya see Sidney Griffith, "Abraham Qîdûnayâ, St. Ephraem the Syrian, and Early Monasticism in the Syriac-Speaking World," *Studia Anselmiana* 140 (2004): 239–64. The translation is my own.

21. Though the quotation comes from a poem by Tennyson, it is widely cited by evolutionary biologists as though it came from the pen of Darwin himself. Evidently this clause captures the spirit of "survival of the fittest" even though it was written before the appearance of *On the Origin of Species.*

22. The term *tsedaqa* ("charity") undergoes a striking transformation in the Bible, for it originally meant "justice." For an excellent account of how this happened, see Avi Hurvitz, "Reshitam Ha-Miqra'it shel Munahim Talmudiyyim—Le-Toledot Tsemihato shel Musag Ha-Tsedaqah'" [Hebrew] in *Mehqarim be-Lashon* 2–3 (1987): 155–60. The word *hesed* also underwent a significant change. In the Hebrew Bible, it most often means "covenantal fidelity." But it developed the extended sense of "mercy toward the poor" in the Second Temple period. For an excellent essay on this development, see Jan Joosten, "*Hesed*, 'bienveillance' et *eleos* 'pitie': Reflexions sur une equivalence lexicale dans la Septante," in *"Car c'est l'amour qui me plait, non le sacrifice . . .": Recherches sur Osée 6:6 et son interprétation juive et chrétienne,* ed. E. Bons (Supplements to the Journal for the Study of Judaism 88; Leiden: Brill, 2004), 25–42.

23. The other five are feeding the hungry, giving drink to the thirsty, clothing the naked, sheltering the homeless, and freeing the captive.

3. A LOAN TO GOD

Epigraphs: The dictionary of Lewis and Short is publicly available at http://perseus.uchicago.edu/Reference/lewisandshort.html. The Talmud quotation is my own translation. The citation of Leo the Great is from *Pope Leo I: Sermons* (Fathers of the Church; Washington, D.C.: Catholic University of America, 1995).

1. *The Letters of Gerard Manley Hopkins to Robert Bridges,* ed. Claude Abbot (London: Oxford University Press, 1935), 60–61.

2. Ibid., 63, 64. Emphasis is mine.

3. *Pirqe Avot* ("The Chapters of the Fathers") is readily available in any translation of the Mishnah. For the text that I shall discuss, see 2.9.

4. Scholars are not sure whether this action took place when the money was first disbursed or only later when the period set for the return of the loan had not been met. See I. Seeligmann, "Darlehen, Bürgschaft und Zins in Recht und Gedankenwelt der Hebräischen Bibel," in *Gesammelte Studien zur Hebräischen Bibel* (Tübingen: Mohr Siebeck, 2004), 319–48, esp. 330–31.

5. James Surowiecki, "Cheat, Pray, Love," *New Yorker,* January 12, 2009, p. 21.

6. The opening paragraph from an unsigned article in the *Economist* ("The Faith That Moves Mammon," *Economist,* October 16, 2008, p. 88) sums this up quite well: "The near-collapse of the banking system has shown just how deep some central parts of economic life are buried. Who, for instance, bothered much about the static interbank market before it seized up in August 2007? The supply of credit is bound up with something even more subterranean: trust. The very word comes from *credere,* to trust, in Latin. When institutions, such as banks, that are supposed to embody trust are shown to be brittle, it leads to concerns about the fragility of the entire economy."

7. Seeligmann, "Darlehen," 323.

8. The German reads: "Da gab es manches saure Wort, ich erinnere mich noch so gut, als wäre es erst gestern geschehen, dass ich durch la religion viel Unannehmlichkeiten erfahren. Wohl sechsmal erging an mich die Frage »Henri, wie heisst der Glaube auf französisch?« Und sechsmal, und immer weinerlicher antwortete ich: »Das heisst le crédit.« Und beim siebenten Male, kirschbraun im Geshichte, rief der wütende Examinator »Er heisst la religion«—und es regnete Prügel, und alle Kameraden lachten. Madame! Seit der Zeit kann ich das Wort religion nicht erwähnen hören, ohne dass mein Rücken blass vor Schrecken, und meine Wange rot vor Scham wird. Und ehrlich gestanden, le crédit hat mir im Leben mehr genützt als la religion—In diesem Augenblick fällt mir ein, dass ich dem Löwenwirt in Bologna noch fünf Taler schuldig bin—Und wahrhaftig, ich mache mich anheischig, dem Löwenwirt noch fünf Taler extra schuldig zu sein, wenn ich nur das unglückselige Wort la religion in diesem Leben nimmermehr zu hören brauche." For the English see *The Harz Journey and Selected Prose,* trans. R. Robinson (London: Penguin, 2006), 110; for the German, *Reisebilder* (Zürich: Diogenes, 1993), 168–69. Also compare Schopenhauer (*Parega und Paralipomena* [Zürich: Haffmans, 1991] vol. 2, § 129, p. 235): "Weiland war die Hauptstütze des Thrones der GLAUBE; heut zu Tage ist es der CREDIT. Kaum mag dem Päpste selbst das Zutrauen seiner Gläubigen mehr am Herzen liegen, als das seiner Gläubiger. Beklage man ehemals die Schuld der Welt, so sieht man jetzt mit Grausen auf die Schulden der Welt und, wie ehemals den jüngsten Tag, so prophezeit man jetzt den universellen Staatsbankrott, jedoch ebenfalls mit der zuversichtlichen Hoffung, ihn nicht selbst zu erleben."

9. In Hungarian the word *hitelezo* can mean "one who issues a loan" and "to believe." For the Akkadian root *qiâpu/qīptu* see the entry in the *Chicago Assyrian Dictionary* (Chicago: University of Chicago Oriental Institute, 1982), 13:93–97.

10. One could also make the argument that vv. 1–13 constitute a single unit divided into three pieces, followed by vv. 14–20. On this view vv. 1–3 introduce the general theme: the command to lend to one's neighbor who is in need. The second section (vv. 4–7) concerns the risks involved in making a loan in the most general of terms, while the third section (vv. 8–13) speaks to the issue of assisting the poor. In any case, the same sharp and surprising division between ordinary loans and loans to the destitute comes to the fore.

I would also like to note that I have relied on my student Brad Gregory's excellent discussion of Ben Sira for this entire chapter though I have not cited each and every point I have drawn from him. See his recently published dissertation, *Like an Everlasting Signet Ring: Generosity in the Book of Sirach* (Berlin: de Gruyter, 2010), 181–203. Also compare the discussion of the chapter as a whole, 133–63.

11. On the origins of this term see Gary A. Anderson, *Sin: A History* (New Haven: Yale University Press, 2009), 139–42. On the use of *eleēmosunē* in the literature of this period, see Patrick Griffin, "A Study of Eleēmosynē in the Bible with Emphasis upon Its Meaning and Usage in the Theology of Tobit and Ben Sira," M.A. thesis, Catholic University of America, 1982. And finally, on the use of *eleos* to translate the Hebrew term *hesed,* see Jan Joosten, "Hesed, 'bienveillance' et *eleos* 'pitie': Reflexions sur une equivalence lexicale dans la Septante," in *"Car c'est l'amour qui me plait, non le sacrifice . . .": Recherches sur Osée 6:6 et son interprétation juive et chrétienne,* ed. E. Bons (Supplements to the Journal for the Study of Judaism 88; Leiden: Brill, 2004), 25–42.

12. The Greek literally reads: "Many will regard a loan as a *found-thing.*" The translation *windfall* construes the sentence as if the loan was a hundred-dollar bill that one spotted lying on the sidewalk.

13. Other texts to consider would be Proverbs 6:1–5, 11:15, 17:18, and 20:16. Also, see the discussion of Seeligmann, "Darlehen," 327–30, and Andreas Scherer, "Is the Selfish Man Wise? Considerations of Context in Proverbs 10:1–22:16 with Special Regard to Surety, Bribery, and Friendship," *Journal for the Study of the Old Testament* 76 (1997): 59–70, esp. 61–64.

14. See Seeligmann, "Darlehen," 325: "Die Bibel kennt lediglich die Sorge um den Schuldner, wogegen sie auf das Risiko des Gläubigers kaum eingeht."

15. Though one should note that this idea is found in Proverbs 19:17.

4. Material Wealth and Its Deceptions

The second epigraph is taken from Cornelius à Lapide's commentary, which can be found at www.catholicapologetics.info/scripture/newtestament/Lapide.htm.

1. I have slightly altered the traditional way in which these two Proverbs have been translated. For example, modern translators render the Hebrew term *tsedaqa* as "righteousness" rather than as "almsgiving"; I have preferred almsgiving because this was the norm in the Second Temple period. This is clear in the Greek translations of Ben Sira and Tobit, where the Hebrew term is rendered *eleēmosunē,* "an act of mercy [shown toward the poor]." Avi Hurvitz has provided good philological reasons for supposing that this was the original sense of the proverb itself. See his "Reshitam Ha-Miqra'it shel Munahim Talmudiyyim—Le-Toledot Tsemihato shel Musag Ha-Tsedaqah'" [Hebrew] in *Mehqarim be-Lashon* 2–3 (1987): 155–60.

2. This is especially true in legal contexts where *le-harshia* means "to declare guilty," while *le-hatsdiq* means "to acquit."

3. What this digression highlights is the fact that almsgiving delivers one from the mundane trials of *this* world. For many this will seem a rather dramatic departure from the claim that almsgiving delivers one from death. Deliverance from death, for most readers, means being saved from eternal damnation. Rabbi Meir's paraphrase "almsgiving delivers us from judgment in Gehenna" (Babylonian Talmud *Baba Bathra* 10a) would seem to be a more accurate rendition. To be delivered from death, however, in the Hebrew Bible rarely refers to the resurrection of the dead at the end of time. Consider, for example, Psalm 30, where we read of an individual who had arrogantly thought himself secure ("I shall never be moved") suddenly subject to divine judgment—perhaps due to a serious illness (see v. 2). Deep in despair he exhorts God to hear his prayer (v. 10) and finds an answer: "You have turned my mourning into dancing; you have taken off my sackcloth and clothed me with joy" (v. 11). This movement from despair to exultation, marked by a move from mourning attire to festal garments, is summarized at the beginning of the Psalm as a movement from death to life: "O Lord my God, I cried to you for help, and you have healed me. O Lord, you brought up my soul from Sheol, restored me to life from among those gone down to the Pit" (vv. 2–3). Ben Sira accents the fact that almsgiving provides salvation in *this* life by glossing the Hebrew term *death* with more conventional attributes. In his view, almsgiving rescues one from "every [kind of] disaster." This means that almsgiving will provide better protection from an enemy than even "a stout shield" or "a sturdy spear." Like a piece of high-quality military equipment, "it will fight for you against the enemy."

4. The translations from Ben Sira and from Proverbs in this section of the chapter are my own.

5. Reading: *'al to'mar.*

6. This recalls what Heinrich Heine purportedly said on his deathbed: "Dieu me pardonnera, c'est son métier" (God will forgive me, that's his job).

7. Bruce Waltke, *The Book of Proverbs, Chapters 1–15* (Grand Rapids, Mich.: Eerdmans, 2004), 453.

8. The sequence "Many have been entrapped by gold, and placed their trust in precious gems, *because* it is a stumbling block for the foolish . . . " provides a tight, logical progression that is compromised by the bracketed clause.

9. Bradley Gregory, *Like an Everlasting Signet Ring: Generosity in the Book of Sirach* (Berlin: de Gruyter, 2010), 52–53.

10. Roland Murphy, "Sin, Repentance, and Forgiveness," in *Der Einzelne und seine Gemeinschaft bei Ben Sira,* ed. R. Egger-Wenzel and I. Krammer (Berlin: de Gruyter, 1998), 265.

11. As scholars have long noted, the idiom of "cleansing from sin" is an economic metaphor that refers to wiping the account books clean of any debt. On this subject see my forthcoming essay "How Does Almsgiving Purge Sins?" which will appear in *Hebrew in the Second Temple Period: The Hebrew of the Dead Sea Scrolls and of Other Contemporary Sources. Proceedings of the Twelfth International Symposium of the Orion Center for the Study of the Dead Sea Scrolls and Associated Literature, Jointly Sponsored by the Eliezer Ben-Yehuda Center for the Study of the History of the Hebrew Language, 29–31 December 2008,* ed. S. E. Fassberg, M. Bar-Asher, and R. Clements (Studies on the Texts of the Desert of Judah; Leiden: Brill, 2013). For now, see the article by J. C. Greenfield, "The 'Defension Clause' in Some Documents from Nahal Heber and Nahal Se'elim," *Revue de Qumran* 15 (1992): 467–71, esp. the table on 468, which documents how various Aramaic terms for "cleansing" refer to the legal idea of clearing one from legal claims.

12. On the theological coordination of the individual Tobit with the people Israel, see George Nickelsburg's short commentary on the book in *The HarperCollins Bible Commentary,* ed. James Mays (San Francisco: HarperCollins, 2000), 719, where he writes, "Parallel to the story of Tobit is the uncompleted story of Israel. Tobit's situation is paradigmatic for the exiled nation. As God has chastised Tobit, so Israel, suffering in exile, is being chastised. But God's mercy on Tobit and his family guarantees that this mercy will bring the Israelites back to their land. Since this event, described only in predictions, awaits fulfillment, one level of the double story is incomplete."

13. I have used the translation of George Nickelsburg and James VanderKam, *1 Enoch: A New Translation Based on the Hermeneia Commentary* (Minneapolis: Fortress, 2004).

14. I would like to thank my colleague James VanderKam for helping me with the Ethiopic original.

15. This should be contrasted with Sirach 31:3–4. It should also be noted that many commentators have suggested the relevance of Sirach 11:18–19 for this pericope: "One becomes rich through diligence and self-denial, and the reward allotted him is this: when he says, 'I have found rest and now I shall feast on my goods!' he does not know how long it will be until he leaves them to others and dies." But the parallel does not quite work. The Rich Fool's mistake is not that he saves up his wealth through self-denial for a day that will never come but rather that he mistakes an economic windfall for true financial security for the future. Though Sirach 11 and Luke 12 share the notion of an unrealized "carpe diem," the motivations for that day of enjoyment are quite different.

16. The recent study of Matthew Rindge, *Jesus' Parable of the Rich Fool: Luke 12:13–34 Among Ancient Conversations on Death and Possessions* (Early Christianity and Its Literature 6; Atlanta: Society of Biblical Literature, 2011), makes a number of very good points on this score. See in particular the discussion entitled "The Folly of Saving for the Future" (209–13).

17. Not all New Testament scholars have noticed these parallels with Israel's wisdom tradition, and as a result some have gone slightly astray in interpreting this literary unit. Abraham Malherbe, for example, in "Christianization of a Topos (Luke 12:13–34)," *Novum Testamentum* 38 (1996): 123–35, puts great emphasis on the fact that in Luke's account, Jesus exhorts the

crowd to be on its guard against "all kinds of greed (*pleonexia*)." Though he is certainly right to point us to the way in which this term functions in Greco-Roman moral discourse, I think that the parallels can also be misleading. For Malherbe, what is fundamentally wrong with the Rich Fool is his desire for more than what is necessary for living (see esp. 131–32). Yet this account misses the more particular focus that we have uncovered: the Rich Fool's mistaken belief that accumulated wealth will secure his future such that he can turn himself with abandon to hedonistic pleasure. Joseph Fitzmyer, on the other hand, concludes that "the amassing of a superabundance of material possessions for the sake of *la dolce vita* becomes the height of folly in the light of the responsibility of life itself and the assessment of it which will take place once it is over"; *The Gospel According to Luke X–XXIV* (AB 28A; Garden City, N.Y.: Doubleday, 1985), 972. This also is not quite right. I have argued that the sin resides not so much in the hedonistic excess ("*la dolce vita*") as in the presumption that wealth will assure one of a rosy future. Fitzmyer also errs in comparing the Lucan account with contemporary Jewish materials that speak about the dangers of unjustly amassing great wealth. As I have repeatedly emphasized, it is not the wealth itself that is bad but how it is assessed *after the fact*. Luke himself seems quite clear on this point—the land returned an enormous profit on this man's initial investment of seed. There is nothing morally wrong here. If anything, we could argue that it is a sign of divine blessing. The Rich Fool goes astray in not distributing his goods to the poor and becoming "rich toward God." This is the only path to follow if the goal is to be assured of a beatific future. Wealth, as Proverbs has taught us, will be of no avail on the day of wrath. Matthew Rindge's recent *Jesus' Parable of the Rich Fool* alertly calls attention to the sapiential motifs embedded in the story and makes a number of good observations about the importance of almsgiving but misses the fundamental significance of Proverbs 10:2.

18. Babylonian Talmud *Baba Bathra* 10a.

19. Gunther Bornkamm, *Der Lohngedanke im Neuen Testament* (Lüneburg: Heliand-Verlag, 1947), 12.

20. New Testament scholars are coming to the realization that German scholars have been in the custom of using the "legalistic" Judaism of Jesus' day as a cipher for anti-Catholic polemics. On this see Jonathan Z. Smith, *Drudgery Divine* (Chicago: University of Chicago Press, 1990), among others.

21. Eudaimonism is the classic moral theory of Plato and Aristotle, which had as its aim the cultivation of the virtues (*aretai*) as a means of achieving happiness (*eudaimonia*). It was adopted by Augustine, came into the work of Thomas Aquinas, and has formed the backbone of Catholic moral teaching.

22. The citation is from paragraph 7. The full text can be found at http://www.vatican.va/holy_father/benedict_xvi/encyclicals/documents/hf_ben-xvi_enc_20051225_deus-caritas-est_en.html. I could also mention the idea that when one makes this practice a habit (a virtue in the Aristotelian sense), a form of alchemy takes place. What began as a concern for self slowly becomes a concern for the other. In Christianity, this is the reason for the cult of the saints. There is much to be learned from how the bare words of Torah are actually carried out in a concrete, human life.

23. Elizabeth Anscombe's famous critique of Kant goes in a different direction; for her, a moral duty implies a duty giver. "Modern Moral Philosophy," *Philosophy*, 33 (1958): 1–19.

5. Deliverance from Death

1. Perhaps the earliest attestation of the idea of a bodily resurrection is found in 1 Enoch 1–36, a work that is often dated to the third century BCE. On the problem of the origin of the concept of the resurrection of the body, see the classic work of George Nickelsberg, *Resurrection, Immortality, and Eternal Life in Intertestamental Judaism* (Cambridge: Harvard University Press, 1972), and the more recent studies of Claudia Setzer, *Resurrection of the*

Body in Early Judaism and Christianity (Leiden: Brill, 2004), and Jon Levenson, *Resurrection and the Restoration of Israel: The Ultimate Victory of the God of Life* (New Haven: Yale University Press, 2006). On the specific problem of resurrection language in the book of Tobit see Beate Ego, "Death and Burial in the Tobit Narration in the Context of the Old Testament Tradition," *The Human Body in Death and Resurrection,* ed. T. Nicklas, F. Reiterer, and J. Verheyden (Berlin: de Gruyter, 2009), 87–103, and Stefan Beyerle, "'Release me to go to my everlasting home . . .' (Tob 3:6): A Belief in an Afterlife in Late Wisdom Literature," *The Book of Tobit: Text, Tradition, Theology,* ed. G. Xerzvits and J. Zsengellér (Leiden: Brill, 2005), 71–88. I am in fundamental agreement with Ego's thesis that Tobit's expression of resurrection is to be understood in this-worldly terms; Beyerle's suggestion that the book of Tobit may imply more than this does not seem accurate in my view.

2. Strikingly, Jerome in his Latin Vulgate translation understands the money that Tobit leaves with Gabael as a form of alms, not a deposit. As such, the return of this money becomes much more important theologically: Tobit's trust that the money will be returned to his son during the journey is now grounded in a specific scriptural promise. God is on record as having promised to repay such deeds (Prov 19:17).

3. This exchange looks very similar to the story of Abraham's near-sacrifice of Isaac. Besides the similarity to the angel's address to Abraham at the denouement of the episode (Genesis 22:11), compare Isaac's exchange with his father when he notes the fire and the wood but no animal for a burnt offering: "Isaac said to his father Abraham, 'Father!' And he said, 'Here I am, my son'" (v. 7). This parallel is not at all surprising in light of the other parallels we shall document below and in the next chapter.

4. For tendency of biblical writers to express emotion through behavior, see Yohanan Muffs, "Joy and Love as Metaphorical Expressions of Willingness and Spontaneity in Cuneiform, Ancient Hebrew, and Related Literatures: Divine Investitures in the Midrash in the Light of Neo-Babylonian Royal Grants," in *Christianity, Judaism, and Other Greco-Roman Cults,* ed. J. Neusner (Leiden: Brill, 1975), 3:1–36. On the specific issue of displaying zeal to fulfill a commandment by rising early and saddling one's own animal, see the midrash found in the *Mekhilta of R. Ishmael* (*be-Shallah* 2, on Exod 14:6) and the discussion of the same in Gary A. Anderson, *A Time to Mourn, A Time to Dance: The Expression of Grief and Joy in Israelite Religion* (University Park: Pennsylvania State University Press, 1991), 103–4.

5. On the matter of Tobit's impurity after handling a corpse, see Ego, "Death and Burial in the Tobit Narration," 89.

6. On the ignominy of being supported by one's wife see Sirach 25:22 and the discussion of this verse by Renate Egger-Wenzel, "'Denn harte Knechtschaft und Schande ist es, wenn eine Frau ihren Mann ernährt' (Sir 25,22)," in *Der Einzelne und seine Gemeinschafte bei Ben Sira,* ed. R. Egger-Wenzel and I. Krammer (Berlin: de Gruyter, 1998), 23–51; see esp. 35–41 and citation of the parallel to the book of Tobit on 39.

7. The literary form of the last testamentary address of the father is found twice in the book of Genesis (Isaac's address to Jacob and Esau in chapter 27 and Jacob's address to Joseph and his two sons in 48 and then to all his sons in 49). In postbiblical literature this type of address is greatly expanded and becomes the occasion for the father to teach his sons Torah. As George Nickelsburg remarks, in "The Bible Rewritten and Expanded," *Jewish Writings of the Second Temple Period,* ed. M. Stone (Philadelphia: Fortress, 1984], 97, this is already evident in the Book of Jubilees. The idea comes to classic expression in the Testaments of the Twelve Patriarchs. For a review of scholarship on the genre, see Anitra B. Kolenkow, "Testaments," in *Early Judaism and Its Modern Interpreters,* ed. R. Kraft and G. Nickelsburg (Philadelphia: Fortress, 1986), 259–67.

8. On the motif of the gall of a fish being used as an agent of healing, see Wolfram von Soden, "Fischgalle als Heilsmittel für Augen," *Archiv für Orientforschung* 21 (1966): 81–82.

9. On the importance of the motif of blindness in the book of Tobit, see Anathea

Portier-Young, "'Eyes to the Blind': A Dialogue Between Tobit and Job," in *Intertextual Studies in Ben Sira and Tobit*, ed. J. Corley and V. Skemp (Washington, D.C.: Catholic Biblical Association, 2005), 14–27, esp. 17–21, and Micah Kiel, "Tobit's Theological Blindness," *Catholic Biblical Quarterly* 72 (2011): 281–98. Both make the good point that blindness symbolizes death, but both err (Kiel, far more grievously) in thinking that Tobit's physical blindness is a cipher for a deeper spiritual blindness. On the motif of blindness in the book of Genesis, see Meir Sternberg, *The Poetics of Biblical Narrative* (Bloomington: Indiana University Press, 1985), 349–54.

10. See his annotation to this Psalm in *The HarperCollins Study Bible, New Revised Standard Version*, ed. W. Meeks (San Francisco: HarperCollins, 1993), 814.

11. See the classic treatment of this problem by Christoph Barth, *Die Errettung vom Tode in den individuellen Klage-und Dankliedern des Alten Testaments* (Zollikon, Switzerland: Evangelischer Verlag, 1947), and the more recent work of Jon Levenson, *Resurrection and the Restoration of Israel* (New Haven: Yale University Press, 2006).

12. Levenson, *Resurrection*, 38–39.

13. See Joseph Fitzmyer, *Tobit* (Berlin: de Gruyter, 2003), 333–34, and Alexander Di Lella, "A Study of Tobit 14:10 and Its Intertextual Parallels," *Catholic Biblical Quarterly* 71 (2009): 497–506. On the figure of Ahikar in the book of Tobit, see Jonas Greenfield, "Ahiqar in the Book of Tobit," *De la Tôrah au Messie,* ed. M. Carrez (Paris: Desclée, 1981), 329–36.

14. The importance of preserving the name after death is seen most clearly in the institution of the levirate marriage (cf. Deut 25:5–10), in which a brother is obligated to have intercourse with his brother's widow in the event that the couple has no male heir. The importance of the son remembering the father after his death is an ancient theme in the Near East and continues long afterward in Jewish ritual. Compare, for example, the role of the son to say kaddish after the death of his father or mother. As Leon Wieseltier shows in *Kaddish* (New York: Knopf, 1998), some postbiblical traditions ascribe to this prayer the ability to facilitate the safe journey of the deceased parent to the heavenly banquet.

15. In the book of Ruth, Naomi loses her husband and both of her sons and must rely on the support of her daughter-in-law Ruth in order to survive. Upon her return to her home in Bethlehem at the end of the first chapter, Naomi is greeted warmly by the women of the town but responds in bitter grief. At the end of the book, when her despair is overturned by the marriage of Ruth to Boaz and the birth of a son, the women again address Naomi. Significantly they remark: "Blessed be the Lord, who has not left you this day without next-of-kin. . . . He shall be to you *a restorer of life* and provide for you in your old age" (Ruth 4:14–15, translation slightly altered). In Isaiah 54:1–8, the exilic plight of Jerusalem is characterized by a barren woman, its restoration by the restoration of her fertility and hence, her children. Levenson (*Resurrection*, 145–47, 156–65) has insightfully compared this vision of restoration to that of Ezekiel's vision of the dry bones (37:1–14); each prophet speaks of resurrection in his own manner.

16. Levenson, *Resurrection*, 67–81.

17. Note the fact that Job *sees* his great-grandchildren at the end of the book and Moses is allowed to *see* the promised land before he dies—hinting that perhaps the land plays a homologous role to that of offspring.

6. Is Charity Always Rewarded?

The citation of Augustine in the epigraph comes from *The Works of Saint Augustine: Expositions of the Psalms, 73–98*, trans. M. Boulding (Hyde Park, N.Y.: New City, 2002), 456. Emphases are mine.

1. I must confess that I do not believe that this is an accurate description of the theology of the Deuteronomist, but this is not the place to make that argument. Given that this assessment is not only accepted by most scholars but also applied to the book of Tobit, I will work within the parameters of this assumption for the purposes of this chapter. For a general overview of the issue, see Joseph Fitzmyer, *Tobit* (Commentaries on Early Jewish Literature; Berlin: de Gruyter, 2003), 47. Also worth consulting are Alexander Di Lella, "The Deuteronomic Background of the Farewell Discourse in Tob 14:3–11," *Catholic Biblical Quarterly* 41 (1979): 380–89; Will Soll, "Misfortune and Exile in Tobit: The Juncture of a Fairy Tale Source and Deuteronomic Theology," *Catholic Biblical Quarterly* 51 (1989): 209–31; and Micah Kiel, "Tobit's Theological Blindness," *Catholic Biblical Quarterly* 73 (2001): 281–98.

2. The links were already noticed by Jerome and accentuated in his Vulgate translation. On this see Vincent Skemp, *The Vulgate of Tobit Compared with Other Ancient Witnesses* (Atlanta: Society of Biblical Literature, 2000), 86–87, 93. But many moderns have noted the same thing. For example, see Robert Pfeiffer, *History of New Testament Times: With an Introduction to the Apocrypha* (New York: Harper and Brothers, 1949), 267–68, Anathea Portier-Young, "'Eyes to the Blind': A Dialogue Between Tobit and Job," in *Intertextual Studies in Ben Sira and Tobit,* ed. J. Corley and V. Skemp (Washington, D.C.: Catholic Biblical Association, 2005), 14–27. See also Devorah Dimant, "Use and Interpretation of Mikra in the Apocrypha and Pseudepigrapha," in *Mikra,* ed. M. J. Moulder and H. Sysling (Philadelphia: Fortress, 1988), 417–19, and her more focused and detailed study, "The Bible Through a Prism: The Wife of Job and the Wife of Tobit," [Hebrew] *Shnaton* 17 (2007): 201–11.

3. Joseph Fitzmyer, for example, asserts that the trial certainly centered around Tobit's blindness, but this takes place long before the arrival of Raphael (Fitzmyer, *Tobit,* 295). This leads him to wonder why Tobit had to be tested again and what that particular test would have amounted to. In my opinion, Fitzmyer has too narrowly centered his focus on the moment of blindness. The larger problem, however, is the issue of theodicy that the blindness sets up. If almsgiving is to deliver one from the realm of darkness then why has it, in this instance, led to darkness? The larger problem, as I see it, is whether Tobit will stick to the truth of that piece of divine teaching or not. And to find the answer to that question, the matter of sending the son on the journey (and finding the requisite companion for the journey) becomes central.

4. Dimant ("Use and Interpretation of Mikra") does a very good job of assembling the parallels between Tobit and Job.

5. One question that goes unanswered is *who* exactly orchestrates the test that Tobit must undergo. The text says that Raphael was the one sent to initiate the test: "And that time when you did not hesitate to get up and leave your dinner to go and bury the dead, I was sent to you to test you. And at the same time God sent me to heal you . . . " (12:13–14a). Are we to presume that the angel of healing is the one responsible for Tobit's blindness? It seems that the shorter Greek text objected to such a view and restructured the verse to accentuate the beneficent characteristics of Raphael (italics mark the differences): "And that time when you did not hesitate to get up and leave your dinner to go and bury the dead, *your good deed did not escape me, but I was with you.* God sent me at the same time to heal you . . . " The Vulgate respects the problem by keeping the idea of a test but leaving its originator unmarked: "and when you left your dinner and hid the dead by day in your house and buried them at night, I offered your prayer to the Lord; because you were acceptable to God, it was necessary that temptation should test you." Clearly at some level, we must affirm that God allows the sparrows to blind Tobit. Whether our author understood Raphael as directly responsible for this test remains unanswered.

6. Dimant ("The Bible Through a Prism") has observed an important development in the Greek translation (Septuagint) of Job. Whereas the Hebrew original has Job's wife

rebuke him with few words and little explanation ("Then his wife said to him, 'Do you still persist in your integrity? Curse God, and die.'"), the Greek version tells us much more (translation from *A New English Translation of the Septuagint* [Oxford: Oxford University Press, 2007]): "Then after a long time had passed, his wife said to him, 'How long will you persist and say, [9a] "Look, I will hang on a little longer, while I wait for the hope of my deliverance?" [9b] For look, your legacy has vanished from the earth—sons and daughters, my womb's birth pangs and labors, for whom I wearied myself with hardships in vain. [9c] And you? You sit in the refuse of worms as you spend the night in the open air. [9d] *As for me, I am one that wanders about and a hired servant—from place to place and house to house, waiting for when the sun will set, so I can rest from the distresses and griefs that now beset me.* [9e] Now say some word to the Lord and die!'" According to the Greek, Job's physical illness required his wife to hire herself out as a day laborer, a motif very similar to what we see in Tobit (2:11–12). Dimant, however, goes too far when she asserts that the author of Tobit presumes that we know one other detail from the Testament of Job, that is, that Job's wife supplemented her wages with sexual favors. In Dimant's view, that is the reason the author of Tobit has Anna bring home a goat as an extra wage from her employers. She claims it is an intertextual echo that recalls the goat that Tamar received from Jacob in exchange for sexual favors (Gen 38). As I shall make clear, I don't agree. Anna remains a person of virtue for the author.

7. It is possible that *eleēmosunai* also derives from this root, but because of the repetition ("Where are your acts of charity [*eleēmosunai*]? Where are your righteous deeds [*dikaiosunai*]?"), it is more likely that the term *charity* derives from the Hebrew root, *hesed*.

8. *Pace* Paul Deselaers, *Das Buch Tobit, Studien zu seiner Entstehung, Komposition und Theologie* (Göttingen: Vandenhoek and Ruprecht, 1982), 27.

9. It is surprising how many readers of the book have missed this simple fact. This in spite of the fact that everyone concedes that the command to give alms is a, if not the, major theme of the book. Sabine Van Den Eynde, for example, understands the trip to collect the deposit to be the result of Tobit's wish to "settle his financial affairs" before he dies ("One Journey and One Journey Makes Three: The Impact of the Readers' Knowledge in the Book of Tobit," *Zeitschrift für die alttestamentliche Wissenschaft* 117 [2005]: 275). Would Tobit expose his son to such risk simply to put his books in order? That seems hard to imagine.

10. Jerome brings the matter into even sharper focus. Whereas the Greek simply records that Tobit had "left ten talents of silver in trust with Gabael" (1:14), the Vulgate records that Tobit "saw Gabelus [=Gabael] in want, a man of his own tribe, and taking a note from his hand, he gave the aforesaid sum of money." Because Gabael is thought to be a man stricken by poverty, the money that is given him is a loan and as such is a form of charity which God has promised to reward: "He who assists the poor makes a loan to God and He shall surely repay him (Prov 19:17)." On this view, the sending of the son is nothing other than an act of faith in the promises of God.

11. So the logic of the conclusion of Tobit's testamentary instruction. After reiterating the matter of the deposit left with Gabael, he says, "Do not be afraid, my son, because we have become poor. You have great wealth if you fear God and flee from every sin and do what is good in the sight of the Lord your God" (4:20–21).

12. One should recall the practice of levirate marriage as described in Deut 25:5–10. According to this law, a surviving brother must engage in sexual relations with his brother's widow in order to provide children for a deceased sibling who lacked offspring.

13. Levenson observes, in *Death and Resurrection of the Beloved Son* (New Haven: Yale University Press, 1993), 162, that Jacob cannot abide the thought that his beloved Benjamin should die and thus will not at first accept the risk involved in sending him on the journey. The problem, of course, is that the famine that has gripped Egypt and spread through the world has threatened the survival of the chosen family. "Only if life is risked," Levenson

writes, "can it continue. . . . The irony is that when Jacob does finally surrender his beloved son Benjamin, he receives anew not only Simeon, but even Joseph, whom he has given up for dead. His courageous willingness to expose Benjamin to the risk of death restores Joseph to him alive."

14. Hugh C. White, "The Initiation Legend of Isaac," *Zeitschrift für die alttestamentliche Wissenschaft* 91 (1979): 17.

15. See the analysis of Levenson, *Death and Resurrection*, 104–10, and Uriel Simon, *Seek Peace and Pursue It: Topical Issues in the Light of the Bible, the Bible in Light of Topical Issues* [Hebrew] (Tel Aviv: Yediot Acharonot, 2002).

16. The fact that Tobias has a hereditary claim that precedes those of all other suitors recalls a similar theme in the book of Ruth (see Tobit 4:12). We will return to the similarities between Ruth and Tobit.

17. Tzvi Novick, "Biblicized Narrative: On Tobit and Genesis 22," *Journal of Biblical Literature* 126 (2007): 755–64.

18. I have modified the translation of the NRSV.

19. Moreover, the uniqueness of this phrase was perceived by other writers in the Second Temple period and was used to mark an explicit reference to the aqedah. See the discussion of Novick, "Biblicized Narrative," 758–59.

20. See Novick, "Biblicized Narrative," 757 n. 5.

21. The linkage between Job and Genesis 22 is also evident in a text from Qumran. On the parallels between the two see James VanderKam, "The Aqedah, *Jubilees*, and PseudoJubilees," in *The Quest for Context and Meaning: Studies in Biblical Intertextuality in Honor of James A. Sanders*, ed. C. Evans and S. Talmon (Leiden: Brill, 1997), 241–61; Joseph Fitzmyer, "The Sacrifice of Isaac in Qumran Literature," *Biblica* 83 (2002): 211–29; and James Kugel, "Exegetical Notes on 4Q225 'PseudoJubilees,'" *Dead Sea Discoveries* 13 (2006): 73–98. On the roles of angels at the aqedah in particular, see Moshe Bernstein, "Angels at the Aqedah," *Dead Sea Discoveries* 7 (2000): 263–91.

22. The translation is that of James VanderKam, *The Book of Jubilees: A Critical Text*, 2 vols. (Leuven: Peeters, 1989), and comes from Jubilees 17:15–18:1.

23. I have adjusted the translation of the NRSV. The crucial term is *aharito*, which the NRSV translated "by how he ends." I have rendered it "by his posterity," as did the Septuagint. For this meaning of the word, see the discussion of Menahem Kister, "Some Blessing and Curse Formulae in the Bible, Northwest Semitic Inscriptions, Post-Biblical Literature and Late Antiquity," in *Hamlet on a Hill: Semitic and Greek Studies Presented to Professor T. Muraoka on the Occasion of his Sixty-Fifth Birthday*, ed. M. F. J. Baasten and W. Th. Van Peursen (Leuven: Peeters, 2003), 313–32, esp. 317–18. Kister shows that this meaning already exists in two Aramaic tomb inscriptions from the seventh century BCE found at Nerab, was evident to the Septuagintal translators, and is confirmed as well in Sirach 16:3. He concludes that the word "has two meanings: it can refer either to the life of the person himself or to his survival by his offspring" (318). Also note Max Kadushin, *A Conceptual Approach to the Mekilta* (New York: Jewish Theological Seminary, 1969), 47, who writes that the concept of the merits of the fathers "is a sub-concept of God's justice, connoting that God rewards children for the good deeds of their fathers. Reflected in this concept is the view that fathers and sons constitute a single personality."

24. On the question of linking one's identity to the larger family unit, see Robert Di Vito, "Old Testament Anthropology and the Construction of Personal Identity," *Catholic Biblical Quarterly* 61 (1999): 217–38.

25. The translation is based on (but not identical to) that of Menahem Kister, "Romans 5:12–21 against the Background of Torah Theology and Hebrew Usage," *Harvard Theological Review* 100 (2007): 394. See Chapter 8 for a full explanation of his reasoning.

26. On the Joban dimensions of Naomi's plight see Yair Zakovitch, *Ruth: Introduction and Commentary* [Hebrew] (Mikra le-Yisrael; Tel Aviv: Am Oved, 1990), 30–31.

7. Charity and the Goodness of Creation

The citation in the epigraph is from *The Works of St. Augustine: The Confessions,* trans. M. Boulding (Hyde Park, N.Y.: New City, 1997), 375.

1. The Septuagint translates the enigmatic Hebrew term *miktam* (often taken as a corruption of *miktab,* "inscription") as *stele,* or "public monument."

8. Can Merits Be Transferred?

1. To be precise, I am speaking of mortal sins in this case. For venial (lesser) sins auricular confession is not required but the Catechism strongly recommends it to enhance one's spiritual disposition. See *The Catechism of the Catholic Church,* §§1458, 1854–64. On the biblical grounds for this, see my discussion of the Elijah and Ahab story later in this chapter and the discussion of David's remorse over his sin with Bathsheba in Chapter 12.

2. In the Aramaic original it is 4:24. The translation is my own and intentionally periphrastic. For a justification, see my *Sin: A History* (New Haven: Yale University Press, 2009), 138–39.

3. On this point, see the essay of Klaus Koch, "Der Schatz im Himmel," in *Leben Angesichts des Todes: Beiträge zum theologischen Problem des Todes. Helmut Thielicke zum 60 Geburtstag* (Tübingen: J. C. B. Mohr, 1968), 47–60.

4. Günther Bornkamm, *Der Lohngedanke im Neuen Testament* (Lüneburg: Heliand-Verlag, 1947).

5. E. P. Sanders, *Paul and Palestinian Judaism. A Comparison of Patterns of Religion* (Philadelphia: Fortress, 1977), 183. Emphasis is that of Sanders.

6. For further details see my discussion in Chapter 12.

7. Sanders, *Paul and Palestinian Judaism,* 196. Emphasis added.

8. Ibid., 197–98.

9. Menahem Kister, "Romans 5:12–21 against the Background of Torah Theology and Hebrew Usage," *Harvard Theological Review* 100 (2007): 391–424, esp. 391–99.

10. The translation here is my own.

11. Though some will be quick to condemn this view as primitive, it is instructive to recall Barack Obama's remark that the "stain of slavery" still afflicts race relations in the United States, several generations after its perpetration (the speech was given in Philadelphia on March 18, 2008). The reach of sin is long indeed. Not even contrition is sufficient to wipe away its effects completely.

12. The translations of 44:10–11 and 13 are my own. I have benefited from the text-critical observations of Kister, "Romans 5:12–21," 394 n. 11.

13. The primary meaning of the commandment "to honor father and mother" is to support them in their dotage and remember their names in prayer after their death. The translation of these verses is my own, following the suggestions of Kister.

14. Kister, "Romans 5:12–21," 394–95. I have lifted the clause "*pace* E. P. Sanders . . ." from his footnote to that sentence. Kister is referring to the exact same portion of Sanders's argument that I cited above.

9. Storing Good Works in Heaven

The first citation in the epigraph is from a translation found in J. Mark Armitage, *A Twofold Solidarity: Leo the Great's Theology of Redemption* (Strathfield, Australia: St. Paul's Publications, 2005), 175. The second quotation of the epigraph is taken from Cornelius à Lapide's commentary. It can be found at www.catholicapologetics.info/scripture/newtestament/Lapide.htm.

1. See the discussion of this problem in Klaus Koch, "Der Schatz im Himmel," in *Leben Angesichts des Todes: Beiträge zum theologischen Problem des Todes. Helmut Thielicke zum 60 Geburtstag* (Tübingen: J. C. B. Mohr, 1968), 47–60. This insightful article provides much of the framework of the present chapter.

2. Following W. D. Davies and Dale Allison, *A Critical and Exegetical Commentary on the Gospel According to St. Matthew*, 3 vols. (New York: T and T Clark, 1988), I have modified the NRSV translation of Matthew 6 in this chapter to bring out the fact that good works constitute a wage that the moral agent earns.

3. Davies and Allison, *Critical and Exegetical Commentary*, 1:582, citing Adolf Deissman, *Light from the Ancient East* (New York: Dolan, 1927), 110–12. I have altered the traditional translation of *misthos* as "reward" to "wage."

4. For the difficult problem of how to relate these verses to their immediate context, see Nathan Eubank, "Wages of Righteousness: The Economy of Heaven in the Gospel According to Matthew," Ph.D. diss., Duke University, 2012, 89–93.

5. The reader will note the close parallels to the treatment of the treasury in heaven in Luke (12:22–34) that we discussed in an earlier chapter. It is likely that both Matthew and Luke have taken their material from a common source, sometimes labeled "Q" by New Testament scholars. For a conjecture about chronological priority, see Chapter 10, note 11.

6. On the grammar of Matt 6:1, see Eubank, "Wages of Righteousness," 81, 87.

7. The translation of this mishna is my own. One should note that the text I have cited is the second half of 1:1; I will discuss the first half of this mishna in Chapter 11. For an excellent treatment of this mishna, see Eliezer Diamond, *Holy Men and Hunger Artists: Fasting and Asceticism in Rabbinic Culture* (New York: Oxford University Press, 2004). The relevant section is the second chapter, "'The Principal Remains for the Next World': Delayed Gratification and Avoidance of Pleasure in Rabbinic Thought." Diamond shows that this mishna teaches that the benefits that accrue to a charitable deed are unlike those of most other commandments. For in the case of the latter, one is entitled to a reward in this world or the next, but not both. Almsgiving is special in that one can enjoy the reward now and be assured that the principal will go untouched.

8. See the discussion of this term at the beginning of Chapter 4. Translating the Greek term as "storeroom" fits the biblical usage quite nicely because the term is used in the Old Testament to refer to a place where weapons, food, clothing, and other such items are kept. In the heavenly storeroom, God keeps safe the rain, snow, and hail that he from time to time releases upon the earth.

9. Tosephta *Peah* 4.18; my citation follows the lead of Koch and strips out the biblical proof texts which are not immediately relevant for our purposes. For a fuller discussion of this text and its several variants in the rabbinic corpus, see Alyssa Gray, "Redemptive Almsgiving and the Rabbis of Late Antiquity," *Jewish Studies Quarterly* 18 (2011): 144–84, esp. 150–54.

10. The translation is from Albert Pietersma and Benjamin Wright, eds., *A New English Translation of the Septuagint* (New York: Oxford University Press, 2007). Emphasis added.

11. Koch, "Der Schatz," 54–58.

12. Translation is that of A. F. J. Klijn and can be found in James Charlesworth, ed., *The Old Testament Pseudepigrapha* (Garden City, N.Y.: Doubleday, 1985).

13. The translation is taken from Michael Stone, *Fourth Ezra* (Hermeneia; Minneapolis: Fortress, 1990), 202–3.

14. Koch, "Der Schatz," 57.

15. Klaus Koch, "Gibt es ein Vergeltungsdogma im Altes Testament?" *Zeitschrift für Theologie und Kirche* 52 (1955): 1–42. Most scholars consult the slightly abridged English translation, "Is There a Doctrine of Retribution in the Old Testament?" in *Theodicy in the Old Testament*, ed. J. Crenshaw (Philadelphia: Westminster, 1983), 27–87. This translation is not altogether dependable.

16. Koch, like many an enthusiast of a new idea, sometimes goes too far in what he believes is the explanative nature of his hypothesis. But in spite of these occasional excesses, it is striking to see how influential his thesis has been for the past several decades. For a critical assessment of how his thesis works in prophetic literature, see Patrick Miller, *Sin and Judgment in the Prophets: A Stylistic and Theological Analysis* (Chico, Calif.: Scholars Press, 1982), 121–39.

17. See the excellent discussion of this "thing-like" quality of sin in Baruch Schwartz, "Term or Metaphor: The Biblical Idiom 'Bearing a Sin'" [Hebrew] *Tarbiz* 63 (1994): 149–71, and my *Sin: A History* (New Haven: Yale University Press, 2011), 3–14.

18. Sebastian Brock, "A Syriac Dispute Between Heaven and Earth," *Le Muséon* 91 (1978): 261–70, see line 11. The manuscript dates to the sixth century CE, but no doubt the text is much older.

19. Diamond, *Holy Men and Hunger Artists.*

20. The discerning reader will have noted that the version of *Peah* cited in the Talmud singles out five commandments. Three of them we can classify as "care for those in need" (honoring parents, charity, hospitality), but the other two (establishing peace, Torah-study) cannot be so easily disposed of. I confess that I have no compelling account as to why these other two commandments found their way into the list. All I can suggest is that as Torah-study rose in stature, it assumed to itself the high value that had earlier attached to charity alone.

10. Prayer, Fasting, and Almsgiving

The citation in the epigraph comes from *St. Leo the Great, Sermons*, trans. J. Freeland (Fathers of the Church; Washington, D.C.: Catholic University of America Press, 1996), 64.

1. For a substantiation of this thesis see my forthcoming article, "How Does Almsgiving Purge Sins?" in *Hebrew in the Second Temple Period: The Hebrew of the Dead Sea Scrolls and of Other Contemporary Sources. Proceedings of the Twelfth International Symposium of the Orion Center for the Study of the Dead Sea Scrolls and Associated Literature, Jointly Sponsored by the Eliezer Ben-Yehuda Center for the Study of the History of the Hebrew Language, 29–31 December 2008*, ed. S. E. Fassberg, M. Bar-Asher, and R. Clements (Studies on the Texts of the Desert of Judah; Leiden: Brill, 2013).

2. NRSV has been slightly modified to bring out the nuance of a memorial (mnēmosunon) and establish the linkage to Acts 10:4; italics mine.

3. Gary Anderson, "From Israel's Burden to Israel's Debt: Towards a Theology of Sin in Biblical and Early Second Temple Sources," in *Reworking the Bible: Apocryphal and Related Texts at Qumran*, ed. E. Chazon et al. (Leiden: Brill, 2005), 1–30.

4. David Lambert, "Fasting as a Penitential Rite: A Biblical Phenomenon?" *Harvard Theological Review* 96 (2003): 479.

5. Ibid., 482.

6. On this aspect of sacrifice, see Baruch Levine, *Leviticus* (Philadelphia: Jewish Publication Society, 1989), 5–6.

7. On this subject see the excellent treatment of Jan Joosten, "*Hesed* 'bienveillance' et *eleos* 'pitie,'" in *Car c'est l'amour qui me plait, non le sacrifice . . .*" *Recherches sur Osée 6:6 et son interpretation juive et chrétienne*, ed. E. Bons (Supplements to the Journal for the Study of Judaism 88; Leiden: Brill, 2004), 25–42.

8. *Genesis Rabbah* 33.3. For an excellent treatment of this text and others like it see Jonathan Shofer's article "Theology and Cosmology in Rabbinic Ethics: The Pedagogical Significance of Rainmaking Narratives," *Jewish Studies Quarterly* 12 (2005): 227–59.

9. The translations of Ben Sira in this paragraph are mine, but I have been guided by the reconstructions suggested by Menahem Kister, "Romans 5:12–21 Against the

Background of Torah-Theology and Hebrew Usage," *Harvard Theological Review* 100 (2007): 394, n. 11.

10. Nathan Eubank ("Wages of Righteousness") has recently argued that the Gospel of Matthew, as a whole, has a more capacious view of what good works generate a wage. He has made a good argument that those who imitate the actions of Jesus will generate a reward that is stored in heaven. If he is correct, then there are several different ways of imagining the consequences of virtuous actions in this Gospel. Matthew 5:11–12, for example, affirms that those who endure persecution on account of their faith in Jesus will receive an ample reward in heaven. Matthew 6, on the other hand, does not say that all good deeds will accumulate in a heavenly treasury (contrary to what Koch claims [see chapter 9, note 1]). In this text, the treasury is limited to the triad of fasting, prayer, and almsgiving.

11. There may be one more benefit to my analysis if it is correct. It might help us solve a crux in the origins of the Q tradition. Scholars have long puzzled over whether the order of the Lukan (anxiety about food and clothing, then funding a treasury in heaven) or Matthean presentation (funding a treasury in heaven, then anxiety about food and clothing) is more original. If I am correct, one could see the redactional reason why Matthew would have put the treasury in heaven material first. It allowed him to advance the view that the traditional triad of pious deeds was equally meritorious and accumulated as stored goods in heaven. On this view, the Lukan order is more original.

12. Lambert, "Fasting," 511.

11. SACRIFICIAL GIVING

The citation of the midrash to Psalm 118 in the epigraph can be found in Midrash Tehillim and was cited in Ephraim Urbach's article "Religious and Social Tendencies in Talmudic Concepts of Charity," *Zion* 16 (1951): 1–27.

1. See the Jerusalem Talmud on *Peah* 1:1 and any of the traditional commentaries on the Mishna. Clement of Alexandria (late second century CE), in his work "Can the Rich Man Be Saved?" also recognizes the need for prudence with regard to how much money ordinary lay people would be expected to part with. But also note that Cyprian (third century CE, from North Africa), in his treatise on almsgiving, believes that God is sufficiently generous that one can be assured that however much one might wish to give, one will be sustained and rewarded in return. See chapters 8–13 of Cyprian's "Works and Almsgiving," in *St. Cyprian, Treaties,* trans R. Deferrari (New York: Fathers of the Church, 1958).

2. Proverbs 19:17 is an exceedingly important biblical text in the early church from the Syriac East to the Latin West. It also appears in the Sybilline Oracles (though it is hard to know whether this represents a Second Temple Jewish usage or a later Christian addition): "Whoever gives alms knows that he is lending to God. Mercy [perhaps better: 'charity'] saves from death when judgement comes." The citation is from John Charlesworth, *Old Testament Pseudepigrapha* (New York: Doubleday, 1983), 1: 347.

3. *Against Heresies,* 4:18; the quotation is taken (with some alteration) from *Ante-Nicene Fathers* (Grand Rapids, Mich.: Eerdmans, 1978), 1:486.

4. Consult, for examples these texts from Clement of Alexandria, Chrysostom, Gregory of Nazianzus, and Ambrose: Clement, *Stromateis, Books One to Three* (Fathers of the Church; Washington D.C.: Catholic University Press, 1991), Book 3.6, p. 290; Chrysostom, *On Repentance and Almsgiving,* trans. G. Christo (Fathers of the Church; Washington D.C.: Catholic University Press, 1998), Homily 7.24, p. 105; Nazianzus, *Select Orations,* trans. M. Vinson (Fathers of the Church; Washington D.C.: Catholic University Press, 2003), Oration 14, pp. 68–70; and Ambrose, *De Tobia: A Commentary, with an Introduction and Translation,* trans. L. Zucker (Patristic Studies 35; Washington D.C.: Catholic University Press, 1933), 71–73.

As Ephraim Urbach has noted ("Religious and Social Tendencies in Talmudic Concepts of Charity," in *The World of the Sages: Collected Studies* [Hebrew] [Jerusalem: Magnes, 2002], 20), this tradition is very close to a tradition found in the Midrash on Psalms. He writes: "There is a great similarity between the teaching of the church in the Apostolic era and the first few centuries afterwards and that of the Rabbis. There can be no doubt that the church was influenced by Jewish thinking. Jesus says: 'Come, those blessed by my father and inherit the kingdom prepared for you. For I was hungry and you fed me, thirsty and you gave me drink, I was a visitor and you took me in, naked and you covered me, sick and you visited me and in prison and you came to me.' This entire list of charitable deeds that the church endeavored to uphold reminds one of an anonymous midrash: "'Open for me the gates of charity [*tsedeq*]" (Psalm 118:19). In the world to come, one will be asked: "What was your work?" If he answers, "I fed the hungry," then they will say, "This is the gate of the LORD" (118:20)—Let the feeder of the hungry enter by it. If he answers, "I gave drink to the thirsty," then they will say: "This is the gate of the LORD"—Let the giver of drink to the thirsty enter by it. If he answers, "I clothed the naked," then they will say, "This is the gate of the LORD" (118:20)—Let the clother of the naked enter by it. And so forth.'" As Urbach has noted, the list of righteous deeds not only overlaps with those of Matthew 25 but derives ultimately from a list in Isaiah 58:6–7.

5. Compare the close of the first chapter in the book of Jonah: the sailors make a freewill offering immediately after the storm is quelled and then vow to offer (presumably) many more animals when they reach shore.

6. The mosaic found on a synagogue floor in Sepphoris has the story of Aaron's first sacrifice (Leviticus 9) in its top register and the binding of Isaac at the bottom. See the discussion in Ze'ev Weiss and Ehud Netzer, *Promise and Redemption: A Synagogue Mosaic from Sepphoris* (Jerusalem: Israel Museum, 1996), 14–31.

7. He is called "the rich young man" only in the Gospel of Matthew; in Mark he is simply a rich man. But given how popular this title is for the story, I will continue to use it for the Markan version as well.

8. *Homilies on Genesis and Exodus,* trans. R. Heine (Fathers of the Church 71; Washington D.C.: Catholic University Press, 1982), Homily 8 on Genesis, paragraph 8, pp. 144–45.

9. Let me clarify a few matters: First, on the question of first and second tables, see the discussion of Philo, *De Dec.* 121: "'The second set' of commandments refers to 'the actions prohibited by our duty to fellow-men' whereas the other 'set of five . . . is more concerned with the divine'" (as cited in Dale Allison and W. D. Davies, *The Gospel According to Matthew* [Edinburgh: T and T Clark, 1997], 3: 43 n. 32). Second, some commentators have puzzled over the understanding of the tenth commandment, "do not *covet* your neighbor's goods," as "do not *defraud.*" But Joel Marcus has pointed to Jewish sources that understood the command this way (*Mark 8–16* [Anchor Bible 27A; New Haven: Yale University Press, 2009], 721–22, 727). Finally, I should note that I have followed the Catholic numeration of the Ten Commandments.

10. Marcus, *Mark 8–16*, 725–26. The Shema proper is to be found in Deuteronomy 6:4, "Hear, O Israel: The LORD is our God, the LORD alone."

11. One way to explain this conundrum is to presume that the man was not completely honest with Jesus about his integrity in keeping the law. Many New Testament commentators have been suspicious of his claim. For example, the eminent British scholar of a generation back, C. E. B. Cranfield, wrote (*The Gospel According to Mark* [The Cambridge Greek Testament Commentary; Cambridge: Cambridge University Press, 1959], 329): "The man's naïve reply makes it clear that he has not understood the Commandments nor ever really taken them seriously. But he was no more mistaken about the law's real seriousness than were his Jewish contemporaries generally." However, it is clear that Cranfield has not come upon this position innocently. His skepticism about the man's honesty is a result of a

specifically Pauline construal of the law. In Paul's mind, it was one thing to know what the law required and another thing to do it. "For we know that the law is spiritual," Paul avers; "but I am of the flesh, sold into slavery under sin. I do not understand my own actions. For I do not do what I want, but I do the very thing I hate. . . . For I know that nothing good dwells within me, that is, in my flesh. I can will what is right, but I cannot do it. For I do not do the good I want, but the evil I do not want is what I do. Now if I do what I do not want, it is no longer I that do it, but sin that dwells in me" (Rom 7:14–15, 18–20). If we begin with the presumption of Paul that keeping the law is an impossibility, then there is really no option but to doubt the veracity of the young man. But surely Joseph Fitzmyer gets it right when he says (in regard to Luke's version of the tale), "Jesus has not denied that the magistrate has actually observed the commandments; he takes the man's answer for what it is and tries to draw him on still further" (*The Gospel According to Luke X–XXIV* [Anchor Bible 28a; New York: Doubleday, 1985], 1197).

12. See Leviticus 19:9–10, 23:22; Deuteronomy 14:27–29 (on the "poor man's tithe," which takes the place of the second tithe in the third and sixth years of the seven-year cycle), 24:19–22.

13. The full form of the opening Mishna in tractate *Peah* is: "These are matters that have no specified amount: peah, first fruits, the festival offering, charitable deeds, and Torah-study. Regarding the following matters, a man may enjoy their fruit in this world and his principal will remain for him in the next: honoring father and mother, charitable deeds, establishing peace between a man and his friend, [but] Torah-study is equal to all of them." We discussed the significance of the latter sentence of this mishna in Chapter 9; our focus in the present chapter is on the former. On the form of this Mishna and its relationship to the Dead Sea Scrolls, see Aharon Shemesh, "The History of the Creation of Measurements: Between Qumran and the Mishna," in *Rabbinic Perspectives: Rabbinic Literature and the Dead Sea Scrolls: Proceedings of the Eighth International Symposium of the Orion Center for the Study of the Dead Sea Scrolls and Associated Literature, 7–9 January, 2003*, ed. S. Fraade, A. Shemesh, and R. Clements (Leiden: Brill, 2006), 147–73. Shemesh argues that among the sect at Qumran the items listed in this first Mishna originally had measures attached to them.

14. Saul Lieberman, *The Tosefta* (Jerusalem: Jewish Theological Seminary, 1992), 41 (first footnote to first line of the mishna), and Hanokh Albeck, *Shishah Sidre Mishna. Seder Zera'im* [Hebrew] (Jerusalem: Bialik, 1959), 41.

15. It should be noted, however, that all commentators on the Mishna—whether traditional or modern—close the door immediately on such a notion. The simple sense of this law—that almsgiving has no limit—must be qualified. One can take the Mishna at face value only for charity that is interpersonal, such as burying the dead, tending the sick, or visiting those in prison. But when it comes to parting with money, strict limits are put in place. One must act prudently so as not to become destitute oneself.

16. Saul Lieberman, "Two Lexicographical Notes," *Journal of Biblical Literature* 65 (1946): 67–72, esp. 69–72. This is an excellent argument for seeing the Tosephta's belief that almsgiving is equal to all the commandments as older than the Mishna's counterclaim for the Torah. Nowhere that I am aware of is Torah-study described as *the* commandment. Rabbinic semantics thus confirms the picture we have seen in Tobit, Ben Sira, and the Gospels.

17. Surprisingly, Lieberman's suggestion was not known by Howard C. Kee in his translation in Charlesworth, *Old Testament Pseudepigrapha*, 1:817. The result is an unintelligible translation: "Someone else commits adultery and is sexually promiscuous, yet is abstemious in his eating. While fasting, he is committing evil deeds. Through the power of his wealth he ravages many, and yet in spite of his excessive evil, *he performs the commandments.*" Since we are dealing with a list of self-contradictory behaviors, Lieberman's suggestion remains much more sensible: he cheats and steals and then uses what he has gained to give alms. For the Greek text, see Marinus de Jonge, *The Testaments of the Twelve Patriarchs: A Critical Edition of the Greek Text* (Leiden: Brill, 1978), 137. It should be noted that de Jonge has

provided very good evidence that the *Testaments* in their final written form were not Jewish but Christian. Lieberman's argument, however, suggests that this particular verse must go back to a Jewish source.

18. In a recent article on this subject, Michael Satlow has argued that the understanding of almsgiving as the commandment is quite late ("'Fruit and Fruit of Fruit': Charity and Piety among Jews in Late Antique Palestine," *Jewish Quarterly Review* 100 (2010): 244–77). Though that is possible, it is important to note that the idea of its centrality is quite early even if the linguistic expression comes later. But I would argue that the linguistic expression is probably early as well. Given its embeddedness in vernacular Hebrew, it cannot be a rabbinic invention.

19. It is also striking that a goodly number of exegetes view the command to give alms as subordinate in importance to the act of following Jesus. Vincent Taylor (*The Gospel According to St. Mark* [London: Macmillan, 1952], 429) speaks for the majority when he writes, "In saying to the man, 'One thing thou lackest,' Jesus does not mean that there is *just one act to perform* in order that he may inherit eternal life, for after the command to sell all that he has He adds 'come and follow me.' It is this 'following' which leads to life; the renunciation of riches and gifts to the poor are actions which in his case following entails." Taylor is clearly uncomfortable with the notion that one would be rewarded for a specific *deed*— that would appear too Pharisaic. Rather, the command to follow indicates that the most important thing is *faith*. Yet Taylor undermines this declaration in part when he later cites with approval the observation that "Jesus Himself appears to have chosen a life of poverty; He wanders to and fro without a settled home (1:39, Lk 9:58), His disciples are hungry (2:23, 8:14), women provide for His needs (Lk 8:3) and His disciples can say, 'behold we have left everything and have followed you' (10:28)" (ibid., 429). But there is nothing intrinsic to the Christian tradition that demands such a low appraisal of the deed itself. Indeed, it seems quite obvious that the possibility of following Jesus turns on the desire to perform this deed. Faith and works are inseparable in this story.

20. There is no need to turn to Paul, as Cranfield did, to explain that the man's claim to have kept the commandments was disingenuous. On the specifically Protestant sources of Cranfield's position, see the excellent exposition of Ulrich Luz, *Matthew 8–20* (Hermeneia, Minneapolis: Fortress, 2001), 521–22. As E. P. Sanders has noted, Jesus may have opposed certain legalistic excesses within the rabbinic movement, but in general he "objects to the Pharisees because they are not righteous enough" (*Jesus and Judaism* [Philadelphia: Fortress, 1985], 277). Strikingly in this narrative about the rich man, Jesus is demanding a strict adherence to the type of legal logic that was preserved in the Mishna.

21. See my article "Sacrifices and Offerings," in the *Anchor Bible Dictionary* (New York: Doubleday, 1992), 5:87–86. I am dependent on the anthropologist Valerio Valeri for this particular gloss of the phrase "do ut des."

22. Justin Martyr, *First Apology*, 67. It can be found in *A Select Library of the Ante-Nicene Fathers of the Christian Church*, 10 vols., ed. Philip Schaff (Grand Rapids, Mich.: Eerdmans, 1978), 1: 186.

23. Rudolf Bultmann, *History of the Synoptic Tradition* (New York: Harper and Row 1963), 124.

24. W. D. Davies and Dale Allison, *Matthew 8–18* (International Critical Commentary; London: T and T Clark, 1991), 642.

12. Deliverance from Purgatory

The second epigraph is from a will found in Judah Galinski, "Jewish Charitable Bequests and the Hekdesh Trust in Thirteenth Century Spain," *Journal of Interdisciplinary History* 35 (2005): 437.

1. The citations of Jerry Walls in this chapter come from his article that appeared in *First Things*, April 2002. One should also consult his recent book, *Purgatory: The Logic of Total Transformation* (New York: Oxford University Press, 2012). A helpful treatment of recent Protestant engagements with the doctrine can be found in Neal Judisch's "Sanctification, Satisfaction, and the Purpose of Purgatory," *Faith and Philosophy* 26 (2009): 167–85. In particular, see the articles he lists at 168 n. 1.

2. Catholics, however, do not distinguish "justification" and "sanctification" in quite the same way as many Protestants. According to the *Catechism of the Catholic Church*, "Justification is not only the remission of sins, but also the sanctification and renewal of the interior man" (§1989, quoting the Council of Trent). I would like to thank my doctoral student John Sehorn for helping me express the distinctiveness of the Catholic position on this question.

3. C. S. Lewis, *Letters to Malcolm: Chiefly on Prayer* (New York: Harcourt, Brace and World, 1964), 108–9. Italics in the original.

4. My approach will be different from conventional approaches that appeal to biblical proof texts such as 1 Maccabees 12:38–45 and 1 Corinthians 3:11–15. On the text from Maccabees—which does support the case I wish to make—see the commentary of Daniel Schwartz, *2 Maccabees* (Berlin: de Gruyter, 2008), 443–44. In his discussion of v. 45, he writes: "The sacrifice was offered due to the fear that, despite the prayer mentioned in v. 42, death was not enough to atone for the sins of the fallen and they were in need of yet more merit, supplied by the sacrifice. The assumption is that if their sin is not atoned they suffer even more, and might even be excluded from resurrection. This implies that sinners are punished after their death, an implication that easily begets the notion of a place where that happens— Gehenna / Purgatory." Schwartz refers to the important article of Elmer O'Brien, "Scriptural Proof for the Existence of Purgatory from 2 Machabees—12:43–45," *Sciences Ecclésiastiques* 2 (1949): 80–108. On 1 Corinthians 3, see the comments of Joseph Fitzmyer, *First Corinthians* (Anchor Bible 32; New Haven: Yale University Press, 2008), 201, who writes: "Verses 14–15 do not speak of a purification or refining fire [for removing sins after death], but rather of a testing of constancy and subsequent deliverance achieved only with great difficulty."

5. The citation is from *Confessions*, 10.29.40. On the surprising similarities between Aquinas and Calvin on the subject of human merit, see Joseph Wawrykow, "John Calvin and Condign Merit," *Archiv für Reformationsgeschichte* 83 (1992): 73–90; and Charles Raith II, "Calvin's Critique of Merit and Why Aquinas (Mostly) Agrees," *Pro Ecclesia* 20 (2011): 135–67.

6. Yohanan Muffs, "Who Can Stand in the Breach? A Study in Prophetic Intercession," in *Love and Joy: Law, Language and Religion in Ancient Israel* (New York: Jewish Theological Seminary, 1992), 9–48.

7. Gary A. Anderson, *Sin: A History* (New Haven: Yale University Press, 2009).

8. The slightly periphrastic translation of Daniel 4:27 is my own. For further information about the figure of Nebuchadnezzar in early Christian thought, see David Satran, *Biblical Prophets in Byzantine Palestine: Reassessing the Lives of the Prophets* (Leiden: Brill, 1995).

9. See the commentary of Jeffrey Tigay on Deuteronomy 6:25 and 24:13 (*Deuteronomy* [Philadelphia: Jewish Publication Society, 1996], 83, 226).

10. Cited from the *Catechism of the Catholic Church*, immediately before §2006. It comes from Augustine's *Commentary on the Psalms* (102:7).

11. Cf. Luke 7:41–47 (widow's son at Nain) and 8:41–42, 49–56 (daughter of Jairus).

12. The translation is from Edward Rebenack, *De Opera et Eleemosynis* (Washington, D.C.: Catholic University of America Press, 1962), 65–67. Italics are mine.

13. I have used the version of the *Apostolic Constitutions* found in the *Ante-Nicene Fathers*, vol. 7 (1885; Grand Rapids, Mich.: Eerdmans, 1978), 8.4.42, p. 498.

14. Stephen Greenblatt notes (*Hamlet in Purgatory* [Princeton: Princeton University Press, 2001], 23) that Henry VII, the father of Henry VIII, had funded many charitable institutions as well as thousands of Masses that were to be said in his name. Henry VIII's suppression of the monasteries where those Masses were to be said was, in Greenblatt's words, "a

son's violent repudiation of his father's attempts to ease his soul's torments." But Henry VIII did not reject all of what the Catholic Church had taught, as is reflected in the words of his last will and testament: "We will and charge our Executors that they dispose and give in alms to the most poor and needy people that may be found (common beggars as much as may be avoided) in as short space as possible they may after our departure out of this transitory life, *one thousand marks* of lawful money of England, part in the same place and thereabouts, where it shall please Almighty God to call us to his Mercy, part by the way, and part in the same place of our burial after their discretions, and to move the poor people that shall have our alms to pray heartily unto God for remission of our offenses and the wealth of our soul" (italics Greenblatt's). Henry VIII, Greenblatt concludes, "does not want to linger in the fires of Purgatory. Thousands of masses will not be sung to haste him toward Heaven, but a thousand marks could purchase the prayer of many poor people. In the unlikely event that he did not go straight to Hell, he would certainly have needed all of them."

15. Gunther Bornkamm, *Der Lohngedanke im Neuen Testament* (Lüneburg: Heliand-Verlag, 1947), 12.

16. Bonaventure, *Commentaria* 4.20.2.5 (4:538). For the translation, see Robert Shaffern, "The Medieval Theology of Indulgences," in R. Swanson, *Promissory Notes on the Treasury of Merits: Indulgences in Late Medieval Europe* (Leiden: Brill, 2006), 35.

17. It is important to note that the Catholic Church puts special emphasis on the suffrage side of any indulged act of charity when it is done on behalf of the deceased. One cannot be fully certain that it will be of assistance; one can only pray on the deceased's behalf. But indulged acts performed by and applied to the faithful are more than simple appeals. They become merit worthy when carried out through the assistance of divine grace. In those cases, God has promised to bestow a reward and he can be trusted to fulfill his word.

18. See the epochal document *Joint Declaration on the Doctrine of Justification* (Grand Rapids, Mich.: Eerdmans, 2000), cowritten by the Lutheran World Federation and the Roman Catholic Church.

19. Galinsky, "Jewish Charitable Bequests," 423–40.

20. Leon Wieseltier, *Kaddish* (New York: Knopf, 1998), and Greenblatt, *Hamlet in Purgatory.*

21. Wieseltier, *Kaddish*, 126–27.

22. Ibid., 127.

23. Greenblatt, *Hamlet in Purgatory*, 7.

24. The story of Mar Uqba can be found in the Babylonian Talmud, *Ketubbot* 67b. The subject of the journey of the dead to their heavenly repose and the role mourning rites, prayer, and almsgiving play in rabbinic Judaism is a subject that warrants further study. For now see the article of Saul Lieberman, "Some Aspects of After Life in Early Rabbinic Literature," in *Harry Austryn Wolfson Jubilee Volume* (Jerusalem: American Academy for Jewish Research, 1965), 2: 495–532.

25. For the original, see B. M. Lewin, *Otzar ha-Geonim*, vol. 4, *Tractate Jom-Tow, Chagiga and Maschkin* (Jerusalem: The Hebrew University Press Association, 1931), 27–28.

26. Greenblatt, *Hamlet in Purgatory*, 9.

27. Ibid., 102–3.

28. C. S. Lewis, *Letters to Malcolm*, 107.

13. Conclusion

The first epigraph comes from Eamon Duffy, *The Stripping of the Altars: Traditional Religion in England, 1500–1580* (New Haven: Yale University Press, 1992), 358. The second comes from Thomas à Kempis, *The Imitation of Christ* (Milwaukee: Bruce, 1949), 2:10. It is in the public domain and available on the World Wide Web.

1. Eric Shuler, "Almsgiving and the Formation of Early Medieval Societies, A.D. 700–1025," Ph.D. diss., University of Notre Dame, 2010.

2. "To cleanse one's account from every sin" is my translation of Tobit 12:9. For a justification of this, see my forthcoming article, "How Does Almsgiving Purge Sins?" in *Hebrew in the Second Temple Period: The Hebrew of the Dead Sea Scrolls and of Other Contemporary Sources. Proceedings of the Twelfth International Symposium of the Orion Center for the Study of the Dead Sea Scrolls and Associated Literature, Jointly Sponsored by the Eliezer Ben-Yehuda Center for the Study of the History of the Hebrew Language, 29–31 December 2008*, ed. S. E. Fassberg, M. Bar-Asher, and R. Clements (Studies on the Texts of the Desert of Judah; Leiden: Brill, 2013).

3. See Chapter 11, note 4, for a discussion of prayers for the dead in 2 Maccabees 12:38–45. For the text of the *Apostolic Constitutions* (Book 8.4.42) see *A Select Library of the Ante-Nicene Fathers of the Christian Church*, 10 vols., ed. Philip Schaff (Grand Rapids, Mich.: Eerdmans, 1978), 7: 498.

4. For a brief discussion of the role of alms in Luther's theses see my *Sin: A History* (New Haven: Yale University Press, 2009), 162–63.

5. All citations are from the translation of Maria Boulding, *The Confessions* (Hyde Park, N.Y.: New City, 2001).

6. The text is taken from "The Enchiridion on Faith, Hope, and Charity," trans. Bruce Harbert. It can be found in B. Ramsey, ed., *On Christian Belief* (Hyde Park, N.Y.: New City, 2005), 316; see paragraphs 71–72.

7. Kempis, *Imitation of Christ*, III:58.

Acknowledgments

The research involved in bringing this book to completion has been supported by numerous sources. I would like to single out the Tikvah Center for Law and Jewish Civilization and the Straus Institute for the Advanced Study of Law and Justice, which supported a marvelous sabbatical year at New York University (2010–11), as well as the Louisville Institute, which also generously supported my project.

Special thanks are owed to Joseph Weiler and Moshe Halbertal of the NYU Law School and all the fellows who helped me frame my argument. I should single out for particular thanks Maoz Kahana, Yair Lorderbaum, Ephraim Shoham-Steiner, and Michael Walzer. As I worked on the subject of charity that year, I was also reading Benedict XVI's encyclical *Deus Caritas Est*. At one point he acknowledges those contributions when he writes, "the real novelty of the New Testament lies not so much in new ideas as in the figure of Christ himself." Jesus does not overturn Jewish teachings on charity; rather, he makes them in manifest in his incarnate life. I hope my book will testify to the deep continuities between church and synagogue on this subject and lead to a greater understanding, respect, and affection between the two. A portion of the second chapter of this book I gave as the ninth annual Caroline and Joseph S. Gruss Lecture in the spring of 2011 at the NYU Law School. I owe Professors Weiler and Halbertal a considerable debt of thanks for all the support and encouragement they gave my work.

Several colleagues have read portions or all of the manuscript in its various stages. These include Josephine Dru, Nathan Eubank, Joel Kaminsky, Jon Levenson, Carol Newsom, Tzvi Novick, Anthony Pagliarini, John Sehorn, and Robert Wilken. Let me also give a special thanks to Jennifer Banks, my editor at Yale, who gave the entire manuscript a careful reading and helped bring it to its final form. These friends and colleagues have saved me from numerous errors. Other colleagues, too numerous to list, have heard portions of the argument in public lectures or casual conversation, and their feedback has helped me find the proper voice for what I want to claim. A slightly different version of Chapter 4 appeared in the journal *Hebrew Bible and Ancient Israel* (2012) and a much briefer form of Chapter 12 appeared in *First Things* (2011). I am grateful to both publications for allowing me to revise these essays and include them in this book.

Nearly all of the quotations from the Bible are taken from New Revised Standard Version. Some, however, are my own translations; I have identified these in the notes.

General Index

R. Akiva, 177–179
R. Eliezer, 37
R. Gamaliel, 30–31, 118
R. Joshua, 37
R. Judah, 134
R. Shemayah, 134
R. Sherira, 179
R. Shimon, 37, 40
R. Tanhuma, 145–46
R. Yohanan, 67
R. Yohanan ben Zakkai, 28, 37
R. Yosi, 37
Rabenau, M., 193n8
Reformation, 69, 3, 8–11, 113, 116, 122,
  162–64, 174–77, 185–86
Rhee, H., 191n1
Rindge, M., 17, 198n16

Sanctification, 164–68
Sanders, E. P., 116–18, 121–22, 174–75,
  211n20
Satlow, M., 191n1, 211n18
Schopenhauer, A., 196n8
Schwartz, B., 207n17
Schwartz, D., 212n4
Seeligmann, I., 40, 51, 194n16, 195n4,
  197n13
Sehorn, J., 194n12, 212n2
Shuler, E., 214n1
Sin, as debt, 1–3, 61, 66, 114–17, 119,
  121–22, 138–39, 168–70, 182,
  187–88

Skemp, V., 201n9, 202n2
Smith, C., 192n8
Smith, J. Z., 10, 199n20
Stark, R., 193n6
Stone, M., 206n13
Surowiecki, J., 38, 40

Teresa, Mother, 4–6
Tithe, 26–28
Treasury in Heaven, 3–6, 25, 29, 32–34, 47,
  49, 52–69, 88–89, 97–99, 105–6, 123–29,
  132–33, 136–38, 147–50, 154, 159–60,
  173–77, 183
Tsedaqa, 19, 33–34, 54–55, 60, 120–21, 144,
  147–48, 169, 195n22, 197n1

Utilitarianism, 5–6

VanderKam, J., 198nn13–14, 24nn21–22
Veyne, P., 15–17
Voltaire, 110
von Rad, G., 27

Walls, J., 162–65
Waltke, B., 58
Wealth, perils of, 53–54, 56–60, 62–66,
  198n15
White, H. C., 92
Wieseltier, L., 177–79, 201n14

Zekut avot ("Merits of the Fathers") , 33–34,
  116–17, 121

Index of Ancient Sources